£1. 15p 17644

Protest, Violence, and Social Change

CANADA

Issues & Options

A series created to stimulate intelligent inquiry into crucial Canadian concerns

Protest, Violence, and Social Change

RICHARD P. BOWLES
Associate Professor, College of Education, University of Toronto

JAMES L. HANLEY
Educator-Producer, History and Social Science,
Ontario Educational Communications Authority

BRUCE W. HODGINS
Professor, Department of History, Trent University

GEORGE A. RAWLYK
Professor, Department of History, Queen's University

p
PRENTICE-HALL ☘ OF CANADA, LTD.
h

Scarborough Ontario

PRENTICE-HALL, INC., ENGLEWOOD CLIFFS, NEW JERSEY
PRENTICE-HALL INTERNATIONAL, INC., LONDON
PRENTICE-HALL OF AUSTRALIA, PTY., LTD., SYDNEY
PRENTICE-HALL OF INDIA, PVT., LTD., NEW DELHI
PRENTICE-HALL OF JAPAN, INC., TOKYO

Library of Congress Catalog No. 74-39625
ISBN 0-13-731406-X
1 2 3 4 5   76 75 74 73 72
PRINTED IN CANADA

Contents

Preface   ix
Acknowledgments   xi
Introduction   xiii

I   THE ISSUE: SOME OPINIONS

  1. Democracy: Change without Violence   1
  2. A Young Radical's View   1
  3. Confrontation on Campus Inevitable   2
  4. Civil Disobedience   2
  5. The Angry Black   2
  6. The Indian Minority: "Guns to Back Demands"   3
  7. Prime Minister Trudeau Comments on Violence   3

II   A CASE IN POINT: CAMPUS SIT-IN

  1. Day One: Police Called in on Demonstration   5
  2. Day Two: U. of T. Senate Occupied   5
  3. Day Two: University President Says Occupiers Must Quit   7
  4. Day Three "We Won," Students Cry   8
  5. And Who Gained?   9
  6. Sit-Ins Are Dangerous   10
  7. Student Apathy Encouraged "All-Purpose Radicals"   12
  8. Dangerous Precedent Created   13
  9. Radicals Have a Right to Be There   13
10. University Should Not Have to Support its
    Students' Children   14
11. Radicals Did Not Take Over Demonstration   14
12. University President Capitulated Says Police Chief   15

III THE CONTEMPORARY PROBLEM

Youth
1. The Student Radical: "We Are Creative"   18
2. The Student Radicals: Do Their Actions Force Us to Think?   19
3. The Quiet Student: Love, not Violence   21
4. Revolt—If You Dig to Lob Bricks   22
5. McGill Students Condemn Rampage at Sir George Williams   23
6. Violence Is Part of the Canadian Way of Life   24
7. Confrontation at Ryerson: Students Squash Sit-In   26
8. Student Revolution: The Marxist Approach   27
9. Student Satire: "Leave Administration Alone"   28
10. Help Stop Campus Riots   29
11. Irving Layton: For My Student Militants   30

The Indian
1. An Indian Moderate: Harold Cardinal   32
2. Indian Reservation: Caughnawaga   33
3. An Indian Radical: Kahn-Tineta Horn   34
4. The Time for Singing Is Past: An Indian Demonstration   37

The Black Canadian
1. In Search of a Sense of Community   42
2. Black Awareness in Halifax   45
3. Rocky the Revolutionary   49

The Radical Left
1. Revolution, not Terrorism   52
2. Election Aims: The Canadian Communist Party   54
3. A Reaction to the Kent State Crisis: The M4 Movement   57
4. The New Left: Voting a Meaningless Ritual   58
5. Canada's Maoists: 300 Who Seek the Revolution   62

The Separatist
1. A Separatist Poet Speaks: L'Afficheur Hurle   64
2. Terrorists Caught in Westmount   65
3. A Marxist's Analysis of Quebec's Troubles   67
4. The Politics of Assassination   70
5. FLQ Manifesto   72
6. Prime Minister Trudeau on the Proclamation of the War
   Measures Act   76
7. René Lévesque Reacts to Kidnappings of October 1970   81
8. René Lévesque: Ottawa and FLQ Are Both Extremist   83
9. Under Attack: The War Measures Act   84
10. FLQ Intellectual Renounces Violence   87

The Poor
1. Discontent of Montreal's Poor Fuels Political Action   90
2. The Poor Will always Be with Us, Eh?   92
3. We Only Get Justice When We Revolt   94
4. We Intend to Push As Far As We Can   95
5. The Poor May Revolt If We Ignore Them   99

The Establishment

1. The Prime Minister and Dissent 100
2. The Minister of Justice: Dissent Must Stop Short of Violence 103
3. The Student As God 104
4. Gallop Poll: 87% Approve of War Measures Act 106
5. We Will Use Horses again If Necessary 107
6. Editorial: Beyond Justification 109
7. Reform in Canada Is Peaceful 110
8. The Establishment Must Not Resort to Violent Backlash 112
9. Would We Really Choose Civil War? 112
10. Why the Public Is Alienated from the Police 115
11. Violence Inevitable When Law Vanishes 116

Our Culture and Violence

1. We're All to Blame for Violence in Sport 119
2. Riot in the Forum 120
3. Violence in Our National Sport 122
4. Comments on the Mass Media: Its Role in Violence 125
5. The *Maclean's*—Goldfarb Report on Canadian Culture and Violence 126

IV THE HISTORICAL EXPERIENCE

The Sons of Freedom

1. How Canada's First Terrorists Were Crushed 132
2. Seek Troops to Halt B.C. Terror Bombs 135
3. Martial Law Urged for B.C. 135
4. Is There a Peaceful Solution? 137

The 1930s

1. A Conservative Journal: "Red" Activities in 1930-31 138
2. Red Meetings Result in May Day Riots 139
3. "Communists" Cause Trouble 141
4. Warfare Breaks Out in Estevan 143
5. Estevan's Black Day 143
6. Estevan: A Poem 144
7. The Senate and Section 98 145
8. Detective Killed in Regina Riot 147
9. An Eyewitness Account of the Regina Riot 148
10. Prime Minister Bennett Comments on the Regina Riot 154
11. Editorial: Mr. Bennett a Hypocrite 155
12. Public Buildings Occupied in Vancouver 156

Cape Breton Unrest

1. Rioters Stone Troops 158
2. Aftermath of Battle 158
3. Troops Called in for Cape Breton Strike 159
4. Steelworkers Surrounded by Enemies 159

The Winnipeg General Strike

1. The Great Unrest 161
2. Mayor Gray Asks Citizens to Avoid Violence 162

3. Strikers Reassure Citizens of Winnipeg   163
4. "No Riots" Veterans Declare   164
5. An Act to Amend the Immigration Act   165
6. Free Press Warns of Violence   166
7. Aliens and Communists Responsible for Winnipeg Strike   168
8. One Killed as Mob Attacks Mounted Police   169
9. Labor News Banned—Editor Arrested   169
10. Government Reacts With Emergency Measures   171
11. Views on the 1919 Winnipeg General Strike   172

The Northwest Rebellion
1. A Letter to Riel   174
2. Riel Answers   175
3. Riel Speaks to his People   175
4. Editorial: Macdonald is to Blame   176
5. Editorial: Law and Order Must Be Maintained   177
6. Blood Stains the Soil   179
7. Louis Riel at His Trial   180

The Rebellions of 1837
1. Will Canadians Shoulder Their Muskets   182
2. Louis-Joseph Papineau to the People of Lower Canada   183
3. British Conciliatory Policy Responsible for Rebellion   184
4. To the Habitants of the District of Montreal   186
5. Proclamation of Martial Law   187
6. The Burning of St. Benoit   188
7. Aftermath of Rebellion in Lower Canada   189
8. William Lyon Mackenzie's Call to Revolution   190
9. Rebellion is Folly   192
10. Mackenzie Justifies the Rebellion   193
11. Toronto in Arms   193
12. Proclamation by Mackenzie   194
13. Anti-Rebel Song   195
14. Arise Canadians   196

The Rebellion Losses Bill
1. Opposition to Rebellion Losses Bill   197
2. Indemnity Sanctioned by Elgin   197
3. The Burning of the Parliament Buildings   198
4. This Shameful Act   200
5. The Last Desperate Struggle of Toryism   200

V   **Conclusion**
1. What Do You Think?   203

Suggested Readings   205

Preface

The *Canada: Issues and Options* series focusses on a number of vital continuing Canadian concerns. Each volume probes the nature of a complex issue in both its contemporary and historical contexts. The issues were chosen because of their relevance to the life of the Canadian teenager as well as the general Canadian public.

Every volume in the series provides a wide variety of primary and secondary source materials. These sources are interdisciplinary as well as analytical and descriptive. They embody many divergent points of view in order to provoke critical in-depth consideration of the issue. They are arranged in a manner designed to personally involve and confront the reader with the clash of opinions and options inherent in the various issues. The historical sources have been carefully selected to provide a better understanding of the roots of the issue under consideration. It is hoped that this method will establish in the reader's mind a meaningful relationship between the past and the present.

The organization is flexible. If a chronological study of the development of the issue is desired, this can be accomplished by treating the historical sources first and later examining the contemporary manifestations of the issue. By reversing this procedure, the reader can first deal with the contemporary section. This approach will provide the reader with a brief overview of the issue, a case study designed to put it into personal and immediate terms, and a more detailed examination of the issue in its contemporary setting, prior to examining its historical roots.

Questions designed to stimulate further research are also included.

These questions do not limit examination or prescribe answers, but raise more questions and suggest aspects of the issue which might be further investigated.

Throughout these volumes, a conscientious effort has been made to avoid endorsing any one viewpoint. No conclusions are drawn. Rather, the reader is presented with information which has been arranged to encourage the drawing of his own tentative conclusions about the issue. The formation of these conclusions involve the use of the skills of inquiry and the examination and clarification of personal values.

Acknowledgments

The authors are indebted to Ken Battle, John Berry, and Keith Walden for their assistance in the assembling of the basic material for this volume.

Particular thanks are due Wendy Cuthbertson and Paul Hunt for their help, advice, and hard work in the final preparation of this material.

The authors also thank the many writers and publishers who have granted them permission to use various materials. Source references are provided with the documents.

Introduction

What forms of protest are legitimate for accomplishing social change in Canada? Is violence an effective tool for accelerating or achieving social reform, or can it be used to prevent the disruption of society? Is its use ever justified to achieve either of these objectives or are there always better alternatives available? Is the use of violence in relation to social change a phenomenon unique to the '60s and '70s? If not, what lessons, if any, are contained in our history?

It would be tempting to try to provide an easy answer to the complex political, moral, and social questions raised by the issue of protest, violence and social change. This volume will not provide such answers. Indeed, it may raise many additional questions. Hopefully, the material presented will cause you to examine your own values and attitudes, and also enable you to eventually try to reach some tentative conclusions.

Recent events in this country have demonstrated the danger of ignoring, or lightly dismissing the crucial issues of our time, and emphasize the importance of having an informed and alert citizenry.

The Issue:
Some Opinions

1. DEMOCRACY: CHANGE WITHOUT VIOLENCE

Dr. Wilder Penfield, the world-famous neurosurgeon, comments in the Montreal *Gazette, February 10, 1969.*

In Canada, we are committed to make our democracy work. We will not close our universities nor will we allow our other establishments to be overthrown by violence. We have chosen freedom, not socialist dictatorship and not undisciplined licence. Democratic freedom allows for change. It welcomes reform from within and hopes for help from each succeeding generation.

2. A YOUNG RADICAL'S VIEW

Editorial comment from the Eye-Opener, *the student newspaper at the Ryerson Polytechnical Institute, October 3, 1968.*

> Mary, Mary
> how should our garden grow?
> with violence—the seeds of discontent.

Who is to say physical violence is to be more abhorred than mental or legislative conflict just because it is so much more obvious?

3. CONFRONTATION ON CAMPUS INEVITABLE

The Toronto Globe and Mail of March 24, 1969 featured an article by Steven Langdon, a prominent figure in the Canadian student movement.

This hard line resistance means that confrontations on campus are inevitable and bound to increase in number next year. Such a situation will require militant student tactics: strikes, sit-ins and the occupation of university buildings will occur, just as they have around similar issues at McGill, Windsor and Simon Fraser.

Violence such as that at Sir George Williams University will not arise, however. The Sir George situation was not typical. The racism issue heightened tension, and the violent atmosphere of present-day Montreal made physical destruction a more believable option than it would be for students anywhere else.

4. CIVIL DISOBEDIENCE

Federal Minister of Justice John Turner's opinion on civil disobedience appeared in the Ottawa Citizen, March 1969.

Civil disobedience by definition involves breaking the law, and those who commit an illegality cannot demand amnesty as the price for refraining from further civil disobedience. Morality does not begin at the barrel of a gun.

5. THE ANGRY BLACK

In the Globe Magazine of February 15, 1969, three young blacks, Jules Oliver, Rocky Jones, and Denny Grant, gave their opinions on protest and violence.

Jules Oliver—Black—Age 23—Halifax

What will happen when blacks are organized and whites still say no to our demands? We will no longer adhere to the system. You've set up the barrier. Politics is war without bloodshed; war is politics with bloodshed.

Rocky Jones—Black—Age 27—Halifax

We can't put any moral judgement on violence; it is fact.

You know when they will listen? When somebody shoots a white woman's kid on the way to school. It's a very sad thing, man, but white people will not listen unless you're violent.

6. THE INDIAN MINORITY: "GUNS TO BACK DEMANDS"

In the Toronto Telegram *of June 8, 1971, a staff reporter related the warnings of an Alberta Indian leader, Mr. Stanley Daniels.*

Ontario's 75,000 Métis and non-status Indians should stress that guns might be necessary to achieve equality if peaceful means don't work, an Alberta Indian leader said yesterday.

Stanley Daniels, president of the Alberta Métis Association, told Ontario leaders they must get tough in dealing with governments and should stage demonstrations to make their demands known.

"Staying at home and crying won't do any good," he said. "Get mad and get what you want. And don't be afraid to make it clear that guns will still be around if the peaceful way doesn't work. But hopefully this route will be avoided.

"The question to be put to government is that the Métis people are prepared to avoid violence—is the Government? I know Canada has enough for everybody's needs, but not for everybody's greeds," Mr. Daniels said.

"When you go to government don't be nice guys. A lot of people hate my guts and that makes me happy—I know I'm doing my job. Always remember that you are the law, you are Canada."

7. PRIME MINISTER TRUDEAU COMMENTS ON VIOLENCE

This is an excerpt from Prime Minister Trudeau's speech to the Liberal Party in Vancouver on August 8, 1969. It was reported in the Toronto Globe and Mail, *August 11, 1969.*

It is perhaps true that it is difficult when you are in a minority to have your point-of-view accepted, but the fact that you are in a minority means that the majority of Canadians think otherwise. They may be wrong, they may be misinformed, but this is the way they think. . . . I think the majority has a right to defend itself and if the laws are wrong, they must be changed. But as long as there is freedom of speech in this country, and as long as a man is free to talk to his neighbour, and to write what he wants, and to form assemblies, and to form up parties and groups, and spread the gospel as he sees it, there is no place for organized violence, or for violent dissent. . . .

What do you think?

1. (a) Of the six statements you have just read, which comes closest to stating your views?
   (b) Which statement seems to you to be the most logical and reasonable?
   (c) Was your choice the same in (a) and (b)?

A Case in Point: Campus Sit-In

In March of 1970 supporters of a day-care centre used by students and faculty of the University of Toronto (and set up in a university-owned building), confronted U. of T. President Claude Bissell with the demand that the university pay for the renovations needed to bring the building up to fire and other licencing standards. When a demonstration failed to evoke response from Bissell, the protestors occupied the U. of T. Senate.

The following documents represent a range of opinion concerning the methods used by the day-care centre supporters to get what they wanted, and the responses of the university administration.

1. DAY ONE: POLICE CALLED IN ON DEMONSTRATION

Wednesday, March 26, 1970, Toronto Telegram.

University of Toronto security guards called for help from Metro police today as a demonstration outside university president Claude Bissell's office got out of hand.

2. DAY TWO: U. OF T. SENATE OCCUPIED

Thursday, March 27, 1970, Toronto Globe and Mail.

Students, parents with children, and outside supporters were still occupying the University of Toronto's administration building early this morning to press their demand that the university guarantee to renovate a day-care centre.

The occupation began at noon yesterday when demonstrators marched into Simcoe Hall to demand that the university give the day-care centre the $2,000 it needs to renovate its Sussex Street house in line with fire and licencing regulations.

Administration officials did not say whether or when they would try to move the demonstrators out. About 20 university police were in the building with the demonstrators but the two groups were observing a cool truce.

The occupation began when an assortment of mothers, babies, teachers and students shoved their way past university security guards into the administration building.

Some of the protestors scuffled with U. of T. police, screamed "Baby haters" at campus guards and forced open the doors of the ornate senate chamber.

As the occupation of the senate chamber began, the black flag of anarchism and red flags flew from the windows, along with a sign, "Join Us Inside."

The original group of mothers and infants was joined throughout the afternoon by student radicals and moderates, feminist groups and young people from Rochdale College and the U.S. exile organizations.

Most of the parents disappeared after the first half hour of the demonstration. Others sat down on steps outside the office of the U. of T. president, Claude Bissell.

One girl fainted in the crush. A youth was hit by a campus guard after he had squared off with another guard.

The march began in a jovial atmosphere with parents carrying balloons and joking with onlookers. But the marchers became angry when four members of the group reported to the crowd that Dr. Bissell would not meet them.

The university president later met a delegation of protesters, assuring them he would ask for funds to renovate the existing day-care centre on Sussex Street. It will cost about $2,000 to bring the building in line with fire regulations.

He later told reporters: "All I said to them was that the university . . . wasn't willing to make an absolute guarantee for this day-care centre because this could mean over the years an increasing amount of money from a limited university budget."

The university, which owns the Sussex Street centre, has agreed to permit its use as a day-care centre until 1972.

While Dr. Bissell was talking with the delegation, a group of unidentified students managed to open the locked doors of the senate chamber upstairs.

The students, by now the leaders of the demonstration, made preparations for a long stay.

They hauled in loaves of bread, peanut butter and jam, cigarets, soft drinks and coffee.

In an almost festive mood, they laid out an impromptu picnic on the blue felt covering the senate tables.

At 6 p.m. in a last attempt to persuade the students to leave, Dr. Bissell said he had been in touch with some directors of the Varsity Fund during the afternoon and they were agreeable to the request.

Dr. Bissell asked the students to leave, and said he was going home "to have a double Scotch" and added he hoped others would do the same. Then he walked out.

But within a few moments, the students voted to continue the occupation until the university gave them a written guarantee that the day-care centre would receive the money for the renovation.

When Dr. Bissell's offer was relayed to the demonstrators, some of them urged acceptance and an end to the occupation.

Lorenne Gordon Smith, a philosophy professor whose small son attends the day-care centre, said Dr. Bissell's offer meant the mothers had a base from which to work for two years.

About 20 faculty members showed up to support the demonstrators, but some were angry at the course of the protest.

History Professor Natalie Davis shouted that the demonstration was handled by people "who have no children and don't intend to."

Some students complained that the demonstration leaders were student radicals and members of the campus Worker-Student Alliance.

By 7 p.m. the occupation of the administration building was firmly under way.

The slogan on the walls of the administration building reads, "Bust Bissell—Power to the Babies."

3. DAY TWO: UNIVERSITY PRESIDENT SAYS OCCUPIERS MUST QUIT

Thursday, March 27, 1970, Toronto Telegram.

University of Toronto President Claude Bissell told the occupiers of Simcoe Hall today they must clear the building before he will seek funds for renovating a day-care centre for them.

About 300 people took over the hall yesterday to enforce demands that a university-owned building be renovated to meet city standards as a day-care centre for children of married students. The work would cost $2,000.

Dr. Bissell said he will recommend strongly to the directors of the Varsity Fund that they make the money available.

"I am not prepared, however, to pursue this proposal under force," he said. "The occupation of Simcoe Hall must cease before I will call for a meeting of the Varsity Fund board of directors and formally submit the proposal to them."

Dr. Bissell said the university is not prepared to accept long term responsibility for the centre at the moment because of the tightness of its budget.

William Schabas, 19-year-old history student, said: "The decision has been made to remain here until our demands are made. It is possible this decision may be changed but I would not say it is probable."

About 150 students occupied the building overnight but about 150 more joined them before 9 a.m. and the number is still rising.

Dr. Bissell told them last night he would present their demand to the Varsity Fund and there was a good chance they would get it.

Dr. Bissell told the jeering, chanting students he was going home to have a "double Scotch" and he suggested they do likewise.

4. DAY THREE: "WE WON," STUDENTS CRY

Friday, March 28, 1970, Toronto Globe and Mail.

Demonstrators occupying the University of Toronto's administration building cheered yesterday as university president Claude Bissell gave in to their demands for money to renovate a day-care centre.

Students, parents and outside supporters yelled "We won, we won" and chanted "Power to the people" after Dr. Bissell promised to raise $2,000 required to bring the Sussex Avenue facility up to licencing and fire-code standards.

"I give you my personal guarantee," Dr. Bissell told more than 500 persons crowded into the building's senate chamber, "that the money for these renovations will be found from whatever sources are available."

Within minutes the chamber, which has been occupied all night by more than 100 demonstrators, was empty except for a few students who remained to sweep up debris that had been scattered during the 22-hour occupation.

By backing down, Dr. Bissell ended what was fast developing into one of the ugliest incidents in the university's history.

All yesterday morning, the original leaders of the demonstration—the parents and Women's Liberation Movement members responsible for the day-care centre—had been losing the initiative to hardline radicals who seemed determined to escalate the conflict.

These radicals—Maoists, Trotskyists and their supporters—set up barriers in Simcoe Hall, questioned persons entering the building and urged other demonstrators to expand the occupation and settle for a long stay.

The administration treated the new situation as a siege. It sent most of its office staff home, and Dr. Bissell issued a statement saying he would not pursue the necessary funds under force of occupation.

Shortly before noon, however, the day-care centre leadership regained the initiative and took steps which helped resolve the crisis.

Lorenne Smith, a philosophy professor whose two children attend the day-care centre, met Dr. Bissell and top academic officials who form the President's Council.

Professor Smith and Natalie Davis, a history professor, asked the officials to guarantee that the money would be raised but explicity relieved the university of responsibility to provide day-care for the children of students and employees.

Dr. Bissell then made his personal guarantee that the money would be raised while at the same time committing the university to a serious investigation of its social responsibilities in the day-care field.

"I think it's marvellous," Professor Smith said, as the occupation broke up.

"Twelve Sussex will continue and will be able to be licenced and we have the assurance that the long-term question of the university's responsibility to day-care will be seriously looked into."

Asked whether she thought the concessions could have been brought about without militant action, Professor Smith answered "No."

The Aftermath

5. AND WHO GAINED?

An editorial from the Toronto Globe and Mail *of March 28, 1970.*

"We won, we won," was the shout that went up after University of Toronto President Claude Bissell promised to raise $2,000 for the renovation of the Sussex Street day-care centre. But who won? And what?

No doubt the organizers of the demonstration and their original band of supporters were cheering because they had won the promise they wanted and could rest assured the centre which at present looks after 22 infants would be able to meet fire and building standards.

However, there were other voices in the triumphant chorus—the voices of demonstrators who, as one participating professor angrily pointed out, had no children and did not intend to have any. The familiar epithets of "pigs" and "lackeys" and cries of "power to the people" told their own eloquent story of conditioned verbal reflexes usually found in the mouths of all-purpose demonstrators.

What had *they* won, those who showed up from the ranks of every activist organization on the campus?

The $2,000 promise by itself meant little; but in obtaining it they had shown that the university authorities could be forced to back down. A short time after Dr. Bissell issued a written statement saying, among other things, that he was not prepared to pursue this proposal (providing funds to renovate the centre) under force, he was giving a personal guarantee that the money would be found.

One could hardly say that the coercive elements in the situation had gone, since he made the announcement to 500 people occupying the senate chamber. Within moments the chamber was empty. Mission accomplished.

Among other lessons to emerge from the 22-hour confrontation was an important one for innocents in the game of demonstration. It should be evident by now that every demonstration that is planned, whether its objectives are just, mischievous or trivial, is vulnerable to seizure by elements that have their own purposes.

The skilled orchestrators of the parasitic element know how to push a situation along much farther and faster than its originators may have intended. It is naive of demonstration planners to suppose otherwise and, in this particular instance, especially reprehensible that they chose to illustrate their plight by taking children into a potentially ugly situation.

Some of the organizers of this affair seemed pleased with results in the end, but the plain fact is that they were lucky. They were fortunate in being able to assert their control eventually and fortunate in dealing with a cool, accommodating man.

6. SIT-INS ARE DANGEROUS

This editorial from the Toronto Globe and Mail *of April 3, 1970, questions the technique of demonstration as a method to achieve change.*

Within a week it has suddenly become fashionable for groups of Ontario students to express their grievances by seizing and holding campus buildings. It began when University of Toronto students and faculty members forced their way into the administration building and held it for 22 hours against its usual occupants, demanding renovations to a day-care centre.

The success of this demonstration—President Claude Bissell agreed to the renovations—may have encouraged others, or it may be only an extraordinary coincidence that this week a group of Ryerson students occupied Administration Hall over the firing of five teachers, and a group of Laurentian University students took over the Great Hall to demonstrate support of the senate against the president. In any case, the technique is now with us.

Is it an acceptable technique?

John T. Scopes, the man once convicted of teaching evolution, described it rather well this week: "It's like the kid that screams and kicks until he gets his lollipop." Certainly both the U. of T. and the Ryerson grievances were minor and both groups were ill-organized and far from united on the purpose underlying their actions. But even when the issue is major, is it an acceptable technique?

We think not. Discounting the question of legality, of the invasion of property, of the interference with other people's rights, of the perverting by a minority of an institution designed to serve the whole, the technique is far too dangerous.

A student sit-in occurs in a highly volatile atmosphere. The demonstrators are often, as at U. of T. and Ryerson, pursuing different purposes by different means. They are cramped into a building that was not designed for living in, eating in, sleeping in. They are in a high state of excitement; even a single individual can precipitate an incident. Only the utmost of discipline could contain the situation for any time at all; and the inner discipline is usually ragged, the outer discipline absent. When pickets parade in the streets, they can be seen to be, or made to be, orderly. Behind the university there is no such authority.

The potential for violence and damage and risk to public safety is altogether too great.

The reasonable approach to student and faculty grievances, as to any other, is the development of a form of institutional government which gives just representation to all and establishes just procedures by which disputes may be settled; and this is a state most educational institutions are working to produce and should continue to work to produce with all possible haste.

In the meantime, an unacceptable technique is being used, and every university president, every community college president, even every high school principal should now determine what he will do if it is used in his institution. He should lay down a code, so that the students will know what will happen if they occupy a building.

A demonstration is frequently signalled, since it can seldom be organized without some leak to the administration. When this happens, the building to be occupied should be locked. If demonstrators break their way in, they should then be charged with break-and-entry under the Criminal Code, as they would be if they were any other criminal breaking into a house or store.

All sit-ins cannot be prevented, however. A technique must therefore be developed for dealing with one that is already under way. Here, the doors could again be locked, all save one marked exit, at which a policeman would be posted. Nobody and nothing would be allowed in: no food, mattresses, record-players, reinforcements.

At this stage there could be variations. The administration could procure a court injunction ordering the occupiers to cease and desist. It could serve notice that the premises would be vacated within X hours, or those remaining within it would become ex-students and ex-faculty members.

Or the administration could take steps to involve the majority of students who seldom have any part in a demonstration, who often fail to recognize the responsibility which their apathy may have for what the minority do. A Ryerson this majority acted on its own and surged in to support President Donald Mordell.

Beyond what the institution's government may do, it must also be recognized that the larger community has a right and role. Where violence occurs, the matter becomes instantly the business of the police chief, as a simple matter of law.

A procedure for dealing with demonstrations needs to be defined and published now, so that all parties will know where they stand. We have seen on campuses to the south what happens when administrations delay and appease.

7. STUDENT APATHY ENCOURAGED "ALL-PURPOSE RADICALS"

The following Letter to the Editor, written by Margaret Hogan, appeared in the Toronto Globe and Mail *of March 31, 1970.*

I am a student at the University of Toronto with three school-age daughters, and an inclination to ardent feminism.

Given my children and my own feelings and experiences of being discriminated against, I was naturally strongly in favor of the planned March 25 day-care demonstration at the university (reported in the March 26 issue of the *Globe and Mail*), and I joined the demonstrators for a time.

It was a totally frustrating experience. The unspeakable apathy of 99 per cent of the student body, much less sensitive, for instance, than the faculty, lots of whom turned up in the initial stages of the demonstration. The overwhelmingly male administrators with so little sense of "community" that they do not consider nurseries—let alone decent nurseries—as a necessary ingredient and responsibility of any large organization, and who seem incapable of facing any situation until the eleventh hour. And most appalling of all, people with a vested interest in the day-care centre actually letting the hardy, all-purpose campus radicals (who printed all the leaflets) organize, direct and fight even this immediate and important battle for them.

(While all this was going on, a group from my college, St. Michael's, mindful of Holy Week, walked a Way of the Cross around campus—in the opposite direction from Sidney Smith Hall, where the day-care demonstration began.)

To crown the day, there was the CBC late national newscast, making sensational hay out of the whole fiasco—another demonstration for students' rights, they said.

8. DANGEROUS PRECEDENT CREATED

This Letter to the Editor, written by Stefan F. Nowina, appeared in the Toronto Globe and Mail *on April 3, 1970.*

As a student at the University of Toronto, I am deeply concerned by the recent occupation of the university administration building, and the dangerous precedents which were set.

In the demonstration, we saw the use of tactics which have become all too familiar in the United States: the use of women and infants as front-line troops, the mindless epithets of "Fascist" and "pig" applied loosely to anyone who opposed them, and a complete disregard for law.

In the administration's surrender to the demonstrators' demands, there is a tacit recognition of the validity of those tactics. Canadian law makes it clear that agreements reached under threat of violence or force are void, and I feel that the administration should not honor its agreement until new negotiations are opened.

At no point during the occupation were the real issues fully discussed by the student body at large. Heroic rhetoric replaced common sense as the criterion for action. The most basic issue, whether or not the university should function as a welfare organization, was quietly ignored.

Perhaps the student demonstrators won their point, but in the face of the damage they did to student-administration relations, was it worth it?

9. RADICALS HAVE A RIGHT TO BE THERE

This Letter to the Editor by Miss Ruth Lerner, one of the "outside agitators," appeared in the Toronto Globe and Mail *on March 29, 1970.*

I am surprised that the *Globe and Mail* would lower its journalistic standards by including in one of its articles Professor Natalie Davis' statement that the University of Toronto demonstration was handled by people "who have no children and don't intend to." (U. of T. Occupied by Mothers, *Globe and Mail*—March 26.) How did Professor Davis discern that the demonstration leaders who don't have children never intend to? Did she ask them? I am sure that many of the demonstrators do not know themselves whether or not they will have children, for many of them are not married. It is certainly very likely that out of over 300 demonstrators *a few* may have children.

Perhaps this is a disguised "outside agitator" argument. Is Professor Davis implying that those who don't have children in the day-care centre don't have a right to fight for better facilities? Are day-care centre volunteers interfering in someone else's business?

10. UNIVERSITY SHOULD NOT HAVE TO SUPPORT ITS STUDENTS' CHILDREN

Mrs. J. de B. Hunt of Toronto, in a Letter to the Editor which appeared in the Toronto Globe and Mail, April 4, 1970, questioned the right of the demonstrators to demand money from the university.

Why do Professor Smith's students feel that they have an unlimited claim on public funds? When people demand subsidies they invite controls. If no one will accept responsibility for the financial support of the children he has chosen to produce, it will not be long before the State regulates who may have children, and it may decide that those who choose to devote only part of their time to study and part to mothering are entitled to neither children nor studies at the taxpayer's expense.

Attitudes can very easily become polarized and there have been revolutions of the right as well as those of the left. Hitler and Mussolini rose to power through the support of those who saw in them the end to chaos in government. The ordinary taxpaying slob may grow tired of the chaos in the universities. The pictures in the newspapers of the sit-in did not offer much proof of academic distinction or responsibility. If it comes to a choice between subsidies for university day-nurseries, or increased old-age pensions so the destitute aged can buy enough to eat, the choice can only go one way.

11. RADICALS DID NOT TAKE OVER DEMONSTRATION

The following Letter to the Editor by Lorenne Smith, a philosophy professor at University of Toronto, and a member of the day-care centre, appeared in the Toronto Globe and Mail on April 4, 1970.

Ross Munro's recent feature on the day-care centre sit-in at the University of Toronto has much to recommend it, but there are some points which must be clarified (Ending a Sit-In With 'A Minimum of Evil'—April 2).

Contrary to the impression created, it is not, and never was, the case that so-called "vanguard parties" of the "radical left" were not welcome at our feast. Many of the volunteers working at the Campus Community Co-operative Day-Care Centre are members of these groups and, as such, had a perfect right to participate.

Thus, the assumption that the "responsible" people from the day-care centre had trouble controlling these groups is utterly false. There was a steering committee made up of people from the day-care centre which made recommendations to the whole group on all major issues. But many persons on the steering committee were also members of these other groups. Andrew Warnock, the "prominent member of the new left" referred to by Mr.

Munro was, for example, a member of this committee. The recommendations of this committee were then voted on by the whole group and it was on the basis of these votes that action was taken.

At no time, and on no issue was it the case that uniquely day-care centre people found themselves out-voted by other groups. In some cases, there was disagreement, but the disagreements did not fall along any group lines, and on the really important questions there was no significant disagreement at all. If some actions appear militant, it is not because they happened to be the actions of some identifiable "militant" group, but because they were felt by all to be necessary in the circumstances.

It would be idle to deny that there was no danger that the sit-in might escalate. This was, particularly on Thursday, a distinct possibility. But it is not the case that this would have been the work of the "vanguard parties." The group, *as a whole,* was determined that some solution must be found which conceded at least some of our demands. And we regarded our position as a negotiable one. However, had it been impossible to achieve a negotiated settlement, whatever action would have been instituted would have been the result of a group decision.

12. UNIVERSITY PRESIDENT CAPITULATED SAYS POLICE CHIEF

The following news item in the Toronto Star, April 11, 1970, reported the comments of Police Chief Harold Adamson on Bissells' actions.

University of Toronto President Claude Bissell "capitulated" to sit-in demonstrators recently when he could have called police to disperse them, Harold Adamson, who will take over as Metro police chief April 24, said last night.

During a panel discussion on demonstrations at Earlscourt Public School, Adamson said the decision rested with the university.

"President Bissell capitulated," he said. "But if the university board of governors had requested it, the police could have been called because the demonstrators were—in law—trespassers."

Several hundred married students occupied the university's administration building last month, demanding improved day-care facilities. They dispersed only when Bissell promised the money to do the job.

What is meant by?

"the black flag of anarchism"
"Trotskyist"
"pig"
"lackey"
"skilled orchestrators of the parasitic element"

What do you think?

1. The slogan on the walls of the administration building read, "Bust Bissell—Power to the Babies."
   (a) In what way does this slogan appeal to reason? to the emotions?
   (b) Does this slogan accurately represent the alternatives available? Why or why not?
   (c) Explain the popularity and the effect of slogans during times of crisis.

2. (a) What alternatives were open to President Bissell when the sit-in began?
   (b) What position did he choose?
   (c) Do you agree with his choice? Why or why not?

3. (a) Do you agree with Police Chief Harold Adamson who said that Bissell "capitulated" to the demonstrators, instead of calling the police to disperse them?
   (b) Why do you think President Bissell decided not to call the police?

4. The articles on pages 5, and 7 are straight news stories; the articles on pages 9 and 10 are editorials.
   (a) What differences do you detect in the two types of writing?
   (b) What is the aim of a straight news story? of an editorial?
   (c) Do you think these aims have always been kept separate in the articles you have just read?
   (d) Is such separation possible?

The Contemporary Problem

3

How is change precipitated in a democratic society?

This question has become particularly critical today when our society is being rapidly transformed by powerful forces which few understand. Some feel that the results of the changes will be anarchy and chaos, while others feel that society will be revitalized and men liberated from drudgery and oppression.

Your situation will affect your point of view on this subject, and your views on the use of violence. If you were a member of a permanent minority, for example, such as the Indian, how would you go about trying to convince the majority to go along with those changes that would be necessary to better your condition?

In the following readings you will encounter some opinions on violence and social change held by people in different situations and with different points of view.

We have chosen the following problem areas to show some of the conflicting opinions:

1. Youth

2. The Indian

3. The Black

4. The Marxist

5. The Separatist

6. The Poor

7. The Establishment

8. Our Culture and Violence

Youth

Are the youth of today unique in their attitudes and actions in relation to achieving social change? Do they perform a function in this regard which their predecessors never performed before? Are there any common concerns regarding social change and the means of effecting it which young people all share?

It is not our intention to examine the youth rebellion as a whole, but rather to provide an analysis of some of the methods advocated by various youth groups for achieving social change.

Where do you stand?

1. THE STUDENT RADICAL: "WE ARE CREATIVE."

This document is an excerpt from an article by Steven Langdon which appeared in the Toronto Globe and Mail, March 24, 1969. Mr. Langdon was a prominent figure in the Canadian student movement.

Student protest is not a conspiratorial product of outside agitators aligned to the Communist Party. It is a serious attempt to change education to meet the needs and desires of the students involved in it and eventually to change the university to meet the needs of the ordinary men and women of Canada.

It may be hard for some to understand why students temporarily occupy a building. In such cases, real issues are always involved and the public should not jump to hasty anti-student conclusions. They should remember the buildings are, after all, part of the university of which students are a major part, and they should not demand that police take action. They must be tolerant about the conflict which seems to them to be hurting the universities for which their taxes pay.

For students are not trying to destroy these institutions, but to change them greatly and for the better so that the people who come out of them and the people who teach in them will be critical, thinking individuals, creative citizens, persons aware of their social responsibilities to the millions of people in this country.

What do you think?

1. *"Student protest is not a conspiratorial product of outside agitators aligned to the Communist Party."*
   (a) *Why would Langdon make this assertion?*
   (b) *What difficulties might be encountered in proving or disproving this statement?*

2. ". . . the public should not jump to hasty anti-student conclusions."
   (a) Would the public be likely to feel "anti-student" after reading the newspaper accounts of the sit-in described in Part I? Why or why not?

3. In what ways could measures such as the occupation of public buildings lead to the development of "critical, thinking individuals, creative citizens, persons aware of their social responsibilities to the millions of people in this country"?

2. THE STUDENT RADICALS: DO THEIR ACTIONS FORCE US TO THINK?

Adèle Lauzon, the author of this article, is a distinguished journalist and broadcaster. This article first appeared in Liberté *and was translated by Patrick Coleman for* Our Generation, *June 1969. The CEGEPs are a government network of post-secondary academic and technical institutions. Some 40,000 students participated in a general strike against the administration of the CEGEPs, boycotting classes and occupying key administrative offices and buildings.*

With the CEGEP crisis, we witnessed for the first time in Quebec, a radical movement proceed *through action* to a fundamental questioning of society. Up to that point, we had seen either reformist leftists working within the system to correct its defects and improve its functioning, or far left movements which identified "action" with a mere verbal expression of their radical opinions.

The occupiers were told by their elders, "Go back to your business, let the machine function; you can protest in your spare time." In other words, accept the realities of society, even though you can denounce them verbally. This gem of advice sums up the history of our impotence.

To recognize, as has been done, that society can be criticized, and to allow the protesters to speak out if they stay in line otherwise, is to demonstrate our own alienation, our own insensitivity, since it is speech that has made up the principal instrument of our alienation.

Having once conceded verbal freedom, instead of going further we have used what should be a weapon in our struggle as a facade to hide our inaction. Freedom of speech has never been a threat to the system. It has been used to consolidate it by absorbing the energies that should have been used to transform reality.

For most of the activists, the action started by reflection on their daily lives. There was a feeling of boredom, of going to college like machines, of being filled up with knowledge like water in a jug, of being passive. The facts about the job problem and social uneasiness in general added to their usual dissatisfaction. First a feeling of insecurity about their future, and then a realization of the awful organization of society and of fundamental injustice. Injustice, and above all a basic hypocrisy: insecurity and poverty masked by abundance, technology and mass consumption; alienation of the individual and of groups by unknown forces beneath an appearance of freedom. From all this, the young people got a feeling of overall *absurdity*, and the desire to break away from that absurdity in order to live in a less competitive, a less difficult, a less anonymous society—to build a society in which human values would dominate over efficiency and profit.

The CEGEP students' revolt, without being bloody, took on a violent and minority character. The occupiers took over by force. If they had, up to a point, the support of the majority, it is clear that this was not for the real goals of the action—which were not hidden but which were misunderstood. But this type of action with all its surrounding explanations, constituted—and this no one denies—a means of awakening people's consciousness and this is the revolutionary part of the movement, that it led many students to a radical position they would have taken years to think out on their own. The minority forced the majority to reflect and to take a stand, but it did not exercise its violence against the majority. On the contrary, it took upon itself the risks of the action—and indeed, it was eventually isolated.

Must we conclude that the student leaders made a mistake in occupying and proclaiming the occupation to be permanent?

The truth points to the opposite conclusion. The majority was not radical, it was inevitable that the occupation would be temporary. But it lasted long enough to greatly swell the ranks of the revolutionary minority, which will be better prepared for new revolutionary actions which will produce more radicals, and so on. It's sometimes said that repression breeds revolutionaries. I don't believe it. *It is revolutionary action that makes revolutionaries,* whether there is repression or not. *Without revolutionary action* repression creates only repressed people.

What is meant by?

"*reformist leftists*"
"*revolutionary*"

What do you think?

1. *Evaluate the author's criticism of existing society and her appraisal of the activists' attitude towards it.*

2. *Why does the author feel the way she does towards constitutional reform and revolutionary action? Why do you agree or disagree with her?*

3. "*Freedom of speech has never been a threat to the system. It has been used to consolidate it by absorbing the energies that should have been used to transform reality.*"

(a) *What does the author mean by this statement? Why do you agree or disagree with her?*

(b) *If, for the sake of argument, there are circumstances when freedom of speech is considered to be a threat to the system, how might those circumstances be defined today? in your grandfather's time? in Canada? in South Africa?*

4. (a) *What are the implications of the author's contention that "it is revolutionary action that makes revolutionaries"?*

(b) *How could revolutionaries overcome the probable backlash they would receive from the majority?*

3. THE QUIET STUDENT: LOVE, NOT VIOLENCE

In a Letter to the Editor in the Toronto Telegram, *August 14, 1969, Drew Milligan, a Grade IX high school student, responded to a previous Letter to the Editor which had advocated a violent and revolutionary overthrow of today's society.*

On July 17 Bryan Larrabee wrote that today's present society should be overthrown by a violent revolution of the young.

I too believe that the ruling class is sick, since today's society is based chiefly on the Almighty Dollar. All important things such as peace, understanding, love and happiness are placed secondary, except when one's self or family is involved.

Politicians are corrupted by local industries, consequently pollution laws are not enforced. Man is slowly using up, destroying or polluting everything vital to the existence of mankind.

Ever since man evolved from a primitive state into a "civilized" state he has talked of peace and murdered his fellow man at the same breath. Today, a war in Vietnam is being fought. Young men, drafted against their will, are being slaughtered daily while generals, sitting comfortably in their Pentagon offices, inform us that they died for peace. What do warmongering generals know about peace?

It is definitely time for change. A revolution is desired but not the type of revolution which Mr. Larrabee proposes. To fight a revolution would be making the same mistake as is being made in Vietnam today. To fight for peace with violence is as absurd as fighting for violence with peace. Such a revolution is doomed to failure.

If a violent revolution occurred, millions would inevitably be killed or wounded. In the end, the younger generation would probably win but only after years of bloody, senseless killing. After our victory the older generation would have to be oppressed in order to avoid a counter-revolution. The hate between generations would be incredible. Murder, street clashes and assassinations would probably occur, even after the war.

If a government's beginning is violent, it has to continue with violence (e.g. United States and Russia). Since the intention of the revolution would be to obtain love, peace, happiness and a better world, the new government would be considered a failure. Power would have an empty meaning.

Peaceful revolution will take longer, but the end results will be a hundred times more successful.

The younger generation has three choices:

(1) To continue with the present sick and materialistic society.

(2) To fight a revolution of hate, violence and turmoil.

(3) A gradual revolution of peace, love and happiness.

I choose the third solution. What is your choice?

What do you think?

1. (a) What do you think the writer means by "a gradual revolution of peace, love, and happiness"?
   (b) In what ways could such a solution be put into practice in Canada? Why or why not?
   (c) What other choices, if any, are there?

4. REVOLT—IF YOU DIG TO LOB BRICKS

The editor of the Martlet, *a student newspaper at the University of Victoria, on December 8, 1968, expressed his views on whether or not violence itself could change the dehumanizing trend apparent in today's society.*

Organized rebellion isn't necessarily a bad thing. It seldom hurts the rebels' cause, but even less often it is the most effective method of promoting that cause. Most especially is this true when the cause is involvement.

True enough, being part of a mob is a certain kind of involvement. There is a certain amount of fellow-feeling—even if the common feeling is anger and fear. But the polarization of forces pro and con, and the organization of those forces into opposing ranks, is a self-defeating paradox; it prevents involvement with the members of the other side, and that's the most important kind of involvement.

In fact, the involvement which organizations like S.D.U. [*Students for a Democratic University*], C.U.S. [*Canadian Union of Students*], and some others ask, is only a commitment to their cause. If you commit yourself in that fashion, even if the revolution is successful you have changed none of the essentials. You have merely replaced one "status quo" with another, and possibly a more militant and restrictive one. All the power structure, all the impersonalization, all the status-symbol-prestige thing remains in a slightly different form. And the change isn't necessarily an improvement.

The change which must come before the dehumanizing trend can be reversed is not a change that can be wrought by force, by external pressure. People can be taught to relate to each other as individuals, to love each other, but they cannot be pushed into it.

Teaching presumes some incentive to learn. The incentive in this case must be a positive one: loving other people makes visible changes in you, one of them being that it makes you happier. Those around you can see that, and some of them will want to be the kind of person you are. And they will learn from you.

That, then, is the solution. And it is probably the only solution. You have to find out for yourself what love is for you, and then you have to put the knowledge to use.

Lobbing bricks in the name of love is no answer. Unless you love broken glass and bloodshed more than you love people.

What is meant by?

"self-defeating paradox"
"status quo"

What do you think?

1. *Does the author feel that people must change first, or that the system must change first for there to be a genuine social transformation? How does he substantiate his argument?*
2. *"You have to find out for yourself what love is for you, and then you have to put the knowledge to use." What are the strengths and weaknesses of the author's argument?*

5. McGILL STUDENTS CONDEMN RAMPAGE AT SIR GEORGE WILLIAMS

Montreal Gazette, February 22, 1969.

On February 18, 1969, the following petition signed by 4,000 McGill students was presented to the McGill Students' Council:

We, the undersigned, wish to express our desire that the students' society of McGill University condemn the actions of the Sir George Williams University students who encouraged and participated in the destruction of university property. Further, the students' society should move to outlaw students' attempts to bypass the existing constitutional channels in seeking to bring about change within the university.

The petition does not oppose change but does oppose some of the current methods being used to try to instigate change. They feel disruption, coercion, and intimidation are not the ways to introduce reform. The students must use constitutional avenues to evoke change and if they do not approve of the available avenues, then the constitution must be amended.

What do you think?

1. *The students who signed the above petition declared themselves to be in favour of change but opposed to violent revolution.*
   (a) Do you agree with their position? Why or why not?
   (b) Are these individuals part of the majority which becomes increasingly radical, as Mlle Lauzon contends, when revolutionary activities increase? Support your answer.

6. VIOLENCE IS PART OF THE CANADIAN WAY OF LIFE

This article from the University of Waterloo student newspaper Chevron of April 14, 1969 was written by Leo Johnson, a professor of history at the university.

When Canadian historians compare Canada to the United States, they unanimously agree that one fundamental difference between the two peoples is the non-violent nature of Canadians in contrast to the crime-ridden, six-gun toting, negro-lynching Americans.

Thus when a computer was smashed and a building damaged during anti-racism protests at Sir George Williams University, Canadian leaders, such as John Diefenbaker, react in shock and anger to this "uncanadian" resort to "mob rule."

"Because Canadians are non-violent people," they concluded, "such violence must have been inspired and carried out by Communists, Marxists, or other paid agitators."

Yet further investigation by police has demonstrated that no such "foreign" (except for the presence of a number of black, foreign-born students) inspiration was present.

Why then did the press and authorities claim that "Communists" and "foreigners" were responsible? A further examination of Canadian history is necessary before any answer can be given.

Is Canada a "non-violent" country. Every labour union member who has faced police-protected strike-breakers, every Canadian Indian who has to break through the barriers of legal discrimination, every French

Canadian who has attempted to exercise his inherited language and cultural rights, knows that violence and repression exist in Canada.

But the authorities who claimed that the result of the protest at Sir George Williams was "uncanadian" were right in one respect at least— Canadian workers and Canadian minorities (including students) have seldom protested against discrimination and oppression in a violent manner. It has been the "authorities"—government, business and civic leaders—who are most often responsible for violence when it occurs.

Moreover, when these authorities declare that extra-parliamentary protests (that is, demonstrations, marches and strikes) are unconstitutional or uncanadian, their leaders cynically neglect to point out that the chief offender against the ideals of the British Constitution in Canada has been the government itself.

This is not to say that such authority-directed violence is necessarily illegal. If anything the opposite is true in Canada. As John Porter pointed out in his book, *The Vertical Mosaic*, a strong stable elite controls the Canadian government, civil service, and judicial system.

The key to this control, of course, is money.

Since both the Liberal and Progressive Conservative parties are dependent upon big business for funds to get into office and remain there, these parties must pass laws satisfactory to their financial backers or be removed from power.

This control, however, does not end with an ability to pour money into election campaigns. Since the elite owns the newspapers and controls the radio and television stations, . . . it can and does distort the news to serve its own selfish ends.

The importance of this control of the government and news media cannot be too strongly stressed. Since the news media shape public opinion, and since our source of information is the media, by concentrated propaganda the public can be persuaded to demand laws which work against its best interest, and destroy its rights and liberties.

What do you think?

1. *"Violence is part of the Canadian way of life."* Do you agree? Why or why not?

2. *"Canadian workers and Canadian minorities (including students) have seldom protested against discrimination and oppression in a violent manner."*
    (a) *Is this true? Why?*
    (b) *Do you feel that there is "discrimination and oppression" in Canada to the degree that violent action is warranted?*

3. *"It has been the 'authorities'—government, business and civic leaders—who are most often responsible for violence when it occurs."*
    (a) *How can this be true?*

(b) What examples of violent activity can be cited to prove this point-of-view?

4. *". . . since our source of information is the media, by concentrated propaganda the public can demand laws which work against its best interest. . . ." Discuss.*

7. CONFRONTATION AT RYERSON POLYTECHNICAL INSTITUTE: STUDENTS SQUASH SIT-IN

The Toronto Telegram, *April 2, 1970, described a split in opinion within the student body over a sit-in at Ryerson Polytechnical Institute.*

A confrontation between engineering and art students ended an all-night sit-in at Ryerson Polytechnical Institute's administration building today.

A group of about 100 engineering students gathered where the occupation by about 100 arts students was taking place and demanded that the protesters leave, saying that they didn't represent the majority of the student body.

Ryerson students yesterday protested faculty hiring and firing procedures. The engineers said that students had no right to criticize the administration over the matter.

A mechanical engineering student said: "We are here to learn, not to dictate who will be hired and fired at this institution."

The art students claimed during a loud shouting match that the engineers' only concern is getting a job when they graduate. They said they aren't interested in improving the school.

The engineers said that when the vote was taken last night to stage the sit-in, only a small group of students were present.

They said that they were tired of a few arts and business students speaking on their behalf. They added that the rift at the sit-in was simply an indication of antagonism between the arts and engineering groups that has been growing for some time.

The students were to present their final demands to Ryerson President Donald Mordell at 11 a.m. but the engineers prevented this.

The engineers said they were pleased with the way Mr. Mordell is carrying on his duties.

Mr. Mordell promised in writing to speed the process by which teachers can appeal a decision to deny them tenure.

When a teacher is granted tenure he cannot be fired except for gross negligence or misconduct.

The dispute began when Ryerson failed to offer five English department teachers permanent contracts after their two-year probationary contracts had expired.

The five—Mrs. A. R. Kaufman, Kay E. Armatage, Alison Acker, Sally Bird and Christopher Dade—have launched appeals under existing grievance procedures.

About 100 Ryerson Polytechnical Institute students staged an all-night sit-in in the administration building yesterday to protest faculty hiring and firing procedures.

The demonstration was to last until 11 a.m. today when final demands were to be presented to President Donald Mordell. The demonstration began when students shouted him down.

The students originally demanded the immediate reinstatement of the five teachers and any others who had been denied tenure since January 1.

What do you think?

1. *In their education the arts students and the engineering students appeared to be seeking different goals. How are their goals different, and how might they be reconciled, if at all?*

8. STUDENT REVOLUTION: THE MARXIST APPROACH

This article is taken from The Revolutionary Party, Students, and Worker-Student Alliance, *a tract published by the Canadian Party of Labour, a militant left-wing group based in Toronto.*

Militant students have come to see that education is part of the "system" and that you cannot change a part of the system without changing the whole. However this realization completely alters the boundaries of a student movement, which will remain the empty abstraction it is, unless it is given real class content. For if what is wrong with the educational system is capitalist society, then it must be apparent that the fundamental social force which will make the socialist revolution and thereby liberate both workers and students is the working class. Moreover, this realization must be more than simply acknowledged and then forgotten in the rush to build a student movement. This realization must infuse every activity of the student move-ment—every leaflet, speech, action and organization. *Only if the student movement comes to see itself as the representative of the working class in the sphere of education will it be able to locate those areas of education which really oppress students and are vital to the survival of capitalism.*

Only if it fights for the interests of the workers in the sphere of education will it win the support of workers. Given the limited sociological base of students and the structural limitations which capitalist society imposes upon educational change, it is clear that students will *not be able to change even education unless they have the support of the working class.*

This means that the construction of a Worker-Student Alliance is a major priority of a revolutionary student movement. Militant rank and file students must struggle with workers in trade unions and general political struggles in order that they become aware of the strength of proletarian culture and action. If students are to see themselves as representative of the working class in the sphere of education, then the anti-working class attitudes and prejudices which education inculcates must be effaced. Attitudes such as these are not willed away but are removed in the course of revolutionary practice. This practice is the Worker-Student alliance.

Political Line:

Struggle:

—Against the bourgeois content of education—the masquerade in which ideology becomes "knowledge."

—Against the system of grades and competitive exams—the means by which bourgeois values are inculcated and the children of Canadian workers are excluded from higher education.

—Against the use of the education system to deprive workers of a social education.

—Against the use of the university resources and its ideologues [*sic*] to attempt to mystify the masses and increase the exploitation of workers.

Struggle:

—For scientific socialism—the ideology of the proletariat.

—For an educational system which serves the interests of Workers.

—For a Worker-Student Alliance.

—For A SOCIALIST CANADA.

What do you think?

1. *What does the author mean by the terms "bourgeois" and "proletariat"? In what way would these differ from your definition of middle class and working class?*
2. *(a) When might the government consider this document a threat?*
   (b) When, and with what effect, has the government banned this type of document?
   (c) What is your opinion on the banning of inflammatory material?

9. STUDENT SATIRE: "LEAVE ADMINISTRATION ALONE"

This editorial is from the Cord Weekly *of November 28, 1968. The* Cord *is a student newspaper at the Lutheran University of Waterloo.*

Students have no right to challenge the right of the university administration in the field of university affairs. It is not their place.

The job of the student at university is to be taught and to study. We think he has no business meddling in the mature world of the administrator since he doesn't have the ability nor the intelligence to run in the world of the adult.

In the world of the adult, the student must realize that he does not have the training to deal with such things as education, administration, and monies.

After university the graduate has the training to enter the adult society and help society prosper. His training at university is priceless and essential. If the radical student spent more time in the classroom and at his desk, he would realize that his training is the most important product and the administration and faculty do know best.

It is a fact that the university curriculum is not as structured as it was in days past. This causes such groups as the Students for a Democratic Society to form and underhandedly operate to ruin the system. If more compulsory courses were made and more time required in the classroom, students wouldn't have time to complain. Besides, if this time was spent, students would easily recognize that the system is a great benefit.

It is up to the faculty and the administration to clamp down on the student movements and force them to see the folly of their ways. If there were more rules and less confrontation with the faculty and the administration, the students would see that nothing could be better than what they have now.

It is time for the students to stop worrying and crying and start to think about what is theirs, like dances, Winter Carnival, Students Council, skiing, and having fun. These things were made for the student, not administration, education systems, faculty, and least of all involvement.

What do you think?

  1. *Why do you think the author of this article is not stating his opinion seriously?*

10.   HELP STOP CAMPUS RIOTS

The Edmund Burke Society, an extreme right-wing group which consists mainly of young people, sponsored an advertisement which appeared in the February 13, 1969 edition of the Toronto Globe and Mail.

HELP STOP CAMPUS RIOTS!

Last Wednesday, scuffling, shouting members of the Toronto Student Movement broke up a public lecture by Clark Kerr. The intolerance of these neo-Red Guards is in contrast to their constant harangues for "liberation." They disgrace themselves and our tax-supported university. One of their leaders, Andy Wernick, has written: "I am asking you to spend the next three or four years systematically blowing the campus apart."

This call to revolution typifies a trend of left-wing violence and disruption in our city. Last October 26th, thirty-four members of the Canadians for the National Liberation Front and other groups of self-styled American "exiles," draft-dodgers, and deserters were arrested for obstruction and other infractions of the laws of our country. They call our Toronto police "pigs"; seek to demolish our free enterprise system; and agitate to reduce our universities to anarchy.

Isn't it time we stopped subsidizing those who want to riot their way through college? Isn't it time to tighten our immigration laws against revolutionaries and deserters from our ally's army? We think so!

We strongly urge you to write your M.P. and M.P.P. and give us your support.

What is meant by?

"neo-Red Guards"

What do you think?

1. (a) *Based upon this advertisement alone, how would you describe the Edmund Burke Society?*
   (b) *To what extent do you agree or disagree with what they have to say?*
2. *To what groups in society do you think the Edmund Burke message might appeal? Why?*

11.   IRVING LAYTON: FOR MY STUDENT MILITANTS

Irving Layton is one of Canada's foremost poets. "For My Student Militants" is from Nail Polish *(Toronto: McClelland and Stewart, 1971).*

history
is not
                histrionics
or hysteria: it is the strict
verdict
                when you are safe and quiet
in your graves
                your children
and grandchildren's skeletons
crumbling beside you
it is reality
                as you could never
see it: its uncompromising purity
no longer raddles your sanity

nor does its intense white light
blind you
                    as it passes over
the arrogance of militant lies
like the sweep of a flashlight
                    in a cellar
or the long electric finger
from the lighthouse tower
                    over heaving waters
listen:
history is reality
dressed for the occasion;
it is the Messiah
                    we all pray for
and reject

now your arms silently at your side
and your mouths stilled forever
you may receive its judgment
There is no appeal
children
for the round bound eye of the camera
is not the eye with which God sees you

What do you think?

1. What is Layton's message for student militants?
2. Under what circumstances is poetry an effective vehicle for the communication of ideas?

The Indian

The white man has regarded the Indian in a variety of ways. He has been seen as a "noble savage" or as a cruel, treacherous and barbarous villain. He was often treated as a soul to save—or as a nuisance to be exterminated. During the Seven Years War, he was treated as an ally; by the middle of the nineteenth century he had become the ward of the federal government.

How have these attitudes of the white man affected the Indian's attitudes and actions in relation to protest, violence, and social change? How does his position as a member of an oppressed and depressed minority affect these attitudes? Do all Indians agree? See if you agree with any of the views, held by Indians, which you will encounter in the following readings.

1. AN INDIAN MODERATE: HAROLD CARDINAL

Mr. Cardinal is considered one of the most prominent Indian spokes-men in Canada. He was the inspiration behind "The Red Paper," the Indian counter proposal to the Trudeau Government's 1968 "White Paper" on Indians. Cardinal has also written The Unjust Society, *a highly critical examination of the treatment Indians have received. The following news item from the Calgary* Herald *of November 4, 1968, is a description of Mr. Cardinal and his views on violence.*

He has spoken at political conventions, national forums and on national television.

People are listening to him. At a recent conference in Toronto, he received a five-minute standing ovation from an audience of 500 whites.

But more importantly, Indians are listening to him and supporting him.

The Indian membership in IAA [Indian Association of Alberta] has risen from 150 to 10,000 during the four months Mr. Cardinal has been president.

*   *   *   *   *

"There's no question that he has the support of Indians throughout the province," commented an Indian leader in Calgary.

His father was a long-time and respected leader of Alberta Indians, and Harold is following in his shoes with the added energy that comes from youth and education.

Mr. Cardinal has completed high school and two years of university. The Department of Indian Affairs financed his education, as is the case with most young Indians who want to continue their education.

"But don't let me hear anyone say we get free education. We paid a high price for any education we get. We gave title to this land and its resources. We also gave up our freedom," the 23-year old asserts.

Mr. Cardinal says he is not a radical.

"The statements I make are really very moderate in view of what has happened to Indians in the past 100 years. My views seem radical because Canadians haven't heard many radical statements from Indians in the past," he explains.

Far from being a radical, Mr. Cardinal says he is working to prevent an upsurge of violence in Alberta.

*   *   *   *   *

"What do we do if we don't get what we want? When people are backed into a corner, what can they do? Sometimes it's difficult for whites to realize the urgency of the situation. I'm rather afraid of what might happen—especially when you see what the Negroes are doing in the United States.

"That's why people like me are involved at this time—to prevent a Watts in Canada. We must work to avoid violence."

* * * * *

Since becoming president, he has increased Indian membership in the IAA one-hundred-fold. The IAA has played an active role in organizing this province's Indians to make their requests and demands effectively.
to make their requests and demands effectively.

Mr. Cardinal interrupted a university course to work with his people here, because the situation is urgent, he said.

Although he does not use the possibility of violence as a threat to get what he wants, he does not hesitate to point out that separatists in Quebec received little public attention for their grievances "until they had popped a couple of bombs in mail-boxes."

What do you think?

1. Harold Cardinal has "spoken at political conventions, national forums, and on national television" and has "received a five-minute standing ovation from an audience of five hundred whites." Why has he received such attention?

2. Mr. Cardinal points out that Indians have said very little during the past 100 years. Is he correct? If so, can you explain this fact?

3. Harold Cardinal asserts that little public attention was paid to the Quebec separatists until some bombs were exploded.
   (a) How would you reply to him?
   (b) Does the fact that terrorist acts in Quebec are publicized increase the likelihood that other groups, such as the Indians, will take violent action in the future?

2. INDIAN RESERVATION: CAUGHNAWAGA

A. M. Klein is a Canadian poet and author. Caughnawaga is located outside Montreal, where Klein spent his childhood. This poem is from Klein's The Rocking Chair and Other Poems *(Toronto: McGraw-Hill Ryerson, 1948).*

Where are the braves, the faces like autumn fruit,
Who stared at the child from the coloured frontispiece?
And the monosyllabic chief who spoke with his throat?
Where are the tribes, the feathered bestiaries?—
Rank Aesop's animals, erect and red,
with fur on their names to make all living things kin—
Chief Running Deer, Black Bear, Old Buffalo Head?

Childhood, that wished me Indian, hoped that
one afterschool I'd leave the classroom chalk,

the varnish smell, the watered dust of the street
to join the clean old outdoors and the Iroquois track.
childhood; but always—as on a calendar,—
there stood that chief, with arms akimbo, waiting
the runaway mascot paddling to his shore.

With what strange moccasin stealth that scene is changed!
With French names, without paint, in overalls,
their bronze, like the nobility expunged,—
the men. Beneath their alimentary shawls
sit like black tents their squaws; while for the tourist's
brown pennies scattered at the old churchdoor
the ragged papooses jump, and bite the dust.

Their past is sold in a shop: The beaded shoes,
the sweetgrass basket, the curio Indian,
burnt wood and gaudy cloth and inch-canoes—
trophies and scalpings for a traveller's den.
Sometimes, it's true, they dance, but for a bribe;
after a deal don the bedraggled feather
and welcome a white major to the tribe.

This is a grassy ghetto, and no home.
And these are fauna in a museum kept.
The better hunters have prevailed. The game,
losing its blood, now makes these grounds its crypt.
The animals pale, the shine of the fur is lost,
bleached are their living bones. About them waver
as though a mist, the pious prosperous ghosts.

What do you think?

1. (a) What feelings are present in this poem?
   (b) How do you react to the poem?
2. What relationship do you see this poem and Miss Horn's views?

3.   AN INDIAN RADICAL: KAHN-TINETA HORN

Kahn-Tineta Horn, an Iroquois Indian from the Caughnawaga Reserve who has become noted for her controversial statements on the Indian situation, was interviewed during a short visit to New Brunswick. The following article is from the St. John Telegraph-Journal, October 23, 1968.

"We are the landlords . . . we don't want anything to do with our tenants. We own this land—you pay the rent."

Kahn-Tineta Horn, the 26-year old raven-haired Iroquois beauty who has been more controversial than the pill, was in Fredericton Tuesday to address the University of New Brunswick community at a teach-in sponsored by the Student Christian Movement.

She was interviewed during her one-day visit to the province, her first in two years.

Miss Horn, a graduate of Sir George Williams University of Montreal, said the Indian in North America is demanding rights accorded in early treaties as well as basic aboriginal claims to the land. She said she expects this demand to be realized.

Following a dispute last year with the National Indian Council, Miss Horn was fired from her posts as chairman of the Indian Centennial Committee and Indian Princess of Canada—but has remained a focal point in North American Indian affairs.

"I have no position, I don't want any position. All I am is a crusader, bringing the Gospel to the infidels. I ask for no power and I am completely independent," she said.

Kahn-Tineta Horn, although just 26, has had a checkered career that spans a long period of controversy.

Proud and arrogant, she lives in a small house on the Caughnawaga Reserve near Montreal, a member of the Six Nations Iroquois Confederacy.

Miss Horn, in some of her more recent escapades, has been convicted for assaulting a Toronto newspaper reporter; brought a dead rat into a meeting of the Indian Affairs Department, and confronted Reverend Ralph Abernathy at Washington, for trying to associate Indians with the Negro movement.

But she says she is not militant, and does not propose a militant attack on the problems facing her people. She says the Indians in Canada would be "stupid" if they tried to defeat 20 million "intruders".

Last week, in Montreal, Miss Horn had a run-in with Black Power advocate Stokely Carmichael, and the two matched words. Carmichael said he would "co-operate" with the "oppressed" Indians.

Miss Horn does not want anything to do with the Negro issues and does not think her people are oppressed. She defines oppressed as being defeated and demoralized, and she thinks her people do not fit in that category.

During the interview she expressed a wide range of philosophies. Among these, she said the Indian was "superior" to all other races. She said she believes in apartheid—racial discrimination. . . . "We don't want our Indian blood contaminated."

Miss Horn said the government should make it illegal for whites to marry Indians, "in order to stop the Whites from draining our finest people from the reserves."

The fiery maiden does not discriminate between Whites, Blacks or Yellows. . . . she thinks of them as equal in their inferiority.

Thus the lack of association with the Black movements. "Everybody who is mad at the Negroes will be mad at us. We don't need any more enemies," Miss Horn said, "we don't care about anybody else, they can pay their rent too."

She calls welfare, education, medical care and Indian allowances as rent being presently paid to the aboriginal race, but says it is not near enough.

She was asked if her radical demonstrations, such as the now famous incident of the rats, have accomplished anything.

"This brought to public attention, the exploitation taking place on the reserve in Canada," she replied.

The incident occurred in September. Miss Horn, and a few followers, in order to protest the use of their reserve—Caughnawaga—being used "as a $2-million garbage dumps which was breeding rats to infest the homes of the residents," brought one dead and many live rats to Ottawa.

Walking in on the deputy minister of Indian Affairs and high-ranking officials, Miss Horn threw the maggot-ridden dead rat on the conference table, but her followers, lost control of the live rats and they ran wild.

Miss Horn lives a Utopian dream—she dreams of a society which recognizes the Indian as master, or landlord, with other inferior people paying rent.

And she claims she speaks the thoughts of most of Canada's Indians. She was asked why she always uses the pronoun "we" instead of "I". "I" am sure that all the Indians agree with every word I say, but I'm a free Indian," she said.

The controversial spokesman had high praise for the leader of New Brunswick Indians, Andrew Nicholas. "Andrew Nicholas is a very, very fine leader . . . one of the great ones that are emerging," Miss Horn said.

She says these leaders are now going to band together to realize the land rights of the Canadian Indians. But she would not say how, when or in what form this revolution will take place . . . she would not allow her dream to be penetrated.

"Mind your own business . . . you wait for our next move," she continually replied to probing questions.

Kahn-Tineta Horn is a very disturbing young lady.

What do you think?

1. "We own this land!" Both Miss Horn and Mr. Cardinal (in the previous reading) make this assertion. On what basis, and for what purpose do you think it was made?

2. "This [Miss Horn's demonstrations] brought to public attention the exploitation taking place on one reserve in Canada." Do you think Miss Horn is accurate in estimating the effect of her actions?

3. "I am sure that all Indians agree with every word I say."
   (a) What evidence is there in the article to support or contradict Miss Horn's statement?
   (b) Why do you agree or disagree with her views?

4. "THE TIME FOR SINGING IS PAST": AN INDIAN DEMONSTRATION

The central figure in this article, which appeared in Weekend Magazine, *April 19, 1969, is Mike Mitchell, a young Indian. The story concerns the actions of Mike and a group of Indians over the abrogation by federal legislation of certain Indian treaty rights dating back to 1794.*

"You've come at a good time," he said, as we approached the longhouse, which is on the U.S. side of the border. (The Indians had been seething ever since the government started to levy duties against personal goods his people purchased in the United States and brought into Canada. The Mohawks claim the Jay Treaty of 1794 assures their exemption from duties but the Supreme Court of Canada has held that new federal legislation, namely, the Migratory Birds Convention Act and Customs Act have, in effect, cancelled these basic Indian rights. When the Customs officers clamped down on them last November, the Indians blockaded the Seaway International Bridge and over 40 of them ended up in jail on charges of obstructing the police.)

"Indians are different," Mike is saying. "We aren't like white people. We don't want to chase the dollars the way you do. We don't want to cut down all the trees for a profit. We want to be able to take off in the summer when it's nice out and take our kids and say, 'Look how beautiful this land is.' And go fishing. *You* don't do that until you have a lot of money. But it's too late then. You're old by then. When we do it you say we're lazy.

"A lot of white people wonder why we want special status but they forget what we gave up. Our forefathers earned these rights and I want to make sure they aren't lost. I can work here or anywhere. For me that border isn't there. I want my kids to be able to work anywhere too, because they're Indians. But every year they take away a little more. The Seaway chopped up our lands. They came and took our lands and when we said, "How much will we get?' they said, 'We'll work something out.' But they didn't take the white lands, oh no, that was too expensive. They would never take the white man's land when they could get ours—after all ours couldn't cost much, there was nothing on it but trees. But we like those trees.

*   *   *   *   *

"They've polluted our air and our water. Our trees are rotting and the cows die and you say *we* were the savages. You still try to get us to give up our culture and our customs. Well I'm going to tell you—on Saturday night the longhouse is filled with the young ones and they are all dancing the dances of their people. We will not give up our Indian ways."

He parked in front of the longhouse. We went in.

Mike walked around the hall, greeting people, happy that many came. The women made coffee. You wonder what time the meeting will get started. Who will be the chairman; will there be an agenda?

Standing Arrow gets up and takes off his hat and starts talking in the Mohawk dialect. You had met him the night before. He had told you the Canadian government was riddled with gangsters—"Why else would they treat the Indians this way?"

"We're fed up," he had said as we sat at Mike's kitchen table. "I'm tired of asking. Look at the blacks, eh? They sat in and they got beat up. They marched and they put the dogs on them. Then they started to burn and only then did the white man start to listen, eh? He said, 'Look, man, these people are hurting us. They are costing us money. We'd better do something about this before we lose any more money.' That's the way I feel now. I can sit up there on the bridge all day long and sing hymns until I'm blue in the face and hold a protest sign and people are going to drive by and look at me and say, 'Look at the crazy Indian.' The time for singing is past."

But right now Standing Arrow is asking the Great Spirit to guide them tonight as they make their plans. You believe the meeting is under way. Standing Arrow finishes, sits down. But nothing happens.

And then a young man gets up and in English warns the people that they should not waste their time fighting the white man for pennies—he was referring to the Customs duties—but should fight whitey on the big stuff. "He's after your land, fight him on that." (He was referring to the fact that the City of Cornwall had annexed Cornwall Island, without the Indians ever knowing it. Cornwall Island is part of the St. Regis reserve and is where most of the 3,000 Mohawks live on the Canadian side of the Canadian-U.S. border. Another 3,000-odd Mohawks live on the American side.)

Somebody else is up and telling the people that there will be a big meeting the next day at 9 a.m. And many Indians from other reserves from both sides of the border will be here.

*   *   *   *   *

Saturday was a cold but sunny day and the longhouse looked good in the sun, set amongst the cedars. Mad Bear Anderson arrived around 10 a.m. and the word got around fast. . . . Mad Bear was representing the Tuscarora Indians from Niagara Falls, New York.

*   *   *   *   *

We all went into the longhouse where it was warm and after a little while one of the old chiefs got up and with his hat in his hand, and his eyes on the floor, he reminded the gathering that the Great Spirit wanted them to act in peace . . . to act like Indians.

They must make plans but they must remember they were Indians. They were a peaceful people. They must make peaceful plans.

After a long coffee break, Mad Bear was out in the middle of the floor.

He told them the time for begging and pleading was done. The Indians had sat back too long.

People all over the world were getting their freedom. Now it was the Indian's turn.

Once they were proud and strong. The prophecy said that when they came back they would be even stronger than before.

The white man said they were savages. Their religion was no good. Their customs were no good. Their government was no good. Nothing that was Indian was any good.

"But the white man lied. And he made a fool of you," Mad Bear told them.

"You went to Ottawa and they laughed at you. They asked you pertinent legal questions and you couldn't answer. They were the specialists, these white people. They were lawyers and they laughed at you."

He said the time had come for the Indian to take his case to an international court. A world court, because the Indian could neither trust the Canadian nor the American governments. And with the sweat running down his nose, Mad Bear told them it was good to be back with his Indian brothers in Akwasasne (the Indian word for the St. Regis reserve, which means Land Where The Partridge Drums).

Another lull. Mumbling and conversation. They know something must be done. They know they have to make a stand. But what? How?

Mike is up.

He points to the old ones.

"You are the wise ones. And you went to Ottawa and then you came back and said we fixed it up. In a little while it might get better, you said. But it never got better. They keep taking away our lands. They annexed Cornwall Island. Well, Cornwall Island doesn't belong to Cornwall or Canada or Ontario or to the United States. It belongs to us. O.K. You made a demonstration. But what did you do after that? Nothing. I went to Ottawa and someone said the trouble with the Indian is that he cries and wails for a little while and then he stops. We can't stop any more. We have to keep it up. We can't go to Ottawa any more. Ottawa must come to us. But they don't. What do we have to do to get them to listen? Blow up the bridges? Kill the Customs officers? We don't want to do that."

Peter Burns, a foreman with a crew of cat-footed Mohawk steelworkers, breaks in: "So what are we going to do, Mike, just take it? Either we do something or we go home, eh? I'm tired of sitting here."

Mike starts up again: "Today the sun shines. It is a good day. Let's do something today. Let's demonstrate again. Let's show Ottawa that we are serious. Let's test them on the Jay Treaty. Let's take some food and clothing across. There are people who need it in Canada. Indian people. In Saskatchewan, where some Indians still live in teepees and the old ones have long hair. They need food. I know, I saw them. I went there."

"And let's put up a sign," somebody says. . . .

Somebody is sent out to buy a paint brush and paint. They find somebody to do the sign-painting. They agree on the wording. But their march forward moves slowly. Theirs is not a well-oiled political machine. The white man's way is not their way. They are a peaceful people and they don't want to go to jail. But they know they must do *something*.

* * * * *

Sunday is another beautiful day and there are more people in the longhouse—and more nerve. Today they are *really* going to do something . . .

They paint some signs: "INDIAN ACT STINKS"

They decide to demonstrate again at the Canadian Customs office. They pile into their cars and head for the border, with a truck loaded down with food and clothing for the "starving" Indians of Saskatchewan.

The Customs officers tell them they must pay duty on the food.

"But this food is for the starving Indians in Canada," they say. Sorry, say the guards. Either the duty is paid or they confiscate the food.

"What are we going to do?" asks Mike. "They want us to pay duty. Do you want to pay?"

"And they shout, "No.""

The guards take away the food.

What are they going to do now?

"We'll stay here till they come down from Ottawa," somebody says. But it is cold out and that could mean a long wait.

A young girl drives a station wagon across the road, blocks the traffic lane, shuts the ignition off and gets out.

A nervous RCMP officer comes out and asks: "Is this a blockade?" She says it is.

But the policeman doesn't want trouble. He'll call his boss and his boss will call his boss and somebody will call Ottawa and maybe the calls will work they way up the bureaucratic ladder until someone, goddammit, decides to do something.

After a while they move the station wagon and block the Seaway International Bridge with human bodies.

And then an old Indian lady is hit by a car. The mood gets nastier. Some youths show up with big sticks. A car tries to run the blockade; some Indian kids get bumped. The Indians are furious. They jump in a car, with Peter Burns in the lead and chase the blockade runners. Mike Mitchell chases them too in a second car. He said he was not the leader but when he left there was no one else to take his place.

*　*　*　*　*

That afternoon, after the blockade was removed, about 200 Mohawks met in an abandoned Customs house with John G. McGilp, regional director of Indian Affairs for Ontario.

They asked him many questions and Mr. McGilp, a specialist in these matters, had the answers. But he didn't have any answers that satisfied the Mohawks. He had white answers to Indian questions and today that wasn't good enough.

Mike got up and talked about all those white millionaires in Montreal and Toronto and New York who never went fishing until they were too old to enjoy it.

And he recalled how Indian Affairs Minister Jean Chretien once said he understood the Indians because he too was a members of a minority group—the French Canadians.

"Well, if it is so much the same," said Mike, "may be we should have a Department of French Affairs, eh? And maybe the minister of that department should be an Indian, eh?"

The crowd loved that.

Mr. McGilp reminded them that the Indian Act was originally designed as a protective device.

But they didn't need that protection any more. They had learned the white man's language. They were educated now. They couldn't be fooled any more.

"We want to run our own show," Mike said. "Indian style."

And Tom Porter got up and asked: "What is the proper way, the legal way, sir, to get Indian Affairs the hell off our land." And then he renounced his Canadian citizenship. "I am a citizen of the Six Nations Confederacy and I'll die that way." And they cheered him.

And Mr. McGilp said: "Surely nobody here would seriously wish to give up their Canadian citizenship . . ."

And Mike and Peter Burns and Standing Arrow and Tom Porter and about 200 other North American Indians laughed and laughed and laughed . . .

What do you think?

1. (a) What did the Indians gain by their demonstration?
   (b) What alternatives for action were possible besides a demonstration? Why were they rejected?
2. Before the demonstration the Indians said, "Let's demonstrate again. Let's show Ottawa we're serious." After the demonstration one of the Indians said, "I am a citizen of the Six Nations Confederacy and I'll die that way."

(a) What change occurred in the Indians' attitude because of the demonstration? Why?

(b) How do your findings substantiate or not substantiate Adèle Lauzon's thesis that revolutionary action makes revolutionaries? Why or why not?

The Black Canadian

There seems to be agreement amongst all blacks, whether moderate or militant, that Canada is not the haven from racial discrimination that many Canadians believe their country to be. With the recent influx of West Indians in particular, the racial issue, which has always existed, may become very serious. Blacks are responding to this developing situation in many different ways.

It is not the intention of this section to attempt a close analysis of the problems faced by black people in Canada, but rather to concentrate on their attitudes towards achieving those changes which would relieve these problems.

1. IN SEARCH OF A SENSE OF COMMUNITY

According to this article from Time, *April 6, 1970, one of the problems that Canadian blacks face in their attempts to combat racial discrimination is the apparent failure so far to achieve a sense of community.*

Far better to breathe Canadian air
Where all are free and well,
Than live in slavery's atmosphere
And wear the chains of hell.

To the runaway slave who wrote those optimistic lines in the 1850s, Canada must have seemed the sort of sanctuary many Canadians still imagine it to be—a society that, in contrast to the U.S., is unfettered by the chains of racial injustice. In the mirror image of today's headlines, the contrast has become blurred. The young Trinidadians who stoned Canadian banks in a recent march through Port of Spain's business district were, in their own minds, demonstrating against an exploitive, racist society, almost as if Canada had become a kind of surrogate for the American South.

The demonstration was inspired by the Montreal trial of the Trinidad Ten, on charges of conspiracy in the sacking of Sir George Williams University's computer center a year ago. As in the case of the Chicago conspiracy trial, the defendants insisted that it was really society itself on trial.

They also seemed convinced that they effectively won a conviction. Said Rosie Douglas, 28, a leader of the Sir George blacks: "We thought about disrupting the trial, but we found we already had the enemy cornered—we exposed Canadian society in the world's eyes as racist."

A complacent man could perhaps write off such charges as just another example of the bitter hyperbole of the times. Yet no one would have to be pressed to concede that all is not well in what, after 100 years, is still not a Just Society in the treatment of its minorities—black, yellow or red. In the case of the black minority, history suggests that Canadians have never had much to feel complacent about.

* * * * *

Today, there are probably 80,000 blacks in Canada (the figure is imprecise, since the Canadian census has not taken note of color since 1961). Yet there is remarkably little sense of a black Canadian community, partly because its members are geographically dispersed, partly because of the divisions between generations as well as between native Canadian blacks and immigrant West Indians whose number is steadily growing. . . .

* * * * *

The relative absence of a sense of black community has left Canadian black people ill-equipped to cope with discrimination that is often more subtle than overt. The distinctive character of white discrimination in Canada has always struck newcomers forcefully. Boubacar Koné, a Senegalese journalist who arrived in Montreal in 1967, says it is like "guerrilla warfare. It's always lurking there in the background. You can't see it and it strikes you when you least expect it. It's subtle." Says Melbourne Thompson, a social science lecturer at Ryerson Polytechnical Institute and president of the Jamaican-Canadian Association: "Toronto is noted for pockets of bigotry rather than open discrimination. There are still literally hundreds of blacks in Toronto unable to use their education and training because they cannot find middle management positions." For many West Indian job applicants, the brushoff is delivered in the form of the apparently innocuous question: "Have you any Canadian experience?" Translation: "No blacks need apply."

In this context, it was hardly surprising that the turmoil at Montreal's Sir George Williams University last year profoundly stirred the consciousness of black Canadians as no single focus ever had before.

* * * * *

The sense of unity that the Sir George affair inspired failed, nonetheless, to survive a conference of black community groups which met in Toronto last October to form a national coalition. The trouble started when a firebrand Montreal caucus, led by Rosie Douglas, the son of a well-to-do legislator on the Island of Dominica, and Kennedy Fredrick of Grenada, attacked the other leaders for being "Oreo cookies"—black outside, white inside. The meeting broke up amid flying elbows and chairs. Locked behind guarded doors, a moderate caucus did manage to form a middle-of-the-road National Black Coalition of 27 organizations. But the overwhelming legacy is one of frustration. For Clarence S. Bayne, a commerce professor at Sir George Williams, the exercise led to the conclusion that "a black community cannot be built on the basis of people who are continually living in a state of returning to the West Indies, who are not committed to making this country their own. Even a revolutionary has to eat and needs to create a community that is friendly to him."

In Montreal, moderate black leadership is emerging from a period of tense, shocked withdrawal that followed the agony of Sir George. Says former President of Negro Citizenship Association Richard Leslie: "The moderates are afraid to make any further protest for fear of becoming identified with the Sir George group—and in so deciding, you automatically become a second class citizen. It's time we began working for our rights again." Mrs. Dorothy Wills, a West Indian housewife and teacher, has become the first black member of Montreal's Board of Catholic Charities, and believes that "the only way we can make progress for the black man is by participating in the community, by showing the white people that we are here to stay as an integral segment of the mosaic." It is not always easy. . . .

Says Horace Campbell, a Jamaican student at York University: "Black people in Canada are suffering from white tokenism. This society is basically racist." In Toronto's Alexandra Park area, which in recent years has attracted black immigrants from the West Indies and Nova Scotia, the new black power consciousness among the young has created uneasy racial tensions. Last summer the park was the scene of an ugly battle between blacks and resentful Portuguese youths, fought out with baseball bats, beer bottles and bicycle chains.

When it comes to assessing their own place within Canadian society many blacks tend to fall back on the same comparison that whites like to make: that things in Canada are at least better than in the United States. Typical is Alfred Hamilton, who sympathizes with the cause of the Black Panthers in the U.S. "I would not like to believe what is happening in the U.S.—the Gestapo-like police raids, people being shot in bed—could happen in Canada. People say Canada is just a suburb of the U.S. but you must have faith in something."

Mingled with this guarded optimism is a growing feeling that Canada's black communities can no longer afford to remain internally divided. Writing in *Contrast,* chairman of the National Black Coalition Dr. Howard McCurdy, of Windsor University, publicly blamed himself for having criticized some black radicals as "transients who had little understanding of the problems of blacks in Canada. Whether we are West Indians, U.S., African immigrants or native Canadians, we are all in the same bag. It is the tragedy of the black community that we are already too much divided."

What do you think?

1. Do you agree with Rosie Douglas, one of the defendants, that the actions of the Trinidad Ten, on trial for the sacking of the Sir George Williams computer centre "exposed Canadian society in the world's eyes as racist."

2. Do you agree with the following statements?
   (a) "The moderates are afraid to make any further protest for fear of becoming identified with the Sir George group—and in so deciding, you automatically become a second-class citizen."
   (b) "Even a revolutionary has to create a community that is friendly to him."

3. How can a "sense of community" be created by Canadian blacks?

2. BLACK AWARENESS IN HALIFAX

"Black awareness. It is in the streets of Halifax now. Afro-cuts. Black pride. Long, colorful African tunics. Black history, A minority within a minority, perhaps, but it is growing. Much of the older generation of Negroes (the young militants insist on being called blacks) has been written off. Black Power."

In this article published by the Globe Magazine, February 15, 1969, the view of moderate blacks like Don Oliver and H. A. J. Wedderburn are seen in comparison with the views of more radical blacks like Jules Oliver.

Don Oliver, a 30-year-old bachelor lawyer with a prestigious Halifax law firm, is not a militant black, although there are plenty of them in Nova Scotia and elsewhere in Canada. He wants to be a good lawyer because he thinks he can contribute more to the movement this way. He is opposed to violence, but he realizes and appreciates the argument of some blacks that it is only thing whites respect. A soft-spoken, polite man, he paused several seconds when asked about the possibility of violence in Halifax. "I don't think the possibility is too great. In fact, I think it's minimal."

   *   *   *   *   *

Oliver said his problem is that he can't understand violence. "I had a case the other day where I was defending a fellow who assaults people. If he told you to take your arms off the table and you said you didn't feel like it, he'd hit you. He's just a violent fellow. . . . Well, I just don't understand violence and I don't understand him. And I don't understand why people want to go out and burn, loot and scare.

   *   *   *   *   *

Stokely Carmichael, recently listed as prime minister of the Black Panther Party for Self Defense, visited Halifax last fall.

Carmichael met Burnley (Rocky) Jones at a Montreal conference and was invited to Halifax to rest before heading back to the United States. He accepted the invitation.

He ate at the Arrow Club in north central Halifax, drove to North Preston, a miserable black slum 15 miles away, and spoke to some school children. He left after about two days.

That was enough. Rumors spread of an invasion of Black Panthers. Maybe 200 of them! Rocky Jones said he is used to hysterical exaggeration in the local press.

*　*　*　*　*

Excluding Carmichael, only two Black Panthers visited Halifax: T. D. Pawley of Boston and George Sams (alias Robert Waddell Smith) of Alabama. They called Rocky Jones a Black Panther. They even called Roosevelt (Rosie) Douglas of Montreal a Black Panther, a suggestion that amused a Toronto friend who remembers Douglas as a rather conservative West Indian student.

"If Rosie's militant," his friend remarked, "it shows how quickly Black Power awareness is setting in here."

*　*　*　*　*

Pawley and Sams attended a meeting of the Nova Scotia Association for the Advancement of Colored People (NSAACP) in November. Too many speakers were white. Pawley got up and suggested that the blacks might feel inhibited. He called for a "black family meeting."

*　*　*　*　*

The all-black meeting was held on November 30 behind closed doors. No press. No whites. About 500 attended. When it ended, Nova Scotia had the Black United Front, a fledgling umbrella organization geared to unite the province's 15,000 blacks.

"BUF wouldn't have gotten off the ground without the Panthers," said Oliver, whose brother, Dr. W. P. Oliver, was chosen as chairman of a seven-member committee to study the need for a united front.

The following week a human rights conference on *The Black Man in Nova Scotia* was to be held at a north central Halifax school. More rumors of Black Panther "invasion." The RCMP actually requested immigration authorities to stop any Negroes crossing the border.

Sams was stopped by police for a minor traffic violation driving Jones' Volkswagen. They arrested him when they found a .38-calibre revolver under the front passenger seat. (They also found three rifles in the car, but, well, Jones is an avid duck hunter.)

Tension mounted.

The day before the conference opened, Jones appeared on television and assured viewers there would be no invasion. It seemed a relief.

*　*　*　*　*

[*Notwithstanding initial protest, the blacks did accept the appointment of a white to lead Nova Scotia's human rights commission.*]

"Black people are funny people," said Oliver, the lawyer. "They would accept you going out into their community much more readily than they would accept me. Because you're white. There is a very very basic mistrust of the black man. . . .

This prevents the rise of effective, indigenous leaders in the black community. No man commands the support of the black community in Halifax or Toronto, Montreal, Dresden, Chatham, North Buxton. It took the Black Panthers, as catalysts, to create BUF.

"If I were to call a meeting they'd say, 'You must be considering running for politics, Donny Oliver. The only way you're going to get a leader is by imposing it on the people—by saying, 'This is good for you, Accept it.' Like your mother used to put down the castor oil."

Jules Oliver, Don's nephew, is one of the most promising black leaders in Halifax, though at 23, he doubts whether he has enough charisma. He hopes to get his Master of Social Work degree at Dalhousie this year, then go on for a Ph.D. He is a militant, but has fair support from moderate blacks.

Halifax Mayor John O'Brien hired him last summer to investigate unfair employment practices in the city. As executive secretary of a committee, he found 128 jobs for black students, 75 of them year-round, part-time jobs. He persuaded the local board of trade to pass a resolution asking members to post fair employment signs. He helped set up a car wash which employed nine black students.

His 18-page report described the employment situation and shocked a somewhat complacent city.

*   *   *   *   *

No matter how much discrimination is denied in Halifax, the report concluded, a simple fact persists: "It is the fuel of protests and revolts." Even Wedderburn of the NSAACP, a rather soft-nosed body, says a race riot in the city "is not inconceivable."

Jules Oliver interprets black independence as a black economic and social base: black business, black culture, black theatre. "What the blacks are saying is we have to get off this integration kick. When we spoke of integration five years ago we meant social, economic and political improvement of our race within this society. Whites thought it mean being dance partners with their daughters.

"We have to get off this kick of human rights conferences, brotherhood weeks. If we spend all our time on this we get only tokenism, gradualism, and hypocrisy. The only alternative is to get among ourselves, unify, organize. Get an identity.

"What will happen when blacks are organized and whites still say no to our demands? We will no longer adhere to the system. You've set up the barrier. Politics is war without bloodshed; war is politics with bloodshed." (Rocky Jones quotes Mao, too.)

Was he advocating his own segregation?

"We're not going to be segregating because segregation is when you confine yourself for reasons that you are superior, for reasons that are harmful to another group of people. We're speaking of black independence.

"Your white system can function as you wish. Black people will function as we wish."

Jules obviously has thought it out. The two societies could get together, he suggested. To solve common problems like air pollution. Whites need not fear Black Power as they do, he said, because the blacks, after years of oppression, are a more compassionate people.

Racism in Canada?

"It's here. The only question is how it manifests itself. I know a man who came up here last summer from Alabama and spent a week and all he could say to me was. 'Man, geez boy, if I was down home I wouldn't even be able to walk through public parks.' But after a week and a half he was saying he felt more uncomfortable here than down home. He didn't know where he stood here. He didn't know what the white man was thinking.

*   *   *   *   *

Says Wedderburn: "There is no reason for Canadians to be smug. The only reason we haven't the problem that they have in the States is because of the smaller concentration of Negroes." Wedderburn, 39, came to Nova Scotia from Jamaica 17 years ago. He admits that the young militants pay little attention to the NSAACP, but he insists it has done more for Nova Scotia Negroes than any other body. It has:

> Sponsored first Negroes for employment in Halifax and
>   Dartmouth stores.
> Won the right in 1946 for Negroes to sit where
>   they like to in movie theatres.
> Integrated nurses' training and placement in 1946.
> Persuaded insurance companies to sell Negroes policies
>   other than for industrial insurance.
> Initiated controversy that resulted in the Dartmouth
>   school board hiring Negroes.
> Integrated barber shops in Dartmouth.

"Fine," says Jules, who acknowledges that the NSAACP has a role to play, "for elderly Negroes, those 35 and up." He sees the NSAACP as taking the old road to integration. "And that's great for that type of people." The young prefer black independence, and they are pinning their hopes on the Black United Front.

Halifax riots? "The probability that it will happen is less than the probability that it will not happen," he says, choosing his words carefully.

"We say, 'Don't waste your time blowing up streets, tearing down the place.' I'm not saying it won't happen. I'm saying there are a lot of frustrated blacks here, and they've got to be dealt with."

What is meant by?

"umbrella organization"
"charisma"

What do you think?

1. *What evidence of racist attitudes in Halifax are presented in this article?*
2. *(a) Compare the goals and the methods of achieving them advocated by Don Oliver, H. A. J. Wedderburn, and Jules Oliver.*
   (b) Whose position do you support? Why?
3. *Why are black militants looking to Africa (African clothing, hairstyles, etc.) for their cultural heritage? Has Canada failed the Canadian black culturally? Is this the reason why blacks have failed to achieve the sense of community mentioned in the previous article?*

3. ROCKY THE REVOLUTIONARY

Burnley (Rocky) Jones is an outspoken and radical leader of the Canadian Black Power movement. An interview with Rocky appeared in the Globe Magazine, February 15, 1969.

Two things people think of when they think of racial trouble in Halifax: Africville and Burnley (Rocky) Jones. Africville is gone now. Its rat-infested slums no longer jar the eye; the rats have the garbage dump all to themselves. . . . But Rocky is still in Halifax. His prestige as a black militant . . . rose a few years ago when newspapers called him "Canada's own Stokely Carmichael." It fell when he was involved in a shooting incident in north central Halifax. It rose last October when Carmichael himself came to Halifax at Jones' request and stayed two days.

I knew I had found Rocky's house because a tiny sticker on his kitchen window said "Revolution." I knocked on the door, like a square, and someone yelled, "Come in!"

"Uncle Sam Wants You, Nigger," screamed a poster on a wall. "Come Let us Build a New World Together," said another. I saw two rifles, a shotgun and a revolver during my four-hour stay. . . .

*   *   *   *   *

At one point in the subsequent interview, I asked what was his attitude to white radicals, and what role whites might have in the ensuing revolution. "The only way to tell is to watch which way their guns are pointed when the shooting starts. We haven't reached that point yet."

Rocky was born 27 years ago in Truro, Nova Scotia, one of a family of seven sisters and three brothers. He left the province when he was 16, joined the army, spent some time in British Columbia and Toronto, then returned to Nova Scotia and Halifax. In 1965 he started working with young blacks in the streets. Now he sees more hope in the militant, Black Panther approach.

A white friend came in from hunting ducks during the evening, picked up his white son, chatted a while and left. Rocky explained this by saying his white friend was a revolutionary. "He'd shoot his own mother. There is no color on a revolutionary." A black friend, Denny Grant, said he didn't like him.

"They're good people," said Rocky.

"They may be good," his friend said, "but as far as I'm concerned right now I have to translate their goodness into evil until black people see white people as monsters."

*   *   *   *   *

The discussion continued later in what turned into a seminar on racism, revolution and Halifax.

Rocky: "The black people today in North America are the revolutionaries, because we are faced with extermination. We are forced to fight."

Grant: "I don't think we're faced with extermination. I think we will be faced with extermination if we decide to fight for what is right, but there won't be extermination if we decide to go on being slaves. We bring on extermination ourselves, but it is a necessary extermination."

*   *   *   *   *

"I don't think 10 per cent of the black people want to completely overthrow the system," said Grant, "I just think that black people want to live like ordinary human beings. Those who want to overthrow the system are those with international minds, or those who have talked with international figures."

"Man," snapped Grant, "there's got to be a revolution. I don't mean quiet revolution. I mean a physical revolution. A physical revolution has to be influenced by a very emotional anger. The mental has to be translated into the physical because it's the only way white people will listen.

"You know when they will listen? When somebody shoots a white woman's kid on the way to school. When a black man shoots her kid on the way to school she'll turn her TV set on and when she sees black people talking she'll sit down and listen.

"It's a very sad thing, man, but white people will not listen unless you're violent."

He hates it when whites say, "We don't treat our Negroes like they do in the States." It sounds like we own them. He visited North Preston, a black community just north of Halifax, and saw black families living with pigs because it was too cold to let the pigs outside. "Pigs sleep with their children, man. Pigs!"

*   *   *   *   *

Rocky (yawning): "There's no peace for the black man. That's why we don't need dope. We're on a constant bad trip."

There are a lot of papers, old speeches, books, newspapers and files in Rocky's den. He rummaged through them expectantly, occasionally pulling something up, scanning it and rejecting it. I asked him how much support he had. He wouldn't say. (Another black man said if he needed help to build a house he could count on about 35 young militants.)

Other blacks said Rocky at heart is a genuinely affectionate man. They contrasted him with George Sams, visiting Alabama Black Panther, who they said was "a real killer." Rocky does kind of grow on you.

Toward the end of the evening, he stood in the middle of the den on his crutches, staring at a handful of yellow papers—an old speech. His wife sat sprawled in a chair. "Hey," said Rocky, "this stuff's great. Dig it." And he recited, sometimes rather eloquently, swaying back and forth on his two crutches:

"You whites who meekly mouth the words of sympathy, understanding and the desire for us to wait just a little longer rank no higher in my estimation than the white bastards who so very methodically put the bullets through the heads of our young black children.

"Uhuru! Freedom now! We shall overcome! Burn, baby, burn! Black power! Words conceived in the womb of black awareness, fathered by frustration and nurtured in despair. . . ."

He swayed on his crutches. I almost had to catch him once. "You should have heard them shout when I got to that part," he said. Finally, he ended: "There is much to be done, but the door of freedom has been thrown open wide. I'm going to sing — no! I'm going to shout, I'm going to demand freedom now!"

What do you think?

1. What is your reaction to Rocky Jones? Do you like him? Dislike him? Why, or why not?

2. When inflammatory statements are given undue prominence in the news media, do you think this tends to glorify the radical dissenter? Does it help to expose the irrationality of his arguments?

3. Do you agree with Denny Grant's statement that ". . . there's got to be a revolution. I don't mean a quiet revolution. I mean a physical revolution . . . the mental has to be translated into the physical because it's the only way people will listen"?

4. Compare the Olivers, Wedderburn, and Rocky Jones with Kahn Tineta Horn with respect to:
   (a) their political, economic and social beliefs,
   (b) the changes they hope to see made,
   (c) their views on violence.

The Radical Left

The radical left is a loosely defined term referring to an assortment of political groups who are interested in seeing fundamental changes made in our society. These groups are usually distinguished from the reform left by the techniques they advocate to effect change, and by the speed with which they want these changes to occur. However, their ideologies, goals, and methods differ so much that they are often in complete disagreement with one another.

The purpose of this book is not to attempt a detailed examination of these divers groups, but to deal only with the attitudes of different factions of the radical left on the place of protest and violence in social change.

1. REVOLUTION, NOT TERRORISM

In its issue of February 24, 1969, the Workers' Vanguard, *a Marxist sheet, attempted to differentiate between revolution and terrorism.*

Everyone is looking to youth—that, is everyone who has any real understanding of our times and any confidence in the future. Certainly socialists who have been swimming against the stream for many years now are inspired by the developing critical mood in the youth of North America, their questioning of everything, their searching and probing, their idealism, their willingness to struggle.

In Quebec, where national consciousness has lent a new dynamic to the class struggle, the recent rash of terror bombings has underscored the urgent need to fuse the lessons of the past with the will to struggle of the present. But not just in Quebec. There is a need on all the campuses.

In Toronto we have student leaders who demonstrate a lofty indifference to the defence of the 114 Simon Fraser defendants and who think it is not at all necessary to place responsibility for the destruction of the computer at Sir George Williams on the dead-end policy of the administration and the police assault on the students. They proclaim proudly that "property is going to have to be attacked at all levels, not just the computers in university buildings but everywhere." All this in a pretense of knowledge of Marxism-Leninism—sometimes actually in its name.

On the contrary Marxism-Leninism was forged in the struggle against the terroristic act, both against individuals of the ruling circle and against property—in fact every revolution, the Russian, the Chinese, the Cuban and even the Vietnamese had to overcome this stage in order to succeed.

By 1909—8 years prior to the October revolution—Trotsky could write that "terrorism in Russia is dead . . . is already a part of the heritage of history."

Bolsheviks reject sabotage and terror as a method of struggle on several important counts.

The power of the ruling class, the capitalist state, rests neither on buildings and equipment nor on individuals, no matter their particular attributes. The class whose interests the state serves always finds new men and new materials to serve its interests. Thus such actions stand condemned first by their powerlessness to achieve what their practitioners anticipate.

Such incidents serve as a useful pretext for the state, under the guise of protecting the public from actions that endanger every passerby, to launch a far-reaching assault on any and all opponents.

But even more—such actions distract the revolutionary class from coming to grips with the essential nature of the problem—that it is the system, a vastly complicated organism with tremendous substitutive and recuperative capacities, that has to be overcome.

Terrorist work, as Trotsky relates in his writings of 1909, "demands such a concentration of energy upon the 'supreme moment,' such an overestimation of personal heroism and lastly, such an hermetically concealed conspiracy as . . . excluded completely any agitational and organizational activity amongst the masses."

To what end are the endeavours of the class struggle, Trotsky asks, if through such simple acts we can achieve our goal? If such minimal material and preparations are capable of solving the problem, where is the need of a class organization? What is the need of meetings, mass agitation, election campaigns? Such individual acts are inadequate precisely because they lower the masses in their own consciousness, reconcile them to impotence and direct their glances and hopes towards the avenger and emancipator who will some day come and accomplish his mission.

What do you think?

1. ". . . Marxism-Leninism was forged in the struggle against the terroristic act, both against individuals of the ruling circle and against property. . . . Bolsheviks reject sabotage and terror as a method of struggle. . . ."
   (a) What is your definition of the term "terrorism"?
   (b) How do you differentiate between terrorism and violence?
   (c) Does this author reject violence?
   (d) Why does the author reject terrorism as a means for achieving change?
   (e) Do you agree with this reasoning?
2. How does this author propose to bring about change?
3. Should publications such as the Workers' Vanguard be suppressed? Why or why not?

2. ELECTION AIMS: THE CANADIAN COMMUNIST PARTY

Article from the Toronto Telegram, September 25, 1971, describes some members of Canada's Communist Party.

Bill Stewart is a stocky, graying man with three children and two mortgages. If he could afford it, he would buy more classical and jazz records, go to all the football games, and drink cognac.

Elizabeth Hill is a 28-year-old, blue-eyed blonde, daughter of a carpenter, wife of a construction worker. She wanted to be an artist but, in her neighbourhood, if you were a girl, you become a typist. And so, Elizabeth did, for a time. She still resents the fact that her father spent his life building houses, but never owned one.

Bill and Elizabeth are both hard-working executives, who put in a lot of night work. They both make the same salary: $100 a week.

That's the way it is, in Ontario's Communist Party. Not much money, a lot of deep-seated resentments, a great deal of quiet, dogged dedication.

Bill Stewart is the leader of the party in Ontario, as well as the provincial organizer. Elizabeth Hill is the full-time secretary of the Young Communist League of Canada.

Both are candidates in the Ontario election, Bill Stewart in Dovercourt and Elizabeth Hill in St. Andrews-St. Patrick. The Communists are running three other candidates: Jack Sweet, Yorkview; Donald Stewart (brother to Bill), Hamilton West; and Jack Clout, Lincoln (St. Catharines).

Don Stewart, like his brother, is a tradesman (both electricians) who became a trade union activist and, eventually, a full-time party worker.

Jack Sweet is a senior engineering clerk with IBM's Don Mills operation, Jack Clout, an auto plant worker.

How did they become Communists? What keeps them going, in the face of the obvious odds? How are they treated by their fellow Ontarians? These are the questions the curious ask, about this obscure, struggling group of politicians.

Another one, of course, is: Are they getting anywhere? Do they ever actually make any headway?

They do, according to Bill Stewart. The Communist Party's membership, like that of other political parties, is a secret. They'll reveal theirs when the others do, he says. But it's growing "quite briskly right now," after a period of decline following the peak years of the Cold War.

Circulation of the Communist publication, the *Canadian Tribune,* which ran about 50,000 after World War II and then nose-dived in the 1950s, is running about 18,000 now and climbing, says Mr. Stewart. The pattern echoes the trend in the U.S., where party membership is currently growing at a faster rate than it has in years.

The reason, in Mr. Stewart's view: People have long memories, and they recognize many of the current programs issued by old-line parties to solve the economic ills of North America as familiar platform planks in old Communist campaigns.

"Put Canada First" was a Communist election slogan in the 1950s, and Stewart is losing no opportunity to remind people of that in 1971, now that the issue has become so much in the forefront of public consciousness.

The question of persecution and discrimination is an old one, with Canadian Communists. Ask any of the three Metro candidates—Stewart, Hill, Sweet—about where their brothers and sisters, wives and children, work, and you get the suddenly closed face, curtained eyes: They can't tell you that, because their relatives might lose their jobs.

Some employers, like IBM, set up no visible barriers. But others make no secret of the fact that they don't want Communists working for them, usually because of a personal patriotic conviction on the part of the man at the top.

It's standard procedure, according to Mr. Stewart, for anyone joining the party to be visited shortly afterwards by the RCMP. The new member, along with members of his family, and friends, are questioned at some length. Forever after, presumably, they are under surveillance.

Mr. Stewart says that even Canadians whose closest connection to the party has been a subscription to a Communist publication have found themselves coming under the watchful eye of the RCMP.

"And there are people who have lived in this country for 25 and 30 years who cannot become Canadian citizens, and will never be Canadian citizens, because of their connection with the left-wing movement."

He says these things, however, without any perceptible note of fervor or indignation. They are statements of fact, accepted, acknowledged and tolerated, in the utter conviction that they will pass.

"It won't last, this discrimination," says Mr. Stewart. "The young people growing up today think differently, and they don't find that kind of thing acceptable."

But are they getting more young people, disenchanted with the system, into the movement? Elizabeth Hill says yes, and certainly Mr. Stewart implies that.

Nevertheless, at Mr. Stewart's kick-off meeting in Kent School this week, one would have been hard put to find five people in the audience of 65 who could be identified as under-30s.

Mostly, they were middle-aged, neatly dressed, lower-income people. A near-solid bloc of what used to be called the working class—and still is, at a Communist Party meeting. Construction workers, factory workers, women in slacks and kerchiefs, a young father wearing a windbreaker and holding a small boy on his knee.

They listened attentively to what Mr. Stewart had to say. Quietly, respectfully, with only an occasional subdued murmur of "hear, hear," and in the question period, they did what they came to do: Air their grievances.

Tax bills. Company lay offs. The school system. Corporate con jobs. The U.S. plan to "phase out the automobile industry in Canada, now that the chips are down, and look after their own first." General Motors. Dunlop. The Toronto *Telegram*. Landlords. Employers. Governments.

All the old villains came under fire, at one time or another during the two-hour meeting. Plus a few new ones. But they could all be lumped together as one, single disenchantment—with The System.

The anger was just a little mechanical, just a little tired. Most of it had been said before, and mostly by the same people.

How do people like Mr. Stewart whip themselves up into any kind of fighting spirit, in an action front so removed from the main arena? How do they inspire their campaign workers? When your party's ideological goals are so unreachable in the immediate future, and the election is now, what do you use for stimulation? Can you fight an election without immediacy?

In fact, as Mr. Stewart points out, the Communists are not advocating an immediate swing to socialism in this country. That's a long-term goal, which the 51-year-old leader expects to see realized in his lifetime. But for now, it's on the shelf.

In the meantime, party policy is to plug for intermediary measures. Economic reform, but within the existing capitalistic structure. The establishment of a Canadian auto industry, upgraded and expanded public and social welfare housing programs, day-care centres and women's rights, curbs on American domination and corporate monopolies, tax reforms.

Winning is not the issue, says Mr. Stewart. He expects the Communist vote to increase (the ridings are chosen mainly on the basis of support in those areas in previous elections), but "whether or not it will increase to the extent that we'll elect a candidate, well . . ."

The real role of the party in this election, he says, is to influence the tone of it. To force issues out in the open that the old-time parties would prefer not to discuss.

Bill Stewart joined the party when he was 18, after listening to some of the early soap-boxers of the Depression years.

Elizabeth Hill was in the Communist youth movement from the age of 15, a party member by the time she was 20.

And Jack Sweet, whose parents were both Communists, is in his 36th year as a party member, at age 54.

The commitment, for each, has never wavered. Mr. Stewart says he read Karl Marx in his teens, thought about it, decided it made sense, and has "never doubted it since."

But, in an atmosphere of sheer irrelevancy, with little encouragement, little money, no glory, and only a far-off hope of victory, what are the personal rewards?

"If you refer to the sweets of office," says Mr. Stewart, "or the heady elixir of victory, it's been pretty slim pickings for us, for a long time.

But if you think of the essential truth of our program, from that point of view, our rewards are high. Whether it's in this election or the next election that reality catches hold, it's not that important.

What do you think?

1. *What is the significance of the Communist Party's participation in an election?*
2. *Do you feel that discrimination against Communists is justifiable?*

3. A REACTION TO THE KENT STATE CRISIS: THE M4 MOVEMENT

The M4 Movement, a Toronto group, is described here in the Toronto Telegram of May 13, 1970.

Their creed is Communism—from Marxism to Maoism.

Their goal is to replace the governments and social systems in Canada and the United States with "people's rule."

This is the background of the May 4 Movement, one of the militant groups taking part in Saturday's clash with police at the U.S. Consulate which ended in 91 arrests.

The M4M group was formed to protest the May 4 deaths of four Kent State University students fired on by Ohio National Guardsmen during an anti-Vietnam war demonstration. They had planned to disband soon, but after Saturday's disturbance, they want to take part in further Toronto protests.

Their headquarters is at Rochdale College.

Although M4M has a common goal—"to fight U.S. imperialism"—the group holds itself aloof from demonstrators like Mad John Free who claims to sleep only 30 minutes a day and eat manna sent from heaven by God.

The M4M members wouldn't give their names.

One M4M leader holds a master's degree in political science from an English university. He is in Canada on a Canadian Government scholarship studying for a doctorate in political theory.

A spokesman for the May 4 Movement, which openly admits its communist attachment, promised:

"It's going to be a long hot summer for Toronto."

Another man added "Peace City is dead" referring to the name Toronto has earned throughout North America among demonstrators.

Police, whose strategy Saturday was to drive a wedge between the M4M and other leftist groups, said they found a Molotov cocktail among bushes near the consulate. They also took a .38 calibre revolver, fully-loaded, from one suspect.

What do you think?

1. *Is it possible to evaluate the real significance of the M4 Movement from this article?*
2. *What details of this article would alarm or outrage a member of the establishment?*

4. THE NEW LEFT: CASTING YOUR VOTE HAS BECOME A MEANINGLESS, MAGICAL RITUAL

The new left is not ideologically rigid, but represents an amalgam of political philosophies, especially anarchism and Marxism. The editor of the new left quarterly Our Generation, *Dimitrios Roussopoulos, in an article in the* Toronto Daily Star *of April 6, 1970, explains why radicals have lost faith in conventional politics.*

Most people in Canada are fed up with "politics"—by which they mean the machinery of political decision-making. At the moment this feeling has no political expression, although anger, despair and frustration expresses itself in many acts of violence.

Our existing political institutions were developed at a time when a far less bureaucratized and centralized society existed. The party system in Canada, for instance, existed before universal suffrage; the parties represented special group interests in existence before the founding of Canada.

Power today is monopolized in immense bureaucracies which have become political institutions by virtue of the role they play in society. The power of the gigantic corporations is informal, to be sure, but there is little doubt that they have drawn off real power from our formal political institutions. Couple this development with the concentration of power at the top of the parliamentary pyramid, and both the legislature and the electorate are reduced to ritual.

This concentration of power, plus the new manipulative methods of conditioning public attitudes and motivation through the mass media, which celebrate the "values" of a society of compulsive consumption, raise in our minds a questioning of the value of the electoral and parliamentary system of representative democracy.

The issues that divided the political parties in this country are artificial—questions of *management* rather than *basic policy*. The important questions of the day—the growth of liberal totalitarianism, the wasteland between people and government, the lack of quality in our lives and the purposelessness of our society, racialism, the arms race, Viet Nam and so on —are not usually put before the people.

Politicians and opinion makers exert strenuous efforts to fix our attention on ritual, in this case the casting of the vote. Voting, as a result, becomes an isolated, magical act set apart from the rest of life, and ceases to have any political or social meaning except as an instrument by which the status quo is conserved. Electoral pageantry serves the purpose of a circus—the beguilement of the populace. The voter is reduced to voting for dazzling smiles, clean teeth, smooth voices and firm handshakes.

If we could vote for those who really control the country—for example the directors of the Royal Bank of Canada, the governors of universities, social welfare agencies, industrial corporations and the shadows behind the ministries—then the trappings of liberal democracy would soon become transparent. The real power centres lie far beyond the people's influence at elections. They remain constant *whatever* party is "in power". So the only possible argument for participating in electoral politics, for voting during federal or provincial elections, is that marginal benefits may be gained.

This is obviously a serious conclusion to reach and to recommend—or at least to sanction—for it implies that the political parties, without exception, cannot operate within the province of deep political concern. This is not to say that "it makes no difference" who wins an election; it is rather to say that the "difference" is so slight or lies in such relatively trivial areas that one might very well bypass the area of electoral politics as being irrelevant to any fresh and profound issue of political circumstance.

To the new left the elaborate procedures and structures of "representative" or parliamentary democracy (which is only one form), born in the 19th century and embroidered on since, stand as ossified caricatures. We live in a society where the majority of people passively consent to things being done in their name, a society of managed politics. The techniques of consultants are polished, but they remain techniques and should not be confused by anyone with participation.

Herbert Marcuse reformulated the libertarian insight that in our type of society any conventional opposition group inevitably assumes the values of the system it opposes and is eventually absorbed by it. In Canada as elsewhere this is the fate of socialists and social democrats.

The object of Canada's power elite and its supporting institutions is clear: It is to muffle real conflict; to dissolve it into a false political consensus; to build, not a participatory democracy where people have power to control a community of meaningful life and work, but a bogus conviviality between every social group. Consensus politics, essential to modern capitalism, is manipulative politics, the politics of man-management, and it is deeply undemocratic. Governments are still elected to be sure, MPs assert the supremacy of the House of Commons, but the real business of government is the management of consensus between the powerful and organized elites.

Consensus politics is intended for any large-scale structural change. It is the politics of pragmatism, of the successful manoeuvre within existing limits. Every administrative act is a kind of clever exercise in political public relations. Whether the manoeuvres are made by a Conservative, Liberal or

New Democrat hardly matters, since they all accept the constraints of the status quo.

The product of this system is an increasing rationalization of the existing sources of power. The banks, corporations, the federations of industrialists, the trade union movement are all given a new and more formal role in the political structure. And to the extent that the "public interest" is defined as including these interests it also excludes what, on the other side, are called "sectional" or "local" interests—namely those of the poor, the low-paid and unorganized workers, youth in general and the backward regions.

All this has thrown socialists into profound confusion. In effect, those who have not turned ideologically to the East, or those who have not accepted a libertarian perspective, have been absorbed by the system. For modern capitalism, in the very process of "surpassing" socialism, takes over many collectivist forms—though none of the content—of freedom. Thus socialists have always believed in planning—and now organized capitalism needs to plan and does. The NDP has opposed the free play of the market— and now organized capitalism transcends the market in its old form. The NDP supports a strong trade union movement—and now organized capitalism needs a strong, centralized trade union movement with which to bargain. It seems easy to turn and say as does the NDP leadership: "We are making socialism, only we call it something else, and we are all in it together."

What we face is not simply a question of programs and ideologies; what we face primarily is a question of institutions. Certain institutions in our society will simply no longer yield fundamental social and political change.

Many people, along with the new left, are concerned with such issues as: the boredom and conformity of life in the midst of a society of cybernetics; the human need for *creative* work; the continued existence of raw, naked exploitation at the work-place and at home; the power of the state over society; of centralized political entities over community, of the older generation over the younger, of bureaucracy over the individual, of parental authoritarianism over youthful spontaneity, of sexual, racial, cultural and imperialist privilege over the unfettered development of human personality.

At the same time, many of us believe that we have a qualitatively new order of possibilities—the possibility of a decolonialized Canada, of a free, non-repressive, decentralized society based on face-to-face democracy, community, spontaneity, and a new sense of human solidarity. This we believe amidst a technology so advanced that the burden of toil and material necessity could be removed from the shoulders of our people.

In the face of this kind of *revolutionary change,* electoral politics are meaningless, for elections are not won on these grounds; they are won amid tried formulas, old slogans and self-fulfilling prophesies. They are won by proposing changes of degree, not of kind; by working for adjustment, not transformation.

So the new left in this country, as in other industrial-technological societies, has concluded that there is no alternative but to withdraw our allegiance from the machines of electoralism, from the institutions of "representative" democracy, to forgo the magic rite of voting and to create instead an extra-parliamentary opposition.

The idea is to build a coalition of individuals and groups with a common critique of liberal democracy. The coalition will range from radicals to revolutionaries—from those who believe it still useful to support candidates but who will, while campaigning, also criticize the inadequacies of the system of representation, to those who seek to encourage the development of new constituencies of the self-organized powerless, of producers who control what they produce, of people who control their environment and neighborhood *directly*. New forms of freedom need to be experimented with—workers' control, participatory democracy (which means control, not consultation), direct democracy—in a period where technology is laying the basis for a decentralized post-scarcity society.

The main thrust of an extra-parliamentary opposition is anti-authoritarianism and self-determination in a society that celebrates individualism. The group and group-process have to be discovered anew in order to piece together our desire for mutual aid and human solidarity. The extra-parliamentary opposition should sever our political dependency on the politicians. It should give hope to the majority of us, powerless and unorganized, and it should also give us the initiative to assert ourselves by taking control of our lives directly, in our own name and without vanguards or representatives.

An extra-parliamentary opposition is primarily an act of negation. To paraphrase the philosopher, Kolakowski, it is a wish to change existing reality. "But negation is not the opposition of construction—it is only the opposite of affirming existing conditions."

What is meant by?

"extra-parliamentary opposition"
"participatory democracy"

What do you think?

1. *What methods is this author advocating for changing society?*
2. *What do you think the effect of this attitude might be in the long run?*
3. *Do you consider that "voting [has ceased] . . . to have any political or social meaning except as an instrument by which the status quo is conserved"?*

5. CANADA'S MAOISTS: 300 WHO SEEK THE REVOLUTION

This item in the Globe and Mail *of August 7, 1970, describes Canada's Maoists, a militant left-wing group who support the concept of a violent revolutionary overthrow of the system.*

At the University of British Columbia in the spring of 1963, a graduate student from India named Hardial Bains started an informal discussion group that he called the Internationalists.

None of us who attended those early Internationalist meetings—which were little more than college bull sessions—ever imagined that the group would evolve into a small but fanatical organization of Maoists whose declared aim is violent revolution.

During the past year, millions of Canadians have heard about the Internationalists, although not by name. They are the "Maoists" who scream at Prime Minister Pierre Trudeau that he is an "imperialist lackey"; they are the ones continually being charged with contempt of court for labelling judges "Fascists"; they are the demonstrators chanting "Escalate people's war" who helped turn an Ottawa anti-war rally in late February into a fiasco.

Today the Internationalists are centred in Toronto and Montreal, with a hard core of 50 to 60 supporters in each city, and have smaller groups in at least seven other Canadian cities. They have outposts in Dublin and Cleveland. Altogether they have about 300 reliable members.

Because of their total dedication to revolutionary action, the Internationalists have an impact out of all proportion to their small numbers. For instance, Prime Minister Pierre Trudeau was persuaded to cancel a vist to Toronto in early June mainly because the Internationalists had planned a potentially violent demonstration. The Security and Intelligence Directorate of the Royal Canadian Mounted Police is characteristically silent about such specifics, but an RCMP spokesman admitted that his force is very much concerned about the Internationalists and are watching them closely.

The 1963 originals were all gone by 1965. In 1966, the Internationalists were no longer functioning except for a small group at Trinity College, Dublin, where Hardial Bains had gone the year before as a lecturer in microbiology. In 1967, the Internationalists emerged as a Maoist group, still under the leadership of Hardial Bains. Not that anyone in the Internationalists will admit it. Working through a jungle of front groups (more than 150 at last count) and issuing statements through "spokesmen" who are not necessarily near the centre of power, the Internationalists are really enthralled with playing the underground revolutionary game.

Hardial Bains, who seven years ago was just another ambitious student politician at UBC (running unsuccessfully for the presidency of three student clubs), now is deliberately cloaked in mystery—never pictured and rarely mentioned by Internationalist publications such as *Mass Line,* their twice-weekly English-language newspaper.

When referred to at all, it is as chairman or director of a Montreal-based outfit with the tongue-twisting name of Necessity for Change Institute of Ideological Studies. From this base, however, he travels around keeping tabs on the various branches of the Internationalists.

(The Internationalists take pains to picture Hardial Bains as a sort of jet-set revolutionary who could be anywhere at any time. They also encourage rumors that he has returned to India to lead a revolutionary struggle there. But in fact he spent a lot of time in the latter half of July right here in Toronto.)

In Canada, the Internationalists' top organizations are the Communist Party of Canada (Marxist-Leninist) and, because they support Quebec separation, the Communist party of Quebec (Marxist-Leninist). They are the bitter enemies of the original Communist Party of Canada, which charges that the Internationalists have stolen its name. Most Internationalists aren't actual party members. The Internationalists parties are both small, restricted groups and probably have fewer than 15 members each. One person who has been a hard-working Internationalist for more than two years told me that he still isn't in the party.

"It's a great honor to be a member of the party," he said, "but I'm not a member."

What is meant by?

"New Left"

What do you think?

1. *Do you think the importance of people like the Maoists has been exaggerated by the press?*
2. *Why do you think the far left wing of politics is prone to factionalism?*

The Separatist

For over a decade French-Canadian separatism has been a headline issue in Canada. Yet many Canadians are woefully ignorant about its origins, grievances, goals and tactics. This lack of comprehension extends so far that moderate separatists like René Lévesque, who abjures violence, are often confused with the violent FLQ. The October Crisis of 1970 illustrated graphically the lack of understanding that many Canadians have about the situation in Quebec.

There is little doubt that a greater understanding of the historical origins and the contemporary development of separatism must be achieved. The purpose of this section, however, is to examine the methods that various separatist groups would use to accomplish the independence of Quebec.

1. A SEPARATIST POET SPEAKS: L'AFFICHEUR HURLE

The author of this poem, which appeared in Our Generation, *November 1966, is Paul Chamberland, a poet, essayist, playwright and philosopher.*

Montréal rhythm of disaster bloated face of a
                    drunkard
Big Brother goon give up two hundred millions of
    anonymous Anglo-Saxons Yankee Hydro formless
    Canadian mass callow with nickel-plated talons
                    Standard Oil General
    Motors I am Cuban Yankee No I am Negro
    I wash the floors in a Texas bordello I am
    Québécois I am regularly fleeced I
    am so gentle a lamb that I dress up on
    Sundays in the Red Ensign and I starve
    throughout the week I am a smudge in
 the margin of My Bank of Montreal of Toronto
I am Cuban I am a Negro a Negro with white
    skin Québécois fleur-de-lys and Canada
    Council I am anger in every tavern
    and in all the vomitoriums for 200 years
I no longer listen to the words of the
    priest his eternal verities and parish
    reports
I no longer stand on guard or screw around
    for thee I do not defend our home and
    native land I do not share the
    comfortable resignation of Our Lord Bishops—
    in—Conference—with—the—Minister I
    speak white and I curse but the alleys of
    the east end and the bordellos on the Main
    are mine
I'd trade this God-forsaken country
    for ten cents worth of undrinkable alcohol
    but he will not give us with his clean
    hand and clear conscience in the bank
    of American democracy we trust in God
    but he had friends with toothpaste smiles
    oh you charming French Canadian
    people but do tell me what so angrily
    unites our two solitudes
He will not give up but we will give him
    fireworks

With his dollars and his Canada we
   will show him the arsenals of our
   anger and dynamite him our refusal . . .

            *   *   *   *   *

Oh people intact whom England could not erase
land comrades
your name Québec like the blazing of comets
   in the sleep of our bones like an
   intrusion of wind in the underbrush
   of our acts

here it is that earth's heart has already upset
   our furrows and streets and our
   heart gives answer in the breaking up
   of old habits
Québec your name cadence written in
   the depth of our need a great clamour
   crosses the forest of our veins and
   raises before the world at the breaking
   of our day
the time of our humanity

What do you think?

1. *How does the author of this poem appeal to emotion?*
2. *Should fiction or poetry, TV or movies, which glorify or encourage violence be suppressed?*

2.   TERRORISTS CAUGHT IN WESTMOUNT

The rise of national consciousness which characterized Quebec in the 60s after the death of long-time premier, Maurice Duplessis, has been called the Quiet Revolution. However, a rash of bombings in the early 60s contradicted this epithet. The following from Le Devoir, May 18, 1963, *is a news account of the random terrorism which took place. Westmount is the wealthy English-speaking district of Montreal.*

Bombs have been deposited in eleven mailboxes in Westmount during the last 24 hours. The explosion of one of these devices wounded someone: a demolition expert in the Canadian army, Sergeant Major Walter Roland Leja.

At the latest report from St. Mary's Hospital, serviceman Leja was in critical condition. Since his arrival in hospital, yesterday morning, a little after 11:30, the doctors have had to amputate his left arm. During the afternoon, he underwent a surgical operation of his chest. He was struck by the full force of the explosion while he was in the midst of defusing the bomb, at the corner of Lansdowne and Westmount Avenues around 10:45 yesterday morning.

The schedule of explosives found during the daytime yesterday was established as follows: six bombs exploded inside mail-boxes, two were defused by serviceman Leja and his companion Lieutenant Douglas Simpson, three others were thrown or dragged up on vacant lots where Westmount police had the responsibility of exploding them.

At rush hour, yesterday evening, hundreds of motorists who wanted to go to the west of the city had to be patient for long hours. As a safety measure, Westmount police had sealed off certain sections of St.Catherine, Dorchester, and the Boulevard Streets from traffic.

During the entire day yesterday, Westmount police rummaged through all the mail-boxes on city streets. In the course of the search the police, assisted by inspectors from the post-office department, found, after the explosion which seriously wounded Sergeant Major Leja, five more bombs.

There is no doubt in the minds of the police, members of parliament in Quebec as well as Ottawa, that the bombs found in Westmount are the work of terrorists from the F.L.Q.

Westmount wasn't the only district of the Metropolitan area touched by terrorism. As early as 11 o'clock, Thursday night, a bomb exploded near a heating oil reservoir of the Golden Eagle Company at Pointe-aux-Trembles. Fortunately, there was only a small amount of oil in the tank. The device made a hole eight inches in diameter in the side of the tank which has a steel covering a quarter of an inch in thickness.

Some combustible oil leaked out which the Company's technicians hurriedly attempted to stop.

From the east of Montreal, the terrorists struck next in the west. Their objective for Friday night—the postal system. First they made known the presence of a bomb in the post-office building on St. Jacques and Windsor Streets. The police evacuated the entire building and made a search without bringing to light the least explosive.

But it was in the west, in Westmount, that terrorists concentrated their efforts. They appear to have performed several manoeuvres during last night. They deposited their dangerous packages—no one knows how many —in mail-boxes in Westmount.

The first bomb exploded at 3 a.m. at the corner of Côle St.-Antoine and Church Hill Streets; then, after an interval of several minutes, the populace of the heart of Westmount was frighted by explosives at the following intersections—Vignal and Sherbrooke; Lewis and Sherbrooke; Sunnyside and Lansdowne; Westmount and Claremont; Lansdowne and Westmount (where the soldier was wounded).

At seven o'clock, Friday evening, at the general headquarters of the Westmount police, all available personnel were on duty for more than 12 hours and there was no question of rest because two bombs remained to be exploded, two bombs placed on vacant lots.

Sergeant Leo Plouffe, of the municipal investigation department, was summoned to Westmount by the police of that municipality after the accident occurred to serviceman Leja. Sergeant Plouffe dismantled a bomb found in a postal box at the corner of Boulevard and Ramsay Streets.

From there, he went to the corner of St. Gregoire and Christophe-Columbe Streets where a bomb had been placed in mail-box not far from a technical services army barracks. Bomb-defusing experts ordered that the said box be taken as far away as Laurier Park, not far from there where, at the dinner hour, Mr. Plouffe exploded the device.

What do you think?

1. *What do you think the terrorists hoped to achieve through these bombings? How successful do you think they were?*
2. *How would the writer of the Workers' Vanguard article on page 52 react to the Quebec terrorists?*

3. A MARXIST'S ANALYSIS OF QUEBEC'S TROUBLES

What follows is the partial text of a speech given by Stanley Gray at Glendon College in Toronto on October 25, 1969. Gray, formerly of McGill University, was a leading member of the Front de Libération Populaire, a Quebec separatist group which was dissolved in July of 1970.

What we've seen in the last year is the convergence in Quebec of two movements or two struggles that had not previously been linked, that is to say, the national liberation struggle in Quebec against Anglo-American colonialism, which originally was very much a phenomenon of the middle-class type of intellectual, small businessmen, some state functionaries, as well as all kinds of media freaks; and also at the same time developing, but not yet linked to it was a fantastically militant rise of the working class as a whole in Quebec.

*   *   *   *   *

It's important to bear in mind what lies behind this. It is the dual status of Quebec, in the sense that it has been on the one hand a colony, a national entity that has been conquered from the outside, which has had imposed on it a language, a culture and economic control. On the other hand, it is a capitalist country in which the relationships of the working class and the bourgeoisie exist; and therefore the working class in Quebec suffers from a dual oppression: exploitation which is a colonial exploitation and oppression, and a specifically capitalist form of exploitation and oppression. And these things are not in reality divorced or dissociated, because the same people who are the oppressors of the workers in most of the plants are also the English.

In fact, the English constitute virtually 90% of the top managerial class in Quebec, and constitute the entire property-holding class, the majority of which is of course controlled by American capital. And therefore everything—the kinds of complaints and grievances that are at the roots of the workers' discontent and increasing militancy include not only what are normally class demands, but also include national demands. It is a fact, for example, that all workers have to speak English in the plant. They suffer a kind of cultural alienation and oppression throughout their whole lives in the plant, in the workshop, in industry, in the consumption sphere and everywhere else. So this is the kind of structural fact about the status of Quebec colonialism and capitalism—that explains the converging of a national consciousness and a class consciousness on a very much more increasingly political and militant scale in the working class in Quebec.

As examples of this, I could go on for a long time in a very detailed way, but just let me give a few examples. A year ago, when they had a national conference of the CSN [Confédération des Syndicats Nationaux: Confederation of National Trade Unions], they adopted a report on political action called, "The Second Front." That document was probably the most radical Marxist document to come out of an official trade union federation on this continent. It had quotes from the Monthly Review and all the established left-wing sources, showing the kind of Anglo-American capitalist control of the economy. It also revealed the nature of the state of Quebec, clearly labelling it a government controlled by and for the capitalist class which must be replaced by a workers' government. A whole series of proposals for militant political action by the trade unions to install a real workers' power were discussed and voted upon. Things which included, for example, the full scale participation of the CSN in all kinds of tenants' associations, citizens' committees, involvement in political action at the local level, and support for what we called Operation Anti-Congress. In August, when the Union Nationale, the present government party in Quebec, held its congress in Quebec City, there was a big march of 3,000–4,000 people which mostly consisted of construction workers on strike, garagemen and civil servants in a clear political protest against the whole policy of the Union Nationale. It ended in a big fight, and for the first time in Quebec, the provincial police and the rest of the pigs used tear gas on the crowds, in the same way it happened in Berkley, from helicopters. But it was not students, nor "anarchists," that were taking the action, it was an action by the working class of Quebec, organized by the CSN.

*   *   *   *   *

As well, in the movements which have tended to have only the national aspect, the actions have more and more tended to incorporate a socialist perspective or a class analysis and perspective as part of the action.

For example, the famous Operation McGill, which we organized last March 28. It came across in the English mass media as lunatic, racist, trying to turn McGill into a French university—for all the reasons that are obvious. But it was as well to turn McGill into a working-class university integrated into Quebec society and serving the majority of people in Quebec, and not the ruling corporations that exploit the Quebec people. And it was very much a program designed to integrate a class perspective and a national perspective at the same time. It was officially supported and financed in part by the CSN. Many workers came on the march and Michel Chartrand of the CSN did a lot of public speaking for the march. This is one of the few times you really saw in action the much talked about worker-student alliance.

        *   *   *   *   *

As an indication of the change of climate in Quebec, at one point [*in the St. Jean Baptiste Day celebrations, June 24, 1969*] the statue of St. Jean Baptiste was overturned by the demonstrators, his head cut off and used as a soccer ball in the streets. That scandalized the editorialists and company, but what it shows is that kids these days and the new movement is very much divorced from the traditional kind of nationalism that characterised some of the nationalist movements in the past in Quebec. Afterwards, horrible, horrible deed—they went down to St. Catherine Street, the main business street, and looted, broke windows and so on until the cops came again. This is another example of the rise in numbers and size of protests in Quebec on the national question, and how it more and more is having a class character.

        *   *   *   *   *

[*Mr. Gray describes government action taken against the protesters, terming it "repressive."*]

The line which is coming out now is shocking even to the liberal bourgeois mind. What is happening in effect is that every form of challenge, of opposition activity—called "contestation" in French—is being called illegal and seditious, and is being equated with terrorism. That is to say, they always mix terrorism and protest marches, leaflets, demonstrations in their denunciations in a very clear way; they're all the same to them. That fits in well with the line that the *Globe and Mail* is taking, that the FLQ and terrorism are behind every form of opposition activity that occurs in Quebec.

        *   *   *   *   *

The reason for this is quite clear: they feel they are increasingly isolated from the population, there's a big wave of popular discontent, the system is incapable of acting in a liberal way, of giving concessions, so the only thing they can use now—and they're certainly using it—is the direct violent repression of all the movement on the left, of all the mass groups, that oppose the government. This is part of the whole situation of polarization that has been occurring—on the one hand, growth in numbers and a rise in militancy on the left and in popular movements; on the other hand, the government is becoming much more reactionary in using repressive means.

What is meant by?

"national consciousness"

"class consciousness"

"colonial oppression"

"capitalist exploitation"

What do you think?

1. *How does Gray attempt to influence his audience? What are the strengths and weaknesses of his technique?*
2. *Gray asserts that there has occurred in Quebec a convergence of the nationalist movement and the working-class movement.*
   (a) If this is true, what might its significance be for the future?
   (b) Will this convergence decrease or increase the likelihood of political violence in Quebec? Explain.
3. *On the basis of this speech do you feel that Gray would approve of violent revolution?*

4. THE POLITICS OF ASSASSINATION

This is part of an article by Patricia Welbourn dealing with the famous filmed interview with two young FLQ terrorists in Jordan. This interview took place shortly before the October Crisis, and appeared in Weekend Magazine on August 15, 1970.

Hidden in the Jordanian mountains, thousands of miles from Quebec, two young Montrealers are learning how to kill. Impatient with the unsuccessful bombing tactics of the Front de Libération Québécois (FLQ), they are learning the art of "selective assassination" to further their dream of an independent Quebec.

Who have they chosen as victims?

"We have their names in our heads," one of them says quietly.

"From the practical point of view, we should really begin by killing the prime minister (Quebec Premier Robert Bourassa), but obviously that's not possible," the other adds. "So we'll begin by getting some of those who've already been aimed at. For example, the head of a syndicate who is really nothing but a stooge for the bosses. We have our eye on a few others who will be tops on the list."

They call themselves Sélim and Salem, borrowed Arab names, and hide their faces behind Bedouin headgear. Thus protected, they were willing one day last June to talk to Montreal television interviewer Pierre Nadeau, who came across them while he was filming life in a Jordanian guerrilla camp for a private Montreal television company, Mondo Vision. The film is produced and directed by Roger Cardinal.

"We are here to get military training which, though we couldn't receive it in Quebec, we can easily put into practice when we get back," Salem says.

"Our goal is the liberation of Quebec," Sélim adds. "Total political and economic independence from the American monster."

Both men were active terrorists and members of the FLQ (they admit to taking part in at least 20 incidents) until April 1969, when terrorist Pierre-Paul Geoffroy was imprisoned for life after a series of bombings, including the Montreal Stock Exchange.

Geoffroy didn't talk, though, and Salem and Sélim were able to slip quietly into the United States until things cooled off. When they parted, Sélim went to Cuba and Salem came back to Montreal to pack, take time out to demonstrate against the Murray Hill limousine firm last October, and fly to Algeria. The two met there and went to Jordan together.

Both dedicated Marxist-Leninists, they are learning military and political strategy, heavy and light arms practice, close-combat fighting and, above all, the art of selective assassination.

"Our training here isn't all that adequate for Quebec," says Sélim, "because first of all the weapons are of Soviet manufacture and difficult to come by in Quebec. They're a little too large for urban guerrilla warfare, and, above all, we wouldn't be able to get bullets. This calibre is unknown in Montreal."

They chose to join the Popular Democratic Front in Jordan because of its reputation as the most leftist of the Jordanian terrorist groups and they are disappointed at how little of the activity is political. However, the practical studies will come in handy for them.

"We are learning more how to kill than how to mobilize popular movements but mobilization action would be difficult for us here in any case—we don't speak Arabic," says Sélim. "We communicate through a French-speaking Lebanese comrade."

Their goal on returning to Montreal is to catch up on what has been happening in the past few months and then to change the face of terrorism in Quebec.

"We want to orient our military tactics towards selective assassination," Sélim explains. "For too long the FLQ has been synonymous with bombs and useless violence. We intend to pick our targets so that the people who are responsible will pay."

The two, who believe themselves to be the only Québécois so far to have taken this training, didn't say when they plan to return. Sélim plans to get in some fighting before he leaves, but for Salem the real battleground must be Quebec. "The Quebec liberation fight is essentially the same as the Palestinian liberation fight," he says. "But I think symbolically my value would be greater in Quebec."

The Mondo Vision film, which will be shown on NBC in the fall, will not be seen in Canada. The CBC may use part of it but not the interview with the two Canadian terrorists. The reason? It's too politically hot.

It's unlikely that Sélim and Salem will worry about that, though. Not when they have murder on their minds.

What do you think?

1. *How would Sélim justify selective assassination as useful violence?*
2. *Do you feel that the CBC was justified in not showing the Mondo Vision film? Why or why not?*

5. FLQ MANIFESTO

This particular FLQ manifesto appeared during the 1970 October Crisis. For a period of time, the publication and distribution of this material was illegal. Arthur, *the student newspaper at Trent University, published the Manifesto in October of 1970.*

THE FRONT DE LIBÉRATION DU QUÉBEC is not a messiah, nor a modern-day Robin Hood. It is a group of Quebec workers who have decided to use all means to make sure that the people of Quebec take control of their destiny.

The Front de Libération du Québec wants the total independence of Quebecers, united in a free society, purged forever of the clique of voracious sharks, the patronizing "big bosses" and their henchmen who have made Quebec their hunting preserve for "cheap labor" and unscrupulous exploitation.

The Front de Libération du Québec is not a movement of aggression, but is a response to the aggression organized by high finance and the puppet governments in Ottawa and Quebec (the Brinks "show", Bill 63, the electoral map, the so-called social progress tax, Power Corporation, "Doctors insurance", the Lapalme boys . . .)

> *The money power of the status quo, the majority of the traditional teachers of our people, have obtained the reaction they hoped for: a backward step rather than the change for which we have worked as never before, for which we will continue to work.*
> René Lévesque, April 29, 1970.

We once believed that perhaps it would be worth it to channel our energy and our impatience, as René Lévesque said so well, in the Parti Québécois, but the Liberal victory showed us clearly that that which we call democracy in Quebec is nothing but the democracy of the rich. The Liberal party's victory was nothing but the victory of the election riggers, Simard-Cotroni. As a result, the British parliamentary system is finished and the Front de Libération du Québec will never allow itself to be distracted by the pseudo-elections that the Anglo-Saxon capitalists toss to the people of Quebec every four years. A number of Quebecers have understood and will act. In the coming year Bourassa will have to face reality: 100,000 revolutionary workers, armed and organized.

Yes, there are reasons for the Liberal victory. Yes, there are reasons for poverty, unemployment, misery and for the fact that you, Mr. Bergeron of Visitation Street and you, Mr. Legendre of Laval who earn $10,000 a year, will not feel free in our country of Quebec.

Yes there are reasons, and the guys at Lord know them, the fishermen of the Gaspé, the workers of the North Shore, the miners for the Iron Ore Company, Quebec Cartier Mining, and Noranda, also know these reasons. And the brave workers in Cabano know all the reasons.

Yes, there are reasons that you, Mr. Tremblay of Panet Street and you Mr. Cloutier, who work in construction in St-Jérôme, that you cannot pay for "vaisseaux d'or" with all the "zizique" and the "fling-flang" as does Drapeau the aristocrat—who is so concerned with slums that he puts colored billboards in front of them to hide our misery from the tourists.

Yes, there are reasons, that you, Mrs. Lemay of St-Hyacinthe, can't pay for little trips to Florida like our dirty judges and parliamentary members do with our money.

The brave workers for Vickers and Davie Ship who were thrown out and not given a reason, know these reasons. And the Murdochville men, who were attacked for the simple and sole reason that they wanted to organize a union and who were forced to pay $2,000,000 by the dirty judges simply because they tried to exercise this basic right—they know justice and they know the reasons.

Yes there are reasons that you Mr. Lachance of St. Marguerite Street, must go and drown your sorrows in a bottle of that dog's beer, Molson. And you, Lachance's son, with your marijuana cigarets . . .

Yes there are reasons that you, the welfare recipients, are kept from generation to generation on social welfare. Yes, there are all sorts of reasons, and the Domtar workers in East Angus and Windsor know them well. And the workers at Squibb and Ayers, and the men at the Liquor Board and those at Seven Up and Victoria Precision, and the blue collar workers in Laval and Montreal and the Lapalme boys know those reasons well.

The Dupont of Canada workers know them as well, even if soon they will only be able to express them in English (thus assimilated they will enlarge the number of immigrants and Neo-Quebecers, favored children of Bill 63). [*The controversial Bill 63 guarantees Quebec parents the right to choose the language they wish their children to use in school.*]

And the Montreal policemen, those strong-arms of the system, should understand these reasons—they should have been able to see we live in a terrorized society because without their force, without their violence, nothing could work October 7.

We have had our fill of Canadian federalism which penalizes the Quebec milk producers to satisfy the needs of the Anglo-Saxons of the Commonwealth; the system which keeps the gallant Montreal taxi drivers in a state of semi-slavery to shamefully protect the exclusive monopoly of the nauseating Murray Hill.

We have had our fill of the system which exercises a policy of heavy importation while turning out into the street the low wage earners in the textile and shoe manufacturing trades in order to provide profits for a clutch of damned money makers in their Cadillacs who rate the Quebec nation on the same level as other ethnic minorities in Canada.

We have had our fill, as have more and more Quebecers, of a government which performs a-thousand-and-one acrobatics to charm American millionaires into investing in Quebec, La Belle Province, where thousands and thousands of square miles of forests, full of game and well-stocked lakes, are the exclusive preserve of the powerful twentieth-century seigneurs.

We have had our fill of the hypocrite Bourassa who reinforces himself with Brinks armor, the veritable symbol of the foreign occupation of Quebec, to keep the poor natives of Quebec in the fear of misery and unemployment in which they are accustomed to living.

We have had our fill of taxes which the Ottawa representative to Quebec wants to give the Anglophone bosses to incite them to speak French, to negotiate in French: Repeat after me: "Cheap labor means manpower in a healthy market."

We have had our fill of promises of jobs and prosperity while we always remain the cowering servants and boot lickers of the big shots who live in Westmount, Town of Mount Royal, Hampstead and Outremont; all the fortresses of high finance on St. James and Wall Streets, while we, the Quebecers, have not used all our means, including arms and dynamite, to rid ourselves of these economic and political bosses who continue to oppress us.

We live in a society of terrorized slaves, terrorized by the large owners like Steinberg, Clark, Bronfman, Smith, Neapole, Timmins, Geoffrion, J. L. Lévesque, Hershorn, Thompson, Nesbitt, Desmarais, Kierans. Beside them Remi Popol, the gasket, Drapeau, the dog, Bourassa, the sidekick of the Simards, and Trudeau, the "tapette [*French slang for homosexual*] are peanuts.

We are terrorized by the capitalist Roman church, even though this seems to be diminishing (Who owns the property on which the stock exchange stands?); by the payments to reimburse Household Finance; by the publicity of the grand masters of consumption like Eaton, Simpson, Morgan, Steinberg, and General Motors.

The number of those who are realizing the oppression of this terrorist society are growing and the day will come when all the Westmounts will disappear from the map.

Production workers, miners, foresters, teachers, students and unemployed workers, take what belongs to you, your jobs, your determination and your liberty. And you, workers of General Electric, it's you who make your factories run, only you are capable of production; without you General Electric is nothing.

Workers of Quebec, start today to take back what is yours; take for yourselves what belongs to you. Only to know your factories, your machines, your hotels, your universities, your unions. Don't wait for an organizational miracle.

Make your own revolution in your areas, in your places of work. And if you do not make it yourselves, other usurpers, technocrats and others will replace the iron fist of the cigar smokers which we know now, and all will be the same again. Only you are able to build a free society.

We must fight, not one by one, but together. We must fight until victory is ours with all the means at our disposal as did the patriots of 1837-38. (Those whom your sacred church excommunicated to sell out to the British interests.)

From the four corners of Quebec, those who have been treated with disdain, the lousy French, and the alcoholics will vigorously undertake combat against the destroyers of liberty and justice. We will banish from our state all the professional robbers, the bankers, the businessmen, the judges and the sold-out politicians.

We are the workers of Quebec and we will go to the end. We want to replace the slave society with a free society, functioning by itself and for itself. An open society to the world.

Our struggle can only be victorious. You cannot hold back an awakening people. Long live Free Quebec.

Long live our comrades who are political prisoners.

Long live the Quebec revolution.

Long live the Front de Libération du Québec.

What is meant by?

"electoral map"
"social progress tax"

What do you think?

1. Analyze the following excerpts from the FLQ Manifesto.
   (a) "The Front de Libération du Québec is not a movement of aggression, but is a response to the aggression organized by high finance and the puppet governments in Ottawa and Quebec."

(b) *"We once believed that perhaps it would be worth it to channel our energy—in the Parti Québécois, but the Liberal victory showed us clearly that that which we call democracy in Quebec is nothing but the democracy of the rich."*

2. Outline, in point form, the grievances of Quebec as catalogued in the Manifesto. To what extent do you agree or disagree with these statements?

3. Give reasons for the FLQ's resentment of Bill 63.

6. PRIME MINISTER TRUDEAU ON THE PROCLAMATION OF THE WAR MEASURES ACT

Pierre Trudeau spoke to the people of Canada at the height of the FLQ kidnapping crisis in October 1970. The occasion was the proclamation of the War Measures Act by the federal government.

I am speaking to you at a moment of grave crisis, when violent and fanatical men are attempting to destroy the unity and the freedom of Canada. One aspect of that crisis is the threat which has been made on the lives of two innocent men. These are matters of the utmost gravity and I want to tell you what the government is doing to deal with them.

What has taken place in Montreal in the past two weeks is not unprecedented. It has happened elsewhere in the world on several recent occasions; it could happen elsewhere within Canada. But Canadians have always assumed that it could not happen here and as a result we are doubly shocked that it has.

Our assumption may have been naive, but it was understandable; understandable because individual liberty is cherished in Canada.

Notwithstanding these conditions—partly because of them—it has been demonstrated now to us by a few misguided persons just how fragile a democratic society can be, if democracy is not prepared to defend itself, and just how vulnerable to blackmail are tolerant, compassionate people.

Because the kidnappers and the blackmail are more familiar to you, I shall deal with them first.

The governments of Canada and Quebec have been told by groups of self-styled revolutionaries that they intend to murder in cold blood two innocent men unless their demands are met. The kidnappers claim they act as they do in order to draw attention to instances of social injustice.

But I ask them whose attention are they seeking to attract. The government of Canada? The government of Quebec?

Every government in this country is well aware of the existence of deep and important social problems. And every government to the limit of its resources and ability is deeply committed to their solution. But not by kidnappings and bombings. By hard work.

And if any doubt exists about the good faith or the ability of any government, there are opposition parties ready and willing to be given the opportunity to govern. In short there is available everywhere in Canada an effective mechanism to change governments by peaceful means. It has been employed by disenchanted voters again and again.

Who are the kidnap victims? To the victims' families they are husbands and fathers. To the kidnappers their identity is immaterial. The kidnappers' purposes would be served equally well by having in their grip you or me, or perhaps some child.

Their purpose is to exploit the normal, human feelings of Canadians and to bend those feelings of sympathy into instruments for their own violent and revolutionary ends.

What are the kidnappers demanding in return for the lives of these men? Several things. For one, they want their grievances aired by force in public on the assumption, no doubt, that all right-thinking persons would be persuaded that the problems of the world can be solved by shouting slogans and insults.

They want more. They want the police to offer up as a sacrificial lamb a person whom they assume assisted in the lawful arrest and proper conviction of certain of their criminal friends.

They also want money. Ransom money.

They want still more. They demand the release from prison of 17 criminals, and the dropping of charges against six other men, all of whom they refer to as "political prisoners".

Who are these men who are held out as latter-day patriots and martyrs? Let me describe them to you.

Three are convicted murderers; five others were jailed for manslaughter; one is serving a life imprisonment after having pleaded guilty to numerous charges related to bombings; another has been convicted of 17 armed robberies; two were once paroled but are now back in jail awaiting trial on charges of robberies.

Yet we are being asked to believe that these persons have been unjustly dealt with, that they have been imprisoned as a result of their political opinions, and that they deserve to be freed immediately, without recourse to due process of law.

The responsibility of deciding whether to release one or another of these criminals is that of the federal government. It is a responsibility that the government will discharge according to law.

To bow to the pressures of these kidnappers who demand that the prisoners be released would be not only an abdication of responsibility, it would lead to an increase in terrorist activities in Quebec.

It would be as well an invitation to terrorism and kidnapping across the country. We might well find ourselves facing an endless series of demands for the release of criminals from jails, from coast to coast, and we would find that the hostages could be innocent members of your family or of your neighborhood.

At the moment the FLQ is holding hostage two men in the Montreal area, one a British diplomat, the other a Quebec cabinet minister. They are threatened with murder. Should governments give in to this crude blackmail we would be facing the breakdown of the legal system, and its replacement by the law of the jungle. The government's decision to prevent this from happening is not taken just to defend an important principle, it is taken to protect the lives of Canadians from dangers of the sort I have mentioned. Freedom and personal security are safeguarded by laws; those laws must be respected in order to be effective.

If it is the responsibility of government to deny the demands of the kidnappers, the safety of the hostages is without question the responsibility of the kidnappers. Only the most twisted form of logic could conclude otherwise. Nothing that either the government of Canada or the government of Quebec has done or failed to do, now or in the future, could possibly excuse any injury to either of these two innocent men. The guns pointed at their heads have FLQ fingers on the triggers. Should any injury result, there is no explanation that could condone the acts. Should there be harm done to these men, the government promises unceasing pursuit of those responsible.

During the past 12 days, the governments of Canada and Quebec have been engaged in constant consultations. The course followed in this matter had the full support of both governments, and of the Montreal municipal authorities. In order to save the lives of Mr. Cross and Mr. Laporte, we have engaged in communications with the kidnappers.

The offer of the federal government to the kidnappers of safe conduct out of Canada to a country of their choice, in return for the delivery of the hostages has not yet been taken up; neither has the offer of the government of Quebec to recommend parole for the five prisoners eligible for parole.

This offer of safe conduct was made only because Mr. Cross and Mr. Laporte might be able to identify their kidnappers and to assist in their prosecution. By offering the kidnappers safe exit from Canada we removed from them any possible motivation for murdering their hostages.

Let me turn now to the broader implications of the threat represented by the FLQ and similar organizations.

If a democratic society is to continue to exist, it must be able to root out the cancer of an armed, revolutionary movement that is bent on destroying the very basis of our freedom. For that reason the government, following an analysis of the facts, including requests of the government of Quebec and the city of Montreal for urgent action, decided to proclaim the War Measures Act. It did so at 4 a.m. this morning, in order to permit the full weight of government to be brought quickly to bear on all those persons advocating or practising violence as a means of achieving political ends.

The War Measures Act gives sweeping powers to the government. It also suspends the operation of the Canadian Bill of Rights. I can assure you that the government is most reluctant to seek such powers, and did so only when it became crystal clear that the situation could not be controlled unless some extraordinary assistance was made available on an urgent basis.

The authority contained in the act will permit governments to deal effectively with the nebulous yet dangerous challenges to society represented by the terrorist organizations. The criminal law as it stands is simply not adequate to deal with systematic terrorism.

The police have therefore been given certain extraordinary powers necessary for the effective detection and elimination of conspiratorial organizations which advocate the use of violence. These organizations, and membership in them, have been declared illegal. The powers include the right to search and arrest without warrant, to detain suspected persons without the necessity of laying specific charges immediately, and to detain persons without bail.

These are strong powers and I find them as distasteful as I am sure do you. They are necessary, however, to permit the police to deal with persons who advocate or promote the violent overthrow of our democratic system. In short, I assure you that the government recognizes its grave responsibilities in interfering in certain cases with civil liberties, and that it remains answerable to the people of Canada for its actions. The government will revoke this proclamation as soon as possible. As I said in the House of Commons this morning, the government will allow sufficient time to pass to give it the necessary experience to assess the type of statute which may be required in the present circumstances.

It is my firm intention to discuss then with the leaders of the opposition parties the desirability of introducing legislation of a less comprehensive nature. In this respect I earnestly solicit from the leaders and from all honorable members constructive suggestions for the amendment of the regulations. Such suggestions will be given careful consideration for possible inclusion in any new statute.

I recognize, as I hope do others, that this extreme position into which governments have been forced is in some respects a trap. It is a well-known technique of revolutionary groups who attempt to destroy society by unjustified violence to goad the authorities into inflexible attitudes. The revolutionaries then employ this evidence of alleged authoritarianism as justification for the need to use violence in their renewed attacks on the social structure. I appeal to all Canadians not to become so obsessed by what the government has done today in response to terrorism that they forget the opening play in this vicious game. That play was taken by the revolutionaries; they chose to use bombing, murder and kidnapping.

The threat posed by the FLQ terrorists and their supporters is out of all proportion to their numbers. This follows from the fact that they act stealthily and because they are known to have in their possession a considerable amount of dynamite. To guard against the very real possibility of bombings directed at public buildings or utilities in the immediate future, the government of Quebec has requested the assistance of the Canadian armed forces to support the police in several places in the province of Quebec. These forces took up their positions yesterday.

Violence, unhappily, is no stranger to this decade. The Speech from the Throne opening the current session of Parliament a few days ago said that "we live in a period of tenseness and unease." We must not overlook the fact, moreover, that violence is often a symptom of deep social unrest. This government has pledged that it will introduce legislation which deals not just with symptoms but with the social causes which often underlie or serve as an excuse for crime and disorder.

It was in that context that I stated in the House of Commons a year ago that there was no need anywhere in Canada for misguided or mis-informed zealots to resort to acts of violence in the belief that only in this fashion could they accomplish change. There may be some places in the world where the law is so inflexible and so insensitive as to prompt such beliefs. But Canada is not such a place. I said then, and I repeat now, that those who would defy the law and ignore the opportunities available to them to right their wrongs and satisfy their claims will receive no hearing from this government.

We shall ensure that the laws passed by Parliament are worthy of respect. We shall also ensure that those laws are respected.

We have seen in many parts of Canada all too much evidence of violence in the name of revolution in the past twelve months. We are now able to see some of the consequences of violence. Persons who invoke vio-lence are raising deliberately the level of hate in Canada. They do so at a time when the country must eliminate hate, and must exhibit tolerance and compassion in order to create the kind of society which we all desire. Yet those who disrespect the law-abiding elements of the community, out of anger and out of fear, will harden their attitudes and refuse to accommodate any change or remedy any shortcomings. They refuse because fear deprives persons of their normal sense of compassion and their normal sense of justice.

This government is not acting out of fear. It is acting to prevent fear from spreading. It is acting to maintain the rule of law without which free-dom is impossible. It is acting to make clear to kidnappers and revolution-aries and assassins that in this country laws are made and changed by the elected representatives of all Canadians—not by a handful of self-selected dictators—those who gain power through terror, rule through terror. The government is acting, therefore, to protect your life and your liberty.

The government is acting as well to ensure the safe return of Mr. James Cross and Mr. Pierre Laporte. I speak for millions of Canadians when I say to their courageous wives and families how much we sympathize with them for the nightmare to which they have been subjected, and how much we all hope and pray that it will soon conclude.

Canada remains one of the most wholesome and humane lands on this earth. If we stand firm, this current situation will soon pass. We will be able to say proudly, as we have for decades, that within Canada there is ample room for opposition and dissent, but none for intimidation and terror.

There are very few times in the history of any country when all persons must take a stand on critical issues. This is one of those times; this is one of those issues. I am confident that those persons who unleashed this tragic sequence of events with the aim of destroying our society and dividing our country will find that the opposite will occur. The result of their acts will be a stronger society in a unified country. Those who would have divided us will have united us.

I sense the unease which grips many Canadians today. Some of you are upset, and this is understandable. I want to reassure you that the authorities have the situation well in hand. Everything that needs to be done is being done; every level of government in this country is well prepared to act in your interests.

What do you think?

1. Discuss the following extracts from the Trudeau speech as they apply to the kidnapping crisis in particular, and to terrorism in general.

   (a) ". . . there is available everywhere in Canada an effective mechanism to change governments by peaceful means. It has been employed by disenchanted voters again and again."

   (b) "To bow to the pressures of the kidnappers . . . would be not only an abdication of responsibility, it would lead to an increase in terrorist activities."

   (c) "If a democratic society is to continue to exist, it must be able to root out the cancer of an armed, revolutionary movement that is bent on destroying the very basis of our freedom."

   (d) "The War Measures Act gives sweeping powers to the government. It also suspends the operation of the Canadian Bill of Rights . . . the criminal law, as it stands, is simply not adequate to deal with systematic terrorism."

   (e) ". . . violence is often a symptom of deep, social unrest."

   (f) "The government is acting, therefore, to protect your life and your liberty."

   (g) "Canada remains one of the most wholesome and humane lands on this earth."

7. RENÉ LÉVESQUE REACTS TO THE KIDNAPPINGS OF OCTOBER 1970

René Lévesque, journalist, a key fighter in the Quiet Revolution and a cabinet minister in the Lesage government, is leader of the Parti Québécois, a separatist party which wants to achieve the independ-

ence of Quebec by gaining an electoral majority in a provincial elec-tion. In the election of 1970 the Parti Québécois won almost one-third of the French-speaking Quebec electorate, although it received only seven seats.

The Toronto Telegram of October 12, 1970, provided Lévesque's reaction to the kidnappings of James Cross and Pierre Laporte.

Others around the world have known this feeling of absurdity and have had to observe, as we do now, the frightening fragility of what we call order or civilization.

We thought we were protected against war, revolution and extreme misery because the great majority of us has something to lose. It could not happen here.

However, it has happened. Two known figures, and with them an entire society, are facing death. And at the same time, I could also see, yester-day, someone learn of the sudden and stupid death of a young man whose doctors, on the eve of their walkout, had postponed treatment to a later date because his symptoms did not make his case one of emergency.

On all counts we are, therefore, passing from a notion of horror, which was far from abstract, to this terrible realization, here and concrete, of the harm men are still capable of doing one another, when unbridled passions topple the lid.

Whatever happens now, we will never be the same. Neither will Quebec. We will carry forever these scars left by the events of recent days and the resulting effects.

The lessons they carry, and which we will have to learn, we could not detect right away. This poisoned climate, as long as it weighs against us, makes us almost totally blind. We feel as if we were in a strange tunnel where life never penetrates.

It is by retreating, and through the return of a certain calm, which appears unthinkable, but which will make itself known, that we will manage to find ourselves.

Meanwhile, there are two things which seem immediately evident to me. First the necessity of an act of individual as well as collective humility (we are no better than the others and not as developed as we thought). And second, the incredible speed at which, these days, the freedom of all of us can be compromised and upset by a few (this freedom, which we as so many others have, must not be forgotten at any cost, before it is too late).

It is from these points that we will have to make a new start.

What do you think?

1. *What does M. Lévesque mean by "collective humility"?*
2. *What purpose might an "act of . . . collective humility" serve?*

8. RENÉ LÉVESQUE: OTTAWA AND THE FLQ ARE BOTH EXTREMIST

Lévesque's reaction to the War Measures Act was reported in the Toronto Star *of October 17, 1970.*

René Lévesque, leader of the separatist Parti Québécois, yesterday issued an "urgent call" to all Quebeckers to organize locally against "repression" by police and troops conducting mass arrests across the province.

Lévesque told a press conference that citizens should band in their local communities, find out who is being arrested, help them obtain legal help and use any other democratic avenues to fight arbitrary government action.

He also said he hopes the kidnappers of British diplomat James Cross and Labor Minister Pierre Laporte have realized by now that they were "in all stupidity the harbingers of the military regime in Quebec and that they have endangered the essential rights of all Quebeckers.

"They must see by now that their gesture has brought nothing but injury to everyone, not only to the hostages and their relatives.

"How many times have we said that neither bombs nor the kidnapping of persons is morally or politically justifiable in a society that still allows the expression and the organization of all desires for change?"

Lévesque called on the kidnappers to accept the government's offer and release the two hostages in exchange for the freedom on parole of five FLQ members currently serving prison terms, and safe exit from Canada for the kidnappers.

"We pray, literally beg, the kidnappers to accept the conditions," he said.

Earlier in the day Quebec police and federal troops arrested more than 200 Quebeckers and conducted hundreds of house searches after the federal cabinet invoked the War Measures Act to help authorities battle terrorists.

Lévesque said that, so far, 36 members of the Parti Québécois had been arrested in the province—excluding Montreal. There was no way of determining how many had been arrested in the city.

Lévesque said in an interview he considers the arrests a "panic reaction" that is both "crazy" and "unjustifiable."

Both he and Claude Ryan, publisher of the influential Montreal daily, *Le Devoir,* deplored the Quebec government's request for declaration of the emergency powers on the grounds it meant relinquishing responsibility that should belong to the provincial cabinet.

Ryan and Lévesque were among 10 prominent Quebeckers who issued a statement Thursday saying the rescue of kidnapping victims Cross and Laporte was solely a provincial responsibility.

They urged Quebec Premier Robert Bourassa to accede to terrorist demands for the release of 23 members of the Front de Libération du Québec if this could save Cross and Laporte.

Lévesque said yesterday that the FLQ is a "basically insignificant" group numbering a few hundred at most.

He felt that the Quebec government might have requested the aid of some federal troops to help in the search for terrorists "but to go smack into wartime measures tramping everyone's basic liberties is crazy."

Ryan said Bourassa has failed to explain "in any satisfactory way," his sudden switch from a policy of trying to negotiate with the kidnappers, to a rigid line and a call for federal military help.

"If he was not absolutely forced to this, he may have committed a major blunder," Ryan said. "He has relinquished his own power by putting the final solution in federal hands."

Lévesque said the provincial government now is "totally non-credible" because it played for six days at negotiating as if the decision was going to be made in Quebec.

"Now we are caught between two bunches of extremists—the extremists in Ottawa and at the other end the FLQ."

What do you think?

1. *"Now we are caught between two bunches of extremists—the extremists in Ottawa and at the other end the FLQ?" Would you agree with Lévesque? Why or why not?*

9. UNDER ATTACK: THE WAR MEASURES ACT

Against overwhelming support for the Government, only 16 of Canada's M.P.'s voted against the War Measures Act in the House. Mr. Tommy Douglas, the leader of the NDP at the time, gave the reasons why his party could not support the Government's move. (House of Commons Debates, October 17, 1970.)

In my opinion the Government has over-reacted to what is undoubtedly a critical situation. Does civil disturbance constitute apprehended insurrection?

AN HON. MEMBER: Yes.

MR. DOUGLAS: We have had civil disturbances in Canada before.

AN HON. MEMBER: Not like this.

MR. DOUGLAS: Well, I recall as a boy the Winnipeg strike and the riot.

EXTERNAL AFFAIRS MINISTER MITCHELL SHARP: But there was no kidnapping then.

FRANK HOWARD (NDP, SKEENA): Why don't you listen, Mitch, and learn.

MR. DOUGLAS: I recall the trek of the unemployed from Vancouver on the way to Ottawa and the riots in Regina. There have been civil disturbances before, and there have been subversive organizations at work in our society before. Governments have been able to secure from Parliament the necessary power and authority to deal with these situations, without invoking the War Measures Act.

This is the first time, to my knowledge, in Canadian history that the War Measures Act has been invoked in peacetime. I want to say so far as the New Democratic Party is concerned that we have been prepared, and are prepared to support enlarging the police powers, if the Government thinks it necessary to give the police greater authority in the matter of searching for dynamite or offensive weapons. They have the power now to search for dynamite and offensive weapons; there is one preclusion, and that is personal dwellings. Certainly, if the Government required the inclusion of personal dwellings for a stated period of time and under some protection, we would certainly be prepared to consider the advisability of giving those additional powers. We are prepared to support the Government in taking whatever measures are necessary to safeguard life and to maintain law and order in this country. But, Mr. Speaker, we are not prepared to use the preservation of law and order as a smokescreen to destroy the liberties and the freedom of the people of Canada . . . . The Government, I submit, is using a sledge-hammer to crack a peanut.

SOME HON. MEMBERS: Oh, oh.

MR. DOUGLAS: This is overkill on gargantuan scale. . . .

. . . Why have we not been asked to supply the Government with the powers to deal with the growing menace which it now says is so tremendous that we must invoke the War Measures Act to deal with an apprehended insurrection? The fact is, and this is very clear, that the Government has panicked and is now putting up a tremendous performance to cover up its own ineptitude . . .

Right now there is no constitution in this country, no Bill of Rights and there are no provincial constitutions. This government now has the power by order-in-council to do anything it wants—to intern any citizen, to deport any citizen, to arrest any person or to decline any organization subversive or illegal. These are tremendous powers to put into the hands of the men who sit on the treasury benches.

SOME HON. MEMBERS: Hear, hear.

MR. DOUGLAS: If my friends will look at the regulations, they will find that if the police in their judgment decide that some person is a member of a subversive organization—not just of the FLQ, but of any organization that the police decide is a subversive organization . . .

SOME HON. MEMBERS: Oh, oh.

MR. DOUGLAS: Or that he contributes to such a party . . .

AN HON. MEMBER: Why is the hon. member scared?

MR. DOUGLAS: Or that he communicates any of the ideas or doctrines of such a party . . .

AN. HON. MEMBER: What has changed you, Tommy?

MR. DOUGLAS: . . . he may be arrested and detained for 90 days. . . .

A person in Canada may be held for 90 days or more without any opportunity to prove his innocence, to prove that he does not belong to a subversive organization or to prove that the organization to which he belongs is not subversive in spite of what may be in the minds of those who arrested him. These regulations give the power to seize property and hold it for 90 days. It is a resurrection of the Padlock Law. These are very serious powers. If the Government requires those kinds of powers, surely in a democracy they should have asked the democratically elected representatives of the people to give them those powers. . . .

I suggest, Mr. Speaker, that the action of the Government constitutes a victory for the FLQ.

SOME HON. MEMBERS: Oh, oh!

MR. DOUGLAS: This is exactly what they want. They want a confrontation between themselves and the Government of Canada. They want to be recognized as a revolutionary force with which the Government of Canada must deal and where the Government of Canada must mobilize all its resources to declare war on them. They want the Government and the people of Canada to consider that we are now engaged in a civil war with the FLQ. This is exactly what they want. The Prime Minister very properly said this morning that these actions fall within the established pattern which is planned by revolutionaries.

What happens if we follow what has happened in other countries? Revolutionary movements begin by associating themselves with the disadvantaged in the community and by espousing their cause. Then follows acts of violence and sabotage, which are responded to by police repression. That gives rise to demonstrations, maybe strikes and further police repression, until bit by bit all the freedom and democracy is pushed aside and there are two armed camps. This is the polarization of confrontation which revolutionary movements in the world have sought to bring about.

The Government has fallen right into the trap. The Government has done exactly what the FLQ hoped they would do. All across this country students, workers and alienated groups will be told "See what happens when we fight on your behalf? The Government immediately brings in repressive measures."

I say to the Government that we cannot protect democratic freedom by restricting, limiting and destroying democratic freedom. . . .

The Government has two tasks before it. I sympathize fully with their desire to cope with civil disturbances and with any anticipated sabotage, but the Government has two tasks to do before they are going to be successful in this regard. The first is that they must use the democratic process in seeking to stop sabotage, kidnapping and acts of violence. They must work within the framework of the democratic system. If we are going to tell people that we value democracy and that democracy is the way of dealing with social change, we must use the democratic procedures and not revert on our part to the very kind of violence which we are condemning on the other side.

MR. SHARP: Do you not condemn it?

MR. DOUGLAS: The second is that stringent measures by themselves, and I agree that stringent measures are necessary, taken through the democratic process, will not cure this situation. We must go back to the root cause. A revolutionary movement has to have a base. Where is the base of the FLQ? The base of the FLQ lies in the disadvantaged and unfortunate people in the province of Quebec. . . .

This Government should know that police action alone will not prevent discontent, will not remove the sense of grievance and injustice which is felt by people. It takes positive measures alongside firm administration of the law. The Government will make a great mistake if it thinks that merely by resorting to wider control powers the problem of the FLQ will go away. It will not go away until we deal with the discontent and the frustration in the hearts of five or six million Canadians. . . .

I say that the Government's action today is an action of panic. In the hysteria which people feel, the Government may, as the Prime Minister has said, get many letters and calls approving what is being done.

But I predict that within six months, when the Canadian people have had time to reflect on what has happened today—the removal of all the protection and liberties presently on the statute books of Canada, a country placed under the War Measures Act, regulations introduced allowing a person to be detained for 90 days without a chance to prove their innocence—when that day comes the Canadian people will look on this as a Black Friday for civil liberties in Canada . . .

What do you think?

1. *Would you agree that the action of the Trudeau Government constituted a victory for the FLQ? Explain.*
2. *Social discontent breeds political violence. Discuss.*

10. FLQ INTELLECTUAL RENOUNCES VIOLENCE

Charged with incitement to crime for his role in the October Crisis, Pierre Vallières, a former associate of Prime Minister Trudeau's, had gone into hiding to evade trial. Vallières had been the intellectual of the FLQ, the man who had provided the rationale for their revolutionary, terrorist activities. But in December of 1971 he renounced violence

as a means to win the independence of Quebec, and urged his col-
leagues in the FLQ to throw their support to the Parti Québécois.
Vallières explained his conversion in a manuscript sent to Le Devoir
which published the statement on December 13, 1971.

Pierre Vallières, the Quebec revolutionary leader, has decided to sever all links with the Front du Libération du Québec (FLQ) and considers the Parti Québécois as the only real alternative to the party in office, and as "the main strategic political force in the Quebec people's struggle for liberation."

Pierre Vallières is doing more than breaking with the FLQ. He is exhorting the "felquistes" [*members of the FLQ*] and their supporters to put an end to the action which began in 1963 and culminated in the October 1970 crisis.

After a vigorous analysis of the present political situation, the action of the FLQ and the dynamics of the Quebec liberation movement, the author of *White Niggers of America* concludes that the action of the FLQ has become in fact the "pretext and opportunity" sought by the government to crush the real strength of the liberation movement, which lies in the Parti Québécois, local branches of the trade unions, and the citizens' committees.

Vallières writes: "But if I accept this responsibility—incumbent on me for more than one reason—for publicly denouncing armed aggression, and at the same time, affirming the necessity for the FLQ to scuttle itself as a group, acronym and myth, as a "terrorist threat", and as theory and practice, I nevertheless have no power of decision over the "felquistes", no mandate to speak on their behalf, and no trick up my sleeve to prevent any-one, including the police, from using the three letters FLQ for any purpose whatsoever."

Thus the most brilliant leader of the Quebec revolutionary move-ment has evolved towards a fundamental realignment. A member of the 1966 "felquiste" faction, imprisoned for more than four years, a political writer, the favourite scapegoat of many in the government, a revolutionary symbol, still sought by police, Vallières a few years ago was advocating armed aggres-sion as the only means of liberation for Quebec.

Vallières emphasizes that the "contents" of independence are defined at the basic level in the trade unions, citizens' committees and local "pe-quiste" [*members of the Parti Québécois*] organisations,—and that these contents must "combine with the political action of the Parti Québécois (the people's party). . . ."

Tackling the burning issue of armed confrontation and electoral contest, Pierre Vallières writes: "In Quebec, there is no doubt that armed agitation has nothing to do with the armed struggle, which is a mass struggle. The FLQ has taken part in armed agitation, it has never committed itself to armed struggle, because in Quebec the mass struggle can use the electoral process, and does so effectively. It cannot simultaneously use the electoral process and armed force, since the mass struggle cannot be bicephalous and bistrategic without denying its own nature. In the nature of things, therefore, the armed struggle of the masses and the electoral struggle of the masses cannot coexist."

At the root of Vallières' realignment we find the October 1970 crisis. On this subject he synthesizes: "The important lesson of October 1970 is the following: the government feels and knows itself to be threatened principally and first of all not by the FLQ, of whose real importance it is well aware, but by the converging activity of the Parti Québécois, the trade union locals and the citizens' committees, a political activity which springs from a radical position because it aims objectively—and more and more consciously —at the dissolution of colonial and imperialist relations which benefit the Anglo-Canadian middle class, its American masters and the fragmentary elites which form the consumptive francophone business class. . . ."

According to Vallières, the government seeks more and more openly a confrontation which would give it the opportunity of crushing the Quebec liberation movement.

"The October 1970 crisis, "writes Vallières, "provided the government with an opportunity for a full-scale rehearsal of this classic scene, at a time when the organization which, by its actions, had triggered off the crisis, possessed no means of sustaining a lengthy offensive against the government, nor of offering the people of Quebec strategy and arms which would have allowed them to resist repression. . . ."

And he goes on: "Had it not been for the combined action of the PQ, the workers' committees and all the progressive forces in Quebec—the FLQ would have gone down in history bearing the odious responsibility for having offered the exploiters of the Quebec people an undreamed-of opportunity for dealing them a blow which could well have proved fatal."

What is meant by?

"bicephalous"
"consumptive francophone business class"

What do you think?

1. What reasons does Vallières give for his assertion that violence is incompatible with constitutionality in a mass movement? Why do you think Vallières is speaking in general terms, or only with reference to Quebec? Discuss the merits of his assertion as a general proposition.

2. If the Parti Québécois had been destroyed in Quebec by the October Crisis, what would Vallières' position have been in the statement to Le Devoir?

3. What incidents would prompt Vallières' accusation that the government was attempting to destroy the non-violent separatist movement in October 1970? Are these incidents sufficient to justify such a charge?
4. Vallières and Prime Minister Trudeau were once allies in the "Quiet Revolution." How can you explain the fact that in October of 1970 they were on opposite sides?

The Poor

The poor have often been referred to as the forgotten minority, the group whose very condition induces apathy and alienation to such an extent that effective protest is almost impossible. Furthermore, poverty has been considered by our social ethic to be shameful, a sign of failure that no one should willingly admit to, and so the poor have not publicized their condition. Many observers have noted that this ethic is changing rapidly; that the poor are beginning to blame the system instead of themselves; that they recognize that the problem is not so much an individual one, as a social one. Consequently, the poor are beginning to demand that society make a determined effort to eradicate poverty. The attitudes of these people towards protest and violence will become increasingly important as their poverty, in contrast to the affluence surrounding it, becomes more and more intolerable.

1.   DISCONTENT OF MONTREAL'S POOR FUELS POLITICAL ACTION

The Toronto Star, October 30, 1970, published this article during the FLQ crisis of 1970.

Behind the political unrest in Montreal in recent weeks is a story of desperation and discontent among the poor who live in Canada's largest city.

It is a story of unemployment, slum housing, illness, and malnutrition.

Some indication of the seething unrest among Montreal's poor has been laid before the Senate Committee on Poverty by poor people's groups in the past year.

The transcripts of committee hearings provide some understanding of the causes and depth of Montrealers' discontent with social and economic development programs which have left Quebec far behind such provinces as Ontario.

The hearings show that poverty problems—housing, welfare rates, jobs, legal aid—are severe across the country, but perhaps nowhere as acute in Quebec and, particularly in Montreal.

A welfare family of four in Montreal received $175 a month. In Toronto, the same family would receive up to $330.

There has been no increase in Montreal welfare allowances since 1962, and during those eight years the allowance rates have been cut by at least 20 per cent by rising cost of living.

Quebeckers total about 25 per cent of Canada's work force, but last year accounted for 41 per cent of the country's unemployed.

Montreal's population is about 75 per cent French-speaking, yet last year a disproportionate 90 per cent of the people on its welfare rolls were French-speaking.

Mrs. Ruth Keatly, a mother of three, was one of the Montreal group to address the Senate committee. She explained she was receiving $170 monthly—after pleading her case to a Montreal alderman and getting a $20 increase—which provides her with less than a malnutrition level existence after paying $80 rent, utilities and other necessities.

She told the senators how she gets by.

"I usually go to Steinberg's and get canned vegetables, a supply of potatoes and a dozen or two eggs for the month. There is no such thing as bacon. In the summer it is cold cereal and soups, bread and the cheaper cuts of meat. If I told you my diet, it might make you all sick."

The Montreal Diet Dispensary has estimated that a family of Mrs. Keatly's size should have been receiving $90 monthly for food. She was getting less than half that.

A package of welfare reforms has been under study and ready for implementation in Quebec for months. But even under them, Mrs. Keatly would still receive less than the nutritionists say is necessary for even the most basic healthy living.

Many Montrealers testifying before the poverty committee have complained about Mayor Jean Drapeau's tendency to provide Montreal with a glittery facade at the expense of the city's poor.

Drapeau's design for the 1976 Olympics call for building 3,000 housing units for athletes that will be made available to low-income families at the end of the games. But to build those units, Drapeau will have to authorize destruction of 3,400 other homes—a net loss to the poor of 400 units.

Mrs. Joan Gordon of the Family Services Association of Montreal gave the poverty committee one family case history of the way the poor are treated by some agencies. The family consisted of a couple with eight children.

"This man is ill," Mrs. Gordon said. "I sent him to the hospital where he spent a whole day, lost a day's pay and was told to go home and take aspirin. A few more weeks would go by and he would be ill again.

"Because of the impossibility of getting this man into a Montreal hospital, we finally had him admitted to a chronic hospital outside Montreal where his wife couldn't see him. We discovered that he was suffering from chronic protein malnutrition and chronic anxiety—the two diseases of the poor.

"His children were being treated with strong psychiatric drugs at the Children's Hospital for bed-wetting—and really they were wetting their beds because they were afraid of cockroaches and had no blankets."

Mrs. Keatly, who, as Montreal poor people go, is hardly an angry militant, told the poverty committee last year that her neighbors in the poor areas of Montreal are fed up with years of government talk and planning and no action.

"Hunger and oppression breed hatred and violence," she said. "Our children are being destroyed by the economic system. Do you expect us to sit idly by and accept your definitions of poverty and your Band-Aid solutions?

"Our children are rebellious now and then turn their anger on their families. When they realize how helplessly we are trapped under present structures, on whom will they turn their anger?

What do you think?

1. "Do you expect us to sit idly by and accept your definition of poverty . . .? How would Mrs. Keatly define poverty? How would the poverty committee? If they differ, why?
2. Is urban poverty more likely to breed violence that rural poverty? Why, or why not?

2. THE POOR WILL ALWAYS BE WITH US, EH?

The following is an excerpt from an article written by Paul Grescoe after a detailed investigation of the attitudes and plight of the poor across Canada. It was published in the Canadian Magazine *of January 30, 1971.*

The poor of Canada might once have been humble, accepting, weak —and silent. No more. They've begun to show muscle and find their voice, and the clamor they're raising today could turn into a clenched fist tomorrow.

More than 350 groups of poor people have been organized across the country in the last couple of years—groups of unemployed men, welfare mothers, deserted wives, the very old and even the young, the children of immigrants. It's Poor Power.

And some day it could swing from peaceful protest to violent confrontation with the suddenness of a summer storm.

For the moment, the poor are testing their new-found voice, and it sounds bitter. Early this winter, for instance, the Greater Victoria Low-Income Group wrote to Queen Elizabeth a letter sarcastically imploring her to postpone her visit to British Columbia this spring because it seemed that the province didn't have enough money to make welfare payments, let alone pay for a royal tour. The group isn't expecting more than a polite acknowledgment from the Queen's secretary, but the press, of course, gave the letter the publicity the Low-Income Group was looking for.

Before that, when the Victoria group discovered a dozen people living on welfare in a single room, it moved them into a provincial museum with sleeping bags; the local welfare supervisor found them a house the same day.

Six welfare mothers in the group marched into Victoria's stodgy Empress Hotel and broke up Premier W. A. C. Bennett's annual dinner for the members of the legislature. The group held a burn-in of hydro bills to protest increased B.C. Hydro rates, a five-day sleep-in of the poor at the provincial parliament building, and even threatened a stomp-in of the flowers around the building—which was cancelled only after scores of complaints from flower-loving citizens.

But such fun and games in Victoria—as in the rest of Canada—may soon be put away as childish things.

"The poor people are getting mad," says Reg Clarkson, a social worker and the group's executive secretary. Clarkson is no hot-blooded young radical: he's 45, has eight kids and some people might remember that he played halfback for the Calgary Stampeders and the Edmonton Eskimos in the early 1950s.

"It might sound funny," he says, "but there really could be trouble. Even here in Victoria we get unemployed people talking about guns (though he admits the talk comes only from an occasional hothead). In the citizens' organizations there are more people prepared for violence. I don't say they're planning it or anything—but it's in them. Confrontations around welfare offices will be the beginning of it: there might be fighting and pushing around, and then that will explode. They're getting mad."

So in otherwise placid Victoria, there's talk of guns. And on a visit to Vancouver, the director of the Senate Committee on Poverty says that unless they make major strides in the next five years, the poor will revolt across Canada. In Prince Albert, Saskatchewan, social scientists working on a federally-financed poverty program, Saskatchewan Newstart, predict that the Canadian poor will use "forceful means" to improve their lives. "Unless better methods of coping with social problems are developed," they say, "these confrontations will be used increasingly to force change and make institutions more responsive, effective and efficient."

And in Toronto, the chief of community psychiatry at the Hospital For Sick Children warns: "There is no doubt it is happening here: poverty, militancy, confrontation and social disruption."

It *is* happening here. In St. Jerome, Quebec, a comparatively depressed city of 35,000 near Montreal, the trouble has begun. Last September, after the visit of Jean Marchand, federal Regional Economic Expansion Minister, and Quebec Premier Robert Bourassa, some workers fought in the streets with provincial policemen, about 500 demonstrated in a park and a few threw Molotov cocktails.

What do you think?

1. "The poor of Canada might once have been humble, accepting, weak—and silent."
   (a) Based upon your knowledge of the Great Depression, do you agree or disagree with the above statement? Why or why not?
   (b) Does this statement describe the poor today?
2. If Mr. Grescoe is correct in his assertion that there has been an upsurge in "Poor Power" recently, how can this be accounted for?
3. Can institutions become "responsive, effective and efficient," or are they inherently slow-moving and inefficient in dealing with the poor? Explain.

3. WE ONLY GET JUSTICE WHEN WE REVOLT

At the time of writing, Mr. E. Dixon, the author of the following Letter to the Editor was living in Trefann Court, a poorer part of Toronto that went through the dislocation of city redevelopment. This letter appeared in the Toronto Star of July 10, 1969.

For an honest day's work, we are entitled to an honest standard of living, regardless of whether that work is sweeping floors, sitting on City Council, writing briefs on poverty, doctoring the sick, ensuring legal justice or driving a truck. If members of council deserve fat salary increases and fat pension plans, then we are entitled to them, too.

We are fed up with politicians, labor leaders, and social workers, etc., who sit fat and comfortable in their ivory towers protecting the status quo while surrounded by poverty and injustice.

We are fed up with a society that can build these ivory towers but cannot provide jobs, homes, hospitals, etc. for the masses.

We are fed up with welfare schemes and charity handouts that allow children to go cold and hungry while their parents hopelessly drink themselves to death.

We are fed up with rich landlords taking more than their fair share in rent for high-rise apartments, public housing or slum tenements.

We are fed up with an education system that tries to con us into believing that our children can enjoy the better life if we just give them a college education when, in fact, they will end up being the same glorified sweepers that their parents and grandparents were.

We are fed up with universities that keep closed shops for the professionals such as doctors, lawyers, dentists and social workers, while the poor wait for medicare, legal and social justice.

We are tired of being a mass of slaves, keeping a small segment of a feudalistic society rich, and we're tired of striving for a standard of living which with modern machinery should give us long hours of leisure but which, in fact, is obtained only by those families with working wives or moonlighting husbands.

We are specially tired and fed up with politicians who promise change while changing nothing.

All through history, justice has been won only when the poor themselves have revolted. The poor have the power to make changes whether it's red, black, white or yellow power. Only by using this power will they find a place in the sun and the Just Society that we are *all* entitled to.

What is meant by?

"*feudalistic society*"

What do you think?

1. *What are the strengths and weaknesses of this writer's style, in presenting his grievances?*
2. *"All through history, justice has been won only when the poor themselves revolted."*
   (a) *What is your reaction to such a statement?*
   (b) *What incidents in history (Canadian or otherwise) can you recall that seem to substantiate this point of view?*
   (c) *Suggest some incidents that seem to prove otherwise.*
   (d) *Some historians have suggested that the poor rarely lead revolts. If this is true, how can you account for it?*

4. WE INTEND TO PUSH EVERYTHING AND EVERYBODY AS FAR AS WE CAN

Civic action groups, poverty groups, local interest associations, and community-oriented centres flourish in Toronto more than in many other North American cities. The following article, written by Hartley Stewart, appeared in the Globe Magazine *of March 27, 1971.*

The government, in fact, had admitted the necessity of the Mike Carsons and the Peter Harringtons in the battle against poverty. Anti-poverty organizations are now eligible in some cases for funds to sustain their organizations. And last January the Department of National Health and

Welfare offered funds for a three-day Poor People's Conference at Toronto's Lord Simcoe Hotel. More than 500 delegates, about 200 more than estimated, responded to an invitation to meet and discuss the causes and solutions for the nation's poverty and to gain the small measure of solace that comes from learning you are not alone in your misery.

The delegates, all poor themselves, were leaders in Canadian anti-poverty organizations. They are the people, like Carson and Harrington, who have decided that Canada's poverty problem is of such magnitude that it is not enough for the individual to "get out" himself, but that they must pull together and find solutions that will make life at the wrong end of Canada's economic scale something more than a fight for survival. They are what Carson calls the "militant evolutionaries".

They are the shock troops and politicians for the four million Canadians who have been living for generations below acknowledged poverty lines and for the time being at least they are willing to contain their fight within society's rules.

"We'll stay within the law," says Harrington, "but just within it. We intend to push everything and everybody as far as we can. It seems to be the only effective way."

With much the same philosophy in mind, Mike Carson begins his day of poverty politicking. A mother calls to say her child has been injured by a car speeding by in front of the house. What can he do about the speed limit? Carson calls the police, OHC [*Ontario Housing Corporation*], city hall, the ward alderman, the traffic commissioner, other area residents. A campaign begins that will take months and will include more phone calls, petitions, perhaps picketing, calls to the press and television, and hopefully in the end a lower speed limit or even a small playground for the children.

An old man calls to say he has received his eviction notice and he doesn't know why. He doesn't know what to do and he has no one else to call.

"They don't know where to turn," Carson says. He calls the OHC offices and after several hours discovers there has been an error and the old man is not only up to date with his rent but because of an adjustment that has never been made, has $28 coming back to him. "It's not even anyone's fault," says Carson. "But someone has to keep after these things."

A mother calls to say she represents six other mothers and they all agree there is a need for a crossing guard on their street. They are starting a petition and they want to know what to do with it. Who to call, how many names to get?

A Newfoundlander calls and asks what can be done for a family of six who has arrived in Toronto and has no place to go; a woman wants to know how she can get medicine for her sick baby; a man wants Carson to talk to his delinquent son; an immigrant has lost his job and wants to know why the welfare office has sent him away; an older woman wants to know why her rent has not been reduced when her income has fallen by $100 a month.

The bureaucracy is just too much for them," says Carson. "And there are still people in positions where they are supposed to help these people who believe that everyone without a job is either stupid or lazy."

"It's getting better," says Harrington, "but sometimes these people are treated cruelly and condescendingly at government agencies."

Harrington's latest long-running battle is with the OHC on behalf of a man named Douglas Upton who lives in the subsidized Scarlettwood Project and is now on strike. His rent is $124 an month and his strike pay is exactly that amount. "The OHC has refused to lower his rent," says Harrington. "If he were locked out by the company they would, but since he is on strike they refuse."

Harrington feels that Upton is taking a perfectly legal action (striking), and since his income is lower because of it, the OHC should lower his rent according to the rent-wage scale in effect at that housing project. "Look," he says, "the Canadian economic system recognizes strikes as a legal way of maintaining a balance between wages and profits, and you can't penalize a man for engaging in this perfectly legitimate form of bargaining."

Furthermore, Harrington points out, even if a striker is against a strike he often has no choice in the matter and must suffer the economic losses no matter how he votes.

"You just can't penalize a man in these circumstances," says Harrington.

In the process of this fight, Harrington has phoned each one of the OHC directors, tracking one of them down to a hospital bed. He also invited former provincial Trade and Development Minister Stanley Randall into court.

Last winter Mike Carson pleaded with housing authorities to find a location for a sick woman who claimed she had to be nearer her doctor. "I told them time and again," he says sadly, "but nothing happened." Lila Curtin was 57 years old and when Carson finally broke into her apartment at neighbors' insistence, she was draped across her couch, dead.

"We even had to bury her," he says. "The York Community Tenants' Association even had to bury the poor woman."

Earlier this winter, Peter Harrington received a request from a non-English speaking immigrant for financial assistance. He instructed the man as best he could and gave him a note for the welfare officer. "I knew even before I sent him downtown I should have gone with him," Harrington says shaking his head. "He came back absolutely bewildered and dejected." Harrington took the man downtown and saw him onto the welfare rolls.

Tactics among the "militant evolutionaries" vary, but common to them all is a persistence and stubborness that suggests they will have their way somehow, sometime. That persistence surfaced obviously at the Poor People's Conference last January. Delegates representing the poor from Newfoundland to British Columbia, with only their poverty as a common bond and with a thousand regional differences to separate them, emerged after three days of meetings as a unified force.

They met in workshops geared to specific poverty problems—unemployment, welfare, housing, Indians, the handicapped—and drafted resolutions that showed a profound understanding of the essence of Canada's poverty problem.

Within the workshops they shared their sympathies and their strategies:

"We find you can't solve major problems through the social workers," advised one delegate from Calgary. "If there is real trouble you have to go above the social worker's head to get any action."

"If you can enlist the support of some of the more liberal professions, it can be helpful," a young woman offered. "We had an architect who drew up renovation plans for our community and when we took them to city council they decided not to send in the bulldozers."

Another young woman from Kingston gave advice on pressuring banks who insist on loaning money to companies who behave in a socially irresponsible fashion. "Get about 200 people," she told them excitedly, "and each one opens up a new bank account with $1. Then an hour later they all withdraw $1. The paper work alone will boggle them."

A workshop on demonstrations heard testimony about the effectiveness and limitations of sit-ins, marches and other forms of protest. "Even two people with signs can have an effect," one man insisted.

But perhaps as important as the emerging unity and shared strategies, was a battle on another front that was taking place at the conference. A battle the poor people's "militant evolutionaries" are fighting with increased regularity these days, and one whose victory carries considerable significance for the rest of Canada. And that is the battle against the revolutionaries; about 40 of whom were present at the conference.

These people, poor as well, have for years pitted their energies against the establishment and have concluded in the end that the establishment must go.

The rest of Canada may take heart, at least for the time being, that the revolutionaries, although they did pass a few radical resolutions concerning the Quebec kidnappings, were routed. They were argued down in the workshops and the main resolutions attested to the fact that this was a battle within the system.

"Violence and action outside the law," Harrington argues, "will only serve to alienate millions of people whose understanding we need. They are the people on the border, who can easily be pushed into the conservative camp by riots and violence."

Mike Carson frowns. "But think of this," he says. "Five years ago there would have been no revolutionaries at a conference of that sort. Think about what that means for the future."

And then he slaps his generous thigh, throws his massive head back and roars like a buffalo. Sometimes.

What is meant by?

"militant evolutionaries"

What do you think?

1. Describe some of the methods used by poverty groups to improve their condition? How effective are they?
2. Can you see a common bond between these people and Canadian blacks and Indians? Could they ever get together? Why or why not?
3. Why would Toronto be an especially active city with respect to community action groups?

5. THE POOR MAY REVOLT IF WE IGNORE THEM

In a news item, which appeared in the Toronto Star of August 25, 1971, two distinguished welfare workers were reported to have said that the poor may turn to violence.

Two Canadian welfare officials warned yesterday that unless Canadians are willing to make some sacrifices to help the country's poor people, the poor may revolt and we will face American-style upheaval.

Dr. John Frei, executive director of the Metro Social Planning Council, said he is not confident that taxpayer resistance to spending money on welfare measures will be overcome soon, but politicians must take the risk of moving ahead faster than public opinion or face the consequences—riots by poor people.

Reuben Baetz, executive director of the Canadian Welfare Council, said public concern about poverty rises and falls in waves and "the threat of violence (by the poor) often seems to have more effect on changing public attitudes for the better than a logical argument."

They were commenting on a speech by John Munro, federal health and welfare minister, who told a Halifax audience last weekend that he does not believe the country is ready for an all-out attack on poverty and pollution because people are not willing to do with less themselves.

Both Frei and Baetz, as well as a number of other social welfare experts and politicians interviewed by the *Star* yesterday, agreed that Munro had zeroed in on a vexing problem.

Frei said Munro's remarks had "opened the door" for ordinary citizens to examine their values and determine if they really want to live in a society that permits one of every five Canadians to live in poverty.

Baetz said most social welfare specialists are aware of public resistance to costly poverty programs and Munro displayed "political guts" in talking about it publicly.

"We've said the same thing before and caught hell for it," he said. "The general public doesn't like to be told that they are selfish and greedy."

John Yaremko, Ontario social and family services minister, said that if the public became acquainted with the miseries of living in poverty in the midst of affluence they would readily support new social welfare programs.

What do you think?

1. *"If the public became acquainted with the miseries of living in poverty in the midst of affluence they would readily support new social welfare programs." Do you agree? Why or why not?*
2. *It has been said that poverty cannot be eliminated without large tax increases. Is this true? What are the alternatives, if any?*

The Establishment

What exactly is meant by the word "establishment"? In this volume this term is used to describe those Canadians who make the vital decisions about our government and economy as well as those who generally support these decisions. In the following articles you will encounter various opinions held by members of the establishment regarding protest, violence and social change. Do any of their opinions reflect your views and attitudes?

1. THE PRIME MINISTER AND DISSENT

These excerpts from a speech by Prime Minister Pierre Trudeau are taken from the Globe and Mail *of August 9, 1969. Trudeau was speaking to a $50-a-plate Liberal Party dinner which followed demonstrations against the Prime Minister outside the Seaford Armories in Vancouver.*

I think that the important thing is that the political processes be encouraged by the citizens in various ways. There are ways of expressing your support. This [*dinner*] is one. There are others. The demonstration that we have outside—it is a form of dissent and I think our society welcomes dissent and it leaves room for dissent.

It is on this basis that ideas in our country and policies are developed. Those who don't agree have a right, indeed they have a duty toward their own consciences to express their feelings and to draw the attention of the authorities to the particular injustices or inequities on which they feel very strongly.

Our society needs this and whether sometimes it comes in a more or less organized way, or whether it be disorganized, the important thing is that people in our society feel that they have the possibility of protesting against the way society is being organized and directed.

I know in some instances I am told that, for instance, the Company of Young Canadians is a disturbing influence and that the federal government shouldn't give funds to an organization which practically takes upon itself to stir up dissension. I must say I don't agree with that. I think that it is a good thing for us to have out there a conscience, a social conscience, which has a right to repeat its disagreements on certain basic options that the Government—society—takes. . . .

I've been to meetings where I am told that the organized dissent was by way of a sign which had been painted on the premises of the Company of Young Canadians and paid for with federal funds.

I am not saying that it's not a little bit annoying, but I think that on balance it's something which we should accept and be prepared to accept. We pay funds to the Opposition so that they should be able to criticize the Government realm. Otherwise the danger to society would be that too many people would feel that they can't express their dissent, too many people would feel that they don't have the tools of changing the orientation of society and the people in power. Those who exercise authority in one way or another have microphones and televisions and so on. But if there were a disinherited part of our society which felt that it couldn't communicate its ideas, that it couldn't express its protest, then our society would be in a very dangerous state indeed.

I repeat there is a place for dissent in our society and we as Liberals welcome it.

I think, however, there is a distinction between civil dialogue and shouting matches. I think that there is a distinction between the free flow of ideas and resorts to violence, whether it be in deed or in word.

This meeting which took place outside, I think, perhaps is a good case study. We were told that they wanted to discuss certain problems, the problem of war in Vietnam. I understand and I respect Canadians or people of other countries who feel this is a sin, a blot on humanity.

So we had agreed to speak to the people outside. It was understood that I would listen to someone explaining their points of view and then I would have a chance to explain the Government's point of view. The strange thing is that a person, and she seemed like a very dedicated and courageous lady, was speaking because she was pleading the cause for Canada doing something about the war in Vietnam, ceasing co-operation with the United States and so on.

But nobody listened to her. They were all shouting. They were all shouting at me. They were shouting at the Government.

They weren't interested even in listening to their own spokesman.

This is not legitimate dissent and this is not the pursuance of a civil dialogue. I think it is important that in our minds as a civilized community we think these things through.

Very often it is a question of class, of color or even of generation and we are told that we must resort to violence, we must disobey the law, we must provoke the police and the authorities because society is corrupt and society is rotten and it must be changed. And I repeat—the people who think this have a right to state their point of view. If they think that society is rotten they are entitled to try and change it. But this recourse to physical and verbal violence is not a proof of high moral conscience. It is not a proof of the rectitude of the ideas.

It is a proof on the contrary, of the low respect in which these people hold the rest of Canadian society.

They think that Canadians are so stupid and so corrupt and so twisted in their minds that the preaching of truth to them will not be understood by Canadians; and that the Canadian people do not deserve democracy, because the Canadian people are not clever enough, are not informed enough, are not intelligent enough, to choose the truth that these people have chosen.

It is part of their system to say: "We can't express ourselves in this society, we are not free. It is run by the imperialists and their lackeys, or it is run by the industrial-military complex, or it is run by the profit motive or it is run by some mysterious devil somewhere. We cannot convince the people, therefore we must tell the people what is good for them. They don't know, we know."

This is the seed of totalitarianism and this is the seed of dictatorship, and this we must fight against and against this we must stand.

What do you think?

1. "I think our society welcomes dissent."
   (a) Do you think that some dissenters would disagree with the Prime Minister's statement? If so, on what grounds do you think they would base their disagreement?
   (b) Is it a matter of a difference of definition as to what constitutes dissent?
   (c) Does dissent become treason in time of war?
   (d) Does dissent become something else when it is accompanied by violence? Explain your reasoning.
2. Mr. Trudeau stated that illegitimate or violent dissent is the seed of dictatorship and of totalitarianism. Explain the reasoning underlying this statement.
3. ". . . if there were a disinherited part of our society which felt that it couldn't communicate its ideas, that it couldn't express its protest, then our society would be in a very dangerous state indeed." What do the disinherited do if they are able to express themselves and are still not heeded, particularly if they are a minority and always will be?

2. THE MINISTER OF JUSTICE: DISSENT MUST STOP SHORT OF VIOLENCE

This document consists of extracts from a talk by federal justice minister John Turner which was reported in the Ottawa Citizen *in March of 1969.*

Let us now posit the guidelines or principles of constructive dissent which must be read together, rather than separately.

(a) One cannot speak of the duty of government to live under the law and the right of an individual to be above the law.

(b) The right to dissent does not mean that all dissent is right. The question is not, may I dissent, but how may I dissent. The right to free speech . . . is not, as Justice Holmes once pointed out, the right to cry "Fire!" falsely in a crowded theatre and thereby cause a panic.

(c) There are several legitimate forms of protest. A person . . . may speak in a public forum, print and distribute pamphlets or leaflets, organize mass meetings and picketing for the same purpose, denounce the political leaders as incompetent or corrupt, and exercise any other form or modality of dissent. Ultimately, there is the power of the ballot box.

(d) Acts of dissent cannot always be expected to express themselves in "polite" dissent or in the conventional forms customarily chosen. Moreover, as more and more dissent emanates from the young and the deprived, it can be expected to be more and more vigorous, and increasingly to take the form of mass demonstrations. Such mass demonstrations have the potential for escalation into violence.

Accordingly, they must be confined to the functions which, as Supreme Court Justice Abe Fortas has pointed out, are: "to communicate a point of view, to arouse enthusiasm and group cohesiveness among participants, to attract others to joining, and to impress upon the public and the authorities the point advocated by the protesters, the urgency of the demand and the power behind it. These forms do not include terror, riot or pillage."

Students often ask me whether the right to dissent goes as far as permitting civil disobedience. . . . There may be exceptional instances where civil disobedience may be justified, but only under the following conditions which must be read together. Moreover, even in those rare situations, where all these conditions are met, it does not make civil disobedience legal.

(a) Every available legal recourse must first be exhausted. If, despite recourse to the law, the evil still abuses the rights of an individual, he may have a persuasive case for resistance—but only in defence of his own personal rights. He must not trespass on anybody else's rights. And what he does does not make it legal. It may make it moral.

(b) The law protested against must itself contain an alleged illegality and be germane to the evil protested. The disobedience of law merely as a tactic of demonstration cannot be condoned.

(c) The evil complained of must be of such magnitude as to present a clear and present danger to the fundamental values of society.

(d) The tactics of civil disobedience in those exceptional cases where it may be justifiable must not involve personal or property damage of any kind. The choice of methods of civil disobedience must not infringe upon the rights or innocence of others.

(e) Civil disobedience by definition involves breaking the law, and those who commit an illegality cannot demand amnesty as the price for refraining from further civil disobedience. Morality does not begin at the barrel of a gun.

It is one thing to say that a society has undemocratic features, to protest legally against them, and in rare instances to commit civil disobedience. But it is quite another to argue that society itself is undemocratic or totalitarian and that it must be destroyed, that an illegality is somehow legal, and that civil disobedience is therefore justifiable.

The rule of law, then, is the essential condition not only of the existence of the state, but of the existence of individual liberty within the state. Freedom is the precondition of liberty, and restraint is the beginning of all freedom. The rule of law is the source and condition of that restraint.

What is meant by?

"civil disobedience"

What do you think?

1. *How effective are the traditional forms of protest when the protesting group is relatively small, poorly organized, and not well-funded? Are there any alternatives open to such a group?*
2. *In this speech Mr. Turner has defined the limits of dissent. Is dissent carried on within these limits likely to be effective? Why or why not?*
3. *Mr. Turner warned that mass demonstrations are potentially violent. Based on your reading of Part II, which described the University of Toronto sit-in, suggest a number of ways in which a demonstration can turn into a riot. Whom do you think would be held responsible? Why?*
4. *"Ultimately there is the power of the ballot box." How effective is this power for members of a permanent minority?*

3. THE STUDENT AS GOD

Dalton Camp, the author of the following article from Campus, *February 1969, is a leading figure in the Conservative Party of Canada and a major political commentator.*

As I watch the activists on their nihilistic rounds, putting the torch to the life's scholarship of a bystanding academic (Columbia), scrawling obscenities on the walls of a newly built political science building (Montreal), turning juice-heads loose at the faculty bar (UBC) [*University of British Columbia*], or in relentless violations of the simple right of others to peace, order and the pursuit of knowledge, I have the uneasy feeling that we are being invaded by a generation seized by the urge to be a puritanical God.

The movement not only reeks of piety, but of paranoia. All our history, to date, is judged to be a conspiracy, and education merely a plot to perpetuate it. The universities, I am told, are not what we have suspected them to be—wherein students are taught to think for themselves and find inspiration in the discovery of others. Nope. Know what? They're part of an industrial-military-Establishment conspiracy, converting wise, creative, independent young minds into computerized drones for service in the hive.

On almost any campus, one detects the presence of a number of intellectual self-immolators, sitting about in darkened rooms in the dim light of candles, calling down curses upon the injustice of it all, antennae out, anxiously awaiting opportunity for confrontation. Sack the president, insult the deans, immobilize the library, picket the head office, push pornography to its limit, raise sex over love—and thereby emancipate the enslaved in the western world.

No one has a greater veneration than I for the right (1) of free assembly, (2) speech, and (3) protest. But I have profound reservations as to whether harrassment for the sake of it, and the calculated destruction of institutions and their officers constitutes anything less than the assertion of a presumptuous right to be irresponsible. We are obliged, apparently, to give sanction to acts of violence, trespass, arson and vandalism to a cult of dieties in our society which claims to be representative of the new majority. We have, in the result, a new tyranny in our midst.

The basic instruments for reform are the political parties. As repulsive as they may look to those whose heroes are Ché Guevara and Stokely Carmichael, they are not only the basic instruments for social change, they are also the best. Given a tenth of the energy now being spent in trying to reform American foreign policy from the sidewalks, or turning out, all dewey-eyed, to "dialogue" with the Prime Minister (or howl him down)—given, as I say, a tenth of all this explosive energy, our political parties would be immeasurably improved, granted the benefit of such a transfusion.

What do you think?

1. Why does Mr. Camp refer to campus activities as "nihilistic" or "intellectual self-immolators"? Do you agree with him? Why or why not?

2. Why are the political parties not seen by youth as vehicles for reform and protest?

4. GALLUP POLL OF CANADA: 87% APPROVE THE INVOKING OF THE WAR MEASURES ACT

Toronto Star, December 12, 1970.

Eighty-seven per cent of Canadians approve the invoking of the War Measures Act in the FLQ crisis. This represents a pinnacle of support for any government action as reported by the poll over many years. Those who feel the action should not have been taken number little more than one-in-20. A very small segment of the public is undecided.

This solid front of support for Prime Minister Trudeau and Quebec Premier Robert Bourassa is at practically the same level among English- and French-speaking Canadians, and only a little lower among those of other ethnic backgrounds, among whom there is a higher degree of indecision.

Approval for introducing the War Measures Act, with the promise that it would be replaced shortly with special legislation giving the government the temporary powers it needs, is at almost a nine-in-10 ratio among those with high school or university backgrounds. Among those with public schooling only, it is about eight-in-10. The question:

"In general, do you approve or disapprove the government's action in bringing in the War Measures Act to handle the FLQ crisis, with the promise that it would be replaced shortly with special legislation to give the government the temporary powers it needs?

	Approve	Disapprove	Undecided
Canada	87%	6%	7%
English-speaking	89%	5%	6%
French-speaking	86%	9%	5%
Other ethnic groups	79%	5%	16%
Public school education	81%	5%	14%
High school/technical	89%	6%	5%
University	89%	7%	4%

Gallup Poll of Canada

What do you think?

1. *How would this poll substantiate the fears of people like black moderate Richard Leslie who said (see page 000): "The moderates are afraid to make any further protest for fear of being identified with the Sir George [Williams] group"? How would this sort of reaction affect the Parti Québécois?*

2. *T. C. Douglas said in the House of Commons (see page 000) that the proclamation of the War Measures Act would be the "Black Friday for civil liberties in Canada." If this poll were taken again today would the results be the same? Why might they be different?*

5. "WE WILL USE HORSES AGAIN IF NECESSARY"

In May of 1970 a clash occurred between the police and anti-war demonstrators who were marching on the U.S. Consulate in Toronto. An account of that incident appeared in the Toronto Telegram, *May 11, 1970.*

Metro Police Chief Harold Adamson today defended use of mounted policemen in breaking up the City's worst anti-Vietnam war riot Saturday and promised they would be used again if necessary.

Several innocent spectators were knocked down by the horses on University Avenue in the wild-swinging melee between police and about 3,000 demonstrators in front of the U.S. Consulate.

Leaders of the anti-war movements protested the use of horses which pushed among their ranks, police who removed identification badges and over-reacted to the demonstration.

There were 91 arrests after the protesters, chased by police, ran rampant through the streets as far as Yonge and Albert Streets, smashing store windows as they ran.

Chief Adamson said the situation would have been much worse without the horses.

"They were used because people wouldn't move," he said. "Nobody was seriously hurt and our men did a fine job."

Police Commissioner Alderman Hugh Bruce said he was not asking for a special inquiry or investigation into the way the Metro police handled the demonstrators on Saturday.

He said he would ask the chief to produce a report collating the numerous incidents involving police and demonstrators during the demonstration.

He said the report is a routine matter and would come forward "in due course."

There were no serious injuries. The only person who required hospital treatment was a policeman whose thumb was broken when he was dragged from his horse.

Deputy Chief Bernard Simmonds, in charge of the police units controlling the demonstration, said the horses were used only after two policemen had been attacked in front of the consulate.

"The men were trying to get the demonstrators to move in an orderly circle when someone jumped on a policeman's back," he said.

"Another officer went to his aid and was hit with a piece of wood from one of the demonstrator's signs. It was then the mounted men moved in to help them."

He said paint was thrown and consulate windows were broken. He said it was decided to split the crowd because "far more violence would have taken place if we hadn't."

Deputy Chief Simmonds said horses were jabbed with sticks and hit with stones. Steel ball-bearings were thrown under their hooves, The deputy blamed the demonstrators for their "defiant attitude."

Acting Deputy Chief Harold Genno said the demonstrators "seemed determined not to let the day go by without a confrontation with the police."

He said he was surprised that three busloads of demonstrators from New York State were able to get across the border.

Police removed their sidearms before they went on the demonstration detail. This was a precaution in the event of trouble. They didn't want pistols falling into the wrong hands if they fell from holsters.

When the clash took place, they removed their badges before moving in to engage the war protesters. Hugh Crothers, a Metro police commissioner, said he was sure this was not done to prevent identity of police in the event of charges of brutality.

"If one of them got hit on the badge it could pierce his chest," Mr. Crothers said.

Executive Alderman Tony O'Donahue, who went to see the riot first hand, said he thought the police handled themselves well.

He said, however, that their order to break up the demonstration at 6 p.m. might have had some influence in making matters worse.

"It's not nice to be called a pig. I'm very satisfied with the way the police behaved," he said.

Alderman Hugh Bruce, also a member of the police commission, said the conduct of the police was "admirable."

The overtime pay for Metro's policemen during Saturday's demontions will cost more than $7,000.

Clayton Ruby, a 28-year-old lawyer who was on hand to arrange bail for any demonstrators arrested, was one of those arrested himself.

He complained he had been held more than three hours without opportunity to contact another lawyer.

The protest was organized by several anti-Vietnam war groups. They gathered outside the consulate to complain about U.S. troops in Cambodia and the four Ohio university students shot to death by the National Guard.

First trouble started when there was a clash between the anti-war demonstrators and the Edmund Burke Society which supports the U.S. action in Vietnam.

The march was organized by the May Fourth Movement, a Rochdale College group describing themselves as "a collection of anarchists, freaks, students and Communists."

Bill King, of the May Fourth Movement, said after: "We believe the majority of the police at the demonstration are ashamed and embarrassed by the department as a whole."

He demanded to know what "pig" had ordered police to remove badges to prevent identification.

Jeff Goodall, of the Burke group, said his members were there "simply to defend democracy and civilization."

He said the main trouble stemmed from the May Fourth Movement and the Maoists.

"Those May Fourth guys, particularly, were talking pretty tough," he said.

The protests outside the consulate began about 3 p.m. At first, there was no trouble. But as more and more protesters arrived there was growing unrest and tension.

Police tried to hold groups on both sides of University Avenue. About 6 p.m., a loud speaker boomed out:

"This demonstration is over. I suggest you all go home."

When the crowd failed to disperse, police moved forward on horseback. Bottles, eggs, dirt and paint descended among the police.

It took more than an hour for police to force the crowd from the consulate to the courthouse across the street.

Traffic in University Avenue was blocked more than once as the melee swirled.

What do you think?

1. How do you feel about the manner in which the police handled this situation?
2. What alternatives were open to the police?
3. Who was responsible for the violence which occurred?

6. EDITORIAL: BEYOND JUSTIFICATION

The destruction of the computer centre at Sir George Williams University at Montreal provoked a national outcry. The following is an editorial from the Edmonton Journal, February 14, 1969.

The senseless violence and destruction of property by militant students at Sir George Williams University in Montreal is the blackest possible mark on the record of student protest in this country.

But, hopefully, it could be a turning point as well, if the lessons it contains are well learned by all Canadians.

In this case, the actions of the students were utterly indefensible. Not only were these actions beyond anything society generally could be expected to tolerate, but the greatest losers were the students themselves. Whatever justice was contained in the students' original charges against the university administration has probably been discredited.

Many of the students involved have been charged with criminal offences and will be dealt with under the law—as anyone else would be, and as they certainly should be.

While the allocation of ultimate blame for the incident is of no relevance in judging the actions of these students, however, the background situation can tell us a great deal about how to prevent similar incidents in the future.

The Montreal incident cannot properly be used as a brush to tar all student dissent. Nor is it the "inevitable" result when students are allowed to be anything but docile and "studious."

The administration of Sir George Williams University must share the blame for the incident because of its apparent adoption over the past year of the traditional, if suicidal, bureaucratic strategy of ignoring a real problem in the hope that it would somehow go away.

The administration, by bottling up student frustration, was almost asking for an explosion. And it came, as it would likely come anywhere under similar circumstances.

Fortunately, the trend at other Canadian universities today is in the opposite direction: toward opening channels of communication between students and administration so that problems can be dealt with before they boil into protest and violence. Such a dialogue is a healthy development and one which, in the long run, could benefit these institutions greatly.

The lesson for students is equally obvious. Society has and will allow wide latitude for student protest, both because it is the students' right and because students have valid arguments to present.

But there is a clear line which protest must not cross. It is a line which society will not allow to be crossed because protest which threatens the very foundations of society is not legitimate protest in any sense of the word.

What do you think?

1. *Do you agree with the last paragraph in its attitude towards protest? Justify your position.*
2. *Are the channels of communication open between students and administration in your school? How might communication be improved?*

7. REFORM IN CANADA IS PEACEFUL

Austin M. Cooper, a prominent Toronto criminal lawyer, commented in the Toronto Star, November 8, 1971, on the way reform is achieved in Canada.

History records that violence is a common component of social change in the countries of the Western world. The people of the United States have always depended heavily on violence to adjust (or maintain) their social order. England's reputation for tranquility is belied by the frequent incidents of mob violence during the last three centuries as a factor in social and economic change.

In Canada, we can remember examples of collective destructiveness in the Doukhobor discontent in British Columbia, the International Woodworkers of America strike in Newfoundland, demonstrations in Toronto at the American Consulate, the malicious damage at Sir George Williams University, and the bombings, robberies and murder by the FLQ.

Historically it would appear, therefore, that some measure of collective violence is inevitable.

However, most important social reforms have been accomplished peacefully in Canada. No noses were bloodied over medicare, reduction of the voting age, unemployment insurance, changes in abortion laws, the Canadian Bill of Rights or redistribution of electoral boundaries. Hopefully, more Canadians will reject mass violence as undesirable and unnecessary. Social change can be effected constitutionally rather than by violent destruction of established patterns.

The electronic age has introduced instant communication among people over wide geographic areas; it has raised their expectations and published their discontents. The result has been the organization of numerous vocal citizens' associations that seek to further their common causes by collective action. They are often characterized by an impatience with bureaucracy and a potentially explosive frustration if their grievances are permitted to fester.

These groups will be less inclined to turn to violence to attain their goals if governments show sensitivity in dealing with their petitions, and conscience and resourcefulness in correcting injustices and inequities. On the other hand, unsympathetic or ossified authority will invite broken bones.

Disorderly gatherings of discontented citizens have been an element in the history of every nation. The current popular passion "to be involved" has prompted more Canadians than ever to assemble publicly to demonstrate their concern—whether it be for women's rights, parochial schools or universal love.

Public demonstrations are vital safety valves for minority dissatisfaction in a political system that reflects the interests of the majority. While they remain peaceful, the law should continue to give them full rein.

The degree to which they may become violent sometimes depends on the manner in which they are handled by those in power. Over-zealous policing may cause more violence than is threatened by the demonstrations being policed. New techniques must be developed and instituted by police forces to enforce legal authority as peacefully as possible when public assemblies threaten to become destructive.

Today, Canadians want more involvement in the processes of government. They seek release from archaic and discriminatory restrictions on their freedoms. They demand honest opportunity to develop their cultural and economic potentials. Canada's political maturity will be measured by the extent to which these goals are achieved peacefully.

What do you think?

1. *"Social change can be effected constitutionally rather than by violent destruction of established patterns." How might a revolutionary refute this assertion?*

2. *"Most important social reforms have been accomplished peacefully in Canada." Why would you agree or disagree with this statement?*

8. THE ESTABLISHMENT MUST NOT RESORT TO VIOLENT BACKLASH

André Laurendeau, the author of this article in Le Devoir, *June 14, 1963, was, until his death in 1968, one of French Canada's most respected voices.*

Violence is not only ill-fated, it becomes useless when democracy functions. The unfortunate thing is that too many men remain silent; whereas, the others miscalculate the seriousness of the drama in which the nation finds itself involved, above all among the younger generation. For example, they don't understand that to have applied against the young terrorists traditional methods (often wrongly) used against criminals of the respectable community is a scandal about which young and positive people are particularly sensitive.

Others believe that we become allied with the FLQ when we insist that her members be treated with justice. They regard them as a nest of snakes, and consider that against terrorists all methods are acceptable.

This blind reaction is one of the by-products of terrorism itself. For violence always threatens to entangle men in a vicious cycle. To try to get out of it, the authorities must plainly show that they will comply with a care for justice, and that they will not abandon themselves to the spirit of vengeance against those who made them afraid.

What do you think?

1. *The author deplores those who feel that "against terrorists all methods are acceptable." Do you agree with him? Why or why not?*

2. *In what ways does M. Laurendeau's position remind you of René Lévesque's remarks about "collective humility" on page 82?*

9. WOULD WE REALLY CHOOSE CIVIL WAR?

This editorial from the Toronto Star of April 17, 1971, comments on the apparent willingness of a plurality of Canadians to go to war if Quebec were to separate from the rest of Canada.

The Gallup Poll published today in the *Star* hints at a frightening deterioration of the public attitudes which sustain "peace, order and good government" in Canada. Who would have thought, even 10 years ago, that Canadians would have been asked whether, under certain circumstances, they favored a civil war in this country?

The question asked by the pollsters should be quoted in its entirety:

"Do you accept the principle that Quebec should have the right to separate from Canada, if the majority of its people want to, or do you think that Quebec should be held in Confederation by force if necessary?"

The wording is thus clear and uncompromising, and it received a surprising answer. A plurality of the Canadians polled—46 per cent across the country—stated that Quebec should be held in Confederation by force if necessary. Forty per cent thought that Quebec should have the right to secede and 14 per cent were undecided.

There were some variations in the results in English-speaking Canada; in the West—which has had secessionist movements of its own—49 per cent would concede Quebec the right to separate. But the most startling results came from Quebec itself, where only 30 per cent believed that the province should have the right to secede, while 50 per cent felt that it should be prevented from doing so, by force if necessary.

This probably represents a revulsion of feeling in Quebec against the violence of the FLQ last fall. To that extent, it must be considered an endorsement of the Trudeau government's hard line policy against separatism.

But it would be unwise to consider it a permanent expression of Quebec opinion. We must set against this fact that, in the provincial election less than a year ago, 30 per cent of the French-speaking population voted for a party openly committed to independence. Nor should it be overlooked that regardless of which political party is in power in Quebec, the drive for greater and greater provincial autonomy goes on, apparently with the full approval of French-speaking public opinion.

We cannot help wondering if those Canadians, whether in Quebec or in English-speaking Canada who supported the use of force to hold Quebec in Confederation, really considered the full implications of their choice.

If a majority of the people of Quebec want to secede from Canada, and elect a government pledged to proclaim independence, they are not likely to be deferred by a mere command from Ottawa to stop this nonsense at once. The separatist government will have to be overthrown and its supporters broken up by military force. This means, simply, civil war.

If anyone is in doubt of what this involves, let him consider the horrifying stories that are slipping through the censorship in Pakistan. There the national army is using force to prevent the people of East Pakistan from seceding—and leaving a trail of wrecked cities and slaughtered people in the process.

A similar horror ended in Nigeria only a year ago, and further back there was the bloodstained annals of the Spanish Civil War and the American Civil War to be read. All war is hell, but civil wars—especially when they are complicated by questions of race and religion—are the most wretched of all. Moreover they are notoriously hard to win permanently. The British government crushed one rebellion after another in Ireland, century after century but a new uprising always rose from the ashes of the last one. The history of Quebec, if held in Confederation by force, could be very similar.

Nor is it by any means certain that Canada could win even the first round. In an article on this page last Thursday, Colonel Strome Galloway pointed out the heavy percentage of French Canadians in the Canadian army, and especially among the infantry officers, on whom the main burden of "pacification" would rest. French Canadians officers and men have fought loyally and gallantly against Canada's foreign enemies. But who knows how they would react if they were ordered to turn their guns on their own people?

The first result of a real civil war might well be the disintegration of the Canadian army—just as the American army almost disintegrated at the outbreak of the U.S. Civil War as its southern officers resigned their commissions. And if anything like this happened there would be no hope of winning the conflict quickly or with a minimum of bloodshed.

The *Star* believes that if things come to a breaking point and if a definite majority of the people of Quebec want to leave Confederation, the Canadian government should seek to negotiate a peaceful separation on terms which protect the vital interests of the rest of Canada. That would be a hard blow for our country, but surely it is preferable to a future of unending bloodshed and terror.

What do you think?

1. Mr. Claude Charron, a Parti Québécois member of Quebec's National Assembly, stated that should Quebec choose independence at the polls then (in an obvious reference to Ottawa) "we will see who the real democrats are."
   (a) What do you think he meant?
   (b) What do you think the average English-speaking Canadian's reaction would be to this statement?
2. If Quebec were to secede from Confederation, what would be the alternatives to civil war?
3. If seven percent of those people who were undecided in this poll had thought that Quebec should be allowed to separate peacefully, then a plurality of Canadians would have rejected civil war. How could the seven percent be converted to an anti-war position?

10. WHY THE PUBLIC IS ALIENATED FROM THE POLICE

Peter Newman, a leading Canadian journalist, in the Toronto Star *of August 9, 1969.*

In this age of moon walks and mass marches, of the new technology and the new left, man is increasingly finding himself in conflict with his social environment. That conflict expresses itself most vividly in his relations with those who symbolize authority, and no one does so more conspicuously than the policeman.

The police officer, no matter how well-meaning, thus finds himself in the psychological front-line of a confrontation he is not prepared to face. He must somehow enforce that delicate balance between order and liberty which has always defined the degree of freedom enjoyed by any society.

Though opinions on police effectiveness differ widely, a growing gap seems to be separating law and justice—and that difference is becoming one of the central issues of our time. The police and the public are both discovering that protecting individual rights and protecting the collective rights of a community are often very different—and even contradictory— assignments.

In many Canadian cities today—and in Toronto more than most— an undercurrent of alienation seems to be separating the police from the citizens. "People no longer seem to think the police are on their side," Judge C. O. Bick, the Metro Police Commission chairman, has said.

There is a kind of burgeoning mistrust, a mutual drawing apart, with many minority groups (such as student radicals) demonstrating increasingly violent resentment of the police. At the same time, many policemen feel themselves to be a misunderstood and beset minority, vilified by the young and hamstrung by "bleeding hearts" who don't appreciate the exigencies of their calling. They tend, at times, to feel they are at war with the society they are charged with protecting.

This alienation arises out of a continuing conflict between the practical ethic of police work ("There are good guys and bad guys and the bad guys should all be tossed in the can"), and the formal judicial ethic of a liberal society which claims that a man is innocent until proven guilty.

Another factor is the general depersonalization of urban living. The neighborhood cop on the beat has virtually disappeared along with the corner store. We just don't *know* our policemen any more.

The historical assignment of the police has been to maintain established authority, public order, prevailing customs and moral values. These seem like unexceptional tasks, even laudable ones. But the lightning changes in our way of life automatically set the community against a police force that considers itself charged with maintaining society in its existing form. The extent of the police problem at any given period in history has been a measure of the velocity of social change. As a result, the police often find themselves ranged not only against wrong-doers, but also against reformers, progressive social elements and those who merely want to be different.

At the same time, are we being fair to our police? The fact is that as a society we demand they do most of our dirty work. They must enforce unpopular and outdated laws often because the rest of us can't agree on what to put in their place. Existing drug laws, for example, have by themselves alienated the police from an entire generation.

What do you think?

1. To what factors does Newman attribute the problems faced by police?
2. Discuss the problem of protecting both individual and collective rights.
3. "The police often find themselves ranged not only against wrong-doers, but also against reformers, progressive social elements and those who merely want to be different." Why?
4. "Existing drug laws, for example, have by themselves alienated the police from an entire generation." Discuss.

11. VIOLENCE INEVITABLE WHEN LAW VANISHES

In the Toronto Telegram, *March 23, 1970, Ron Haggart, a leading Canadian reporter and journalist, commented on what can happen when the establishment itself steps outside the law. The first incident he describes is an event from the famous Pipeline Debate of 1956. It has been alleged that the Speaker of the House, whose position has traditionally been impartial, bowed to the wishes of the Liberal Party and illegally called "closure" on the debate. The second part of the article deals with the controversial Lapalme postal workers' strike in Montreal in 1970.*

Fourteen years ago in the Canadian House of Commons, many honorable gentlemen rose to their feet to cry out in anger, to shriek at the robed figure in tricorn hat who stood at their head.

When the Speaker of the Canadian House of Commons stands up, everyone else save the page boys sits down. This is the fundamental law of the place where laws are made; it is the central rule for preserving order in the place which brings order to the nation.

René Beaudoin stood up, but the honorable gentlemen did not sit down. Instead, they streamed as one angry mob into the central aisle where ordinarily, if they go at all, they go only to bow from the waist.

"Order, order," cried René Beaudoin, but there was no order because at that moment there was no law. René Beaudoin had seen to that.

They marched down the aisle toward him, shaking their fists and swearing and screaming. Men who loved the rules of Parliament in a way few others can understand, who respected those rules for the freedom which is bestowed by order, found themselves hurled forward in a passionate unruly rabble.

Had the scene occurred anywhere else, wrote Harvey Hickey of the *Globe and Mail*, the police would have been called.

"I have never understood revolution," said John Diefenbaker later that weekend, "but now I do."

René Beaudoin, chosen to be the impartial arbiter of the laws which govern Parliament, had done the bidding of the Liberal Party. He made a ruling whose complexities are unimportant now but which had the effect of making a liar of clock and calendar, of suspending the law so that the Government of the day might achieve its objective, which happened to be the building of a gas pipeline from Alberta to Ontario.

There was no law in the House of Commons at that moment that René Beaudoin spoke and, as always happens when justice fails, men turned to violence, even the honorable gentlemen of the Canadian House of Commons. That is what John Diefenbaker meant when he said he now understood revolution, that men cannot rely on the orderly processes of law when no law exists.

Many of those who were in the House of Commons on that terrible Friday in front of the Speaker's Throne are in Parliament still, but no member, whether new or old, has failed to hear and to absorb the lessons and the legends which were swept into the history of Canada with the riotous behavior of the honorable members.

The scene has not been repeated in Parliament, which makes it all the more incredible that the Government now in power, forgetting nothing and learning nothing, has tormented a handful of men in Montreal into the alternative of violence by the willful suspension of the ordinary rules of decency and natural justice.

Men who have invested their sweat and small skill in the driving of postal trucks now see the investment of their labor being expropriated without recompense, without a second thought, by a Government in Ottawa so arrogant it refuses even to discuss the catastrophe, on the shallow pretext that it is now receiving the study it should have received in the first place.

True to its long tradition of managerial government, the Liberals in Ottawa are bent upon their task of making the Post Office more "efficient" and less of a "burden" on the taxpayer, those words which have such an appealing, if hollow, political tinkle.

In pursuit of this goal, the contract to distribute the mail in Montreal is being transferred from one large company to five smaller ones. One week from today, if nothing changes in the interim, the present employees of G. Lapalme Ltd. will have to line up for their jobs all over again; they will have to re-form their union and renegotiate their wages and re-invest their labor for the small perquisites of seniority.

The job functions remain as always: The mail must be taken from post office to post office, and from post office to carrier walk. The job functions remain, but not the jobs.

The Liberal Government scrupulously calls for tenders to establish the property value of a mail route; it spends not a moment, if we are to judge from results, in considering the accumulated value of a man's investment in his job. The five contractors will inherit the mail routes but they can do as they wish with the drivers, including nothing at all. As the Confederation of National Trade Unions so eloquently puts it: How would you like to fight for your job every year?

Abandoned by the law and by the ordinary standards of natural justice, the postal drivers of Montreal turned to slashing tires, just as the honorable gentlemen of the House of Commons erupted, when the law deserted them, into a violence which was, when judged within the context of their own decorous rules of behavior, a bloody riot.

These considerations lie behind the explosive words of Michel Chartrand, the Montreal labor leader who went to Ottawa this week to call the Prime Minister a liar and a whore. Not pretty, perhaps, but the violent words and the violent acts were sadly predictable because there is nothing quite so dangerous as a Government which is at the same time both cold-blooded and inept.

What do you think?

1. *Under what circumstances does this author feel that violence becomes inevitable? Why?*
2. *Can an alternative action for groups such as the Lapalme drivers be found in the discussion of dissent by John Turner on page 103?*

Our Culture and Violence

In a collection of readings such as this it is not our intention to thoroughly analyze all the manifestations of cultural violence. However, it is hoped that the following selections will, at least, pose questions concerning the nature of our society and its tendency to embrace violence in its athletics (particularly our national game) and in its mass media.

1. WE'RE ALL TO BLAME FOR VIOLENCE IN SPORT

Dr. John Farina, author of the following article in Weekend Magazine, *November 1969, professor at the School of Social Work of the University of Toronto, is an outspoken critic of violence in sport.*

Every time some professional sports performer gets a nasty bash editors recall some "bleeding heart", "kill-joy", "do-gooder" or "academic dreamer" who may make the appropriate and timely noises. I apparently fit, in the case of *Weekend's* story in this issue, "What Football Fans Don't See." Such recall, of course, in itself represents the generally cynical and essentially commercial reaction of the fourth estate to the legalized mayhem termed professional sport.

It has been intimated by many who report athletic entertainment that such protests come from bitter, frustrated, non-athletes somewhat lacking in manly virtues—clearly a projection. Yet indeed there seems to be futility in railing against players, coaches, managers and owners of teams. Most responsible sports writers have themselves criticized current standards of conduct and control over the violent young athletes. It seems to be an exercise in futility.

Professional or spectator sports cannot significantly affect the attitudes and responses of adults towards sportsmanship and fair play. Rather what goes on in the arena or on the field to a large extent reflects and confirms the attitudes of the spectator. Thus the mediaeval religious attitudes of spectators in Glasgow, Scotland, are confirmed when the Celtics and Rangers, two soccer teams, hack at each other; the underlying primitiveness of the Boston Bruins spectator is reflected in the play of Bobby Orr; the aggressive hostility of the alienated Torontonian finds expression in the frustrating end-of-the-game battle of their tough little Argonaut and a large Saskatchewan Roughrider.

There are many instances of the effort of spectators to participate in the sporting spectacle and to act in concert with the immature behaviour of the performers. Italy gives us several examples, but the most disastrous perhaps was the war between Guatemala and Honduras precipitated by a soccer match. As Reuel Denney, a sociologist who specializes in the study of sport, notes: ". . . the sports public often responds with an ugly eagerness to the promotion of sports sadism and masochism. Perhaps it even brings to the sports arena . . . a brutishness that reminds us of lynch law, Texan male compulsives, and child-hating antivivisectionists. Slaps on the wrists of venal promoters are less likely to improve conditions than is a change of heart in the public itself."

This statement suggests that the characteristic unsportsmanlike behavior in professional athletic performances will not be more strictly controlled. Promoters, who are not sportsmen but businessmen, react to market demand, not to social values. NHL president Clarence Campbell has reacted to a veritable tattoo of wrist slaps with a bland aplomb that would do credit to the grade four delinquent publicly chastised before his classmates. Any twinge of sports ethics he may feel is quickly anaesthetized by club owners.

Yet perhaps the blood lust of the spectator is a true reflection of the values of society. Is the exaggerated emotionalism of the spectator a safety valve or a true representation of a socially immature population struggling to achieve self-realization in a technically sophisticated society?

Let us lay off Campbell and the players in various sports and examine ourselves. What values are we transmitting to the next generation? Do our families, schools and communities demonstrate a different value system than that manifested in the arena?

What do you think?

1. *Do you agree or disagree with the following comments by Dr. Farina? Explain your answer.*
   (a) *"It has been intimated by many who report athletic entertainment that such protests [against violence] come from bitter, frustrated, non-athletes somewhat lacking in manly virtues."*
   (b) *". . . what goes on in the arena or on the field to a large extent reflects and confirms the attitudes of the spectators."*
2. *Dr. Farina concludes his article with two questions. How would you answer them?*

2. RIOT IN THE FORUM

In 1955, in the Montreal Forum a riot broke out which was ostensibly caused by the suspension of Maurice Richard, the star of the Montreal Canadiens. In the following essay which appeared in Saturday Night, *April 9, 1955, Hugh MacLennan, novelist and essayist, analyzed the situation.*

It was a wild improbability that a deskbound, more or less solitary individual like myself should have a ring-side seat at one of the most disgraceful riots in Canadian history, but when the famous tear gas bomb exploded in the Montreal Forum on March 17, I was sitting within four and a half feet of it.

By this time, of course, everyone in Canada who sees a newspaper has read and re-read the factual account of the happenings of that night, and it has been rightly pointed out that it was a bitter misfortune that Frank Selke's rink should have been the scene of them. He is a wise, kindly man who loves hockey for its own sake, who has yet to make an inflammatory statement and who deplores more deeply than most of us the Roman atmosphere which has invaded the game in recent years.

I was about twenty yards from Clarence Campbell's seat and I saw him isolated, unprotected by the police because nearly all the police were outside in the street holding a mob of hoodlums at bay, apparently afraid of losing their popularity by turning the firehoses on them. Mr. Campbell, the league president, must have felt like a bear at the stake, his position all the more shameful because dozens of photographers, both official and amateur, stood coldly snapping every change in his expression as the deluge of rotten fruit, programs, rubbers and abuse poured down on him. The viciousness was insensate.

Insensate, but not inexplicable. As I watched that riot build up, I realized that I was present at one of those situations in which all the explosive ingredients in a segment of society were ripe for a denouement. They had been growing and fermenting for years in our urban life and in our national game. On the night of St. Patrick's they all met in a critical mass at exactly the right temperature.

Every riot known to history has been the result of some imbalance in our society or institution in which it has occurred. The fundamental moral imbalance behind this particular one has been evident for two and a half decades.

When Tex Rikard first began to promote hockey in New York, he lined up ambulances outside Madison Square Garden as a come-on for the crowds who knew nothing about the Canadian national game, it being his idea that if the public of New York would not enjoy hockey they could at least be persuaded to enjoy the mayhem which hockey was likely to produce. "If you can't lick them in the alley, you can't lick them in the rink" has become a famous saying in English-speaking Canada, and quite a few perennial adolescents, who like to think Canadians are exceptionally tough people, lick their lips with pleasure when they repeat it. Unfortunately the adage has been taken literally by thousands of kids too ignorant to understand how untrue it is. I have seen plenty of plug-uglies who could have licked a small man like Howie Morenz in the alley, but I have yet to see one who could have licked him in the rink unless he used illegal tactics.

Crude violence has been deliberately encouraged by some business men who think it pays off at the box office, and by one or two coaches and managers whose teams are so crude they know they could not hope to win without it. Inevitably this has placed real hockey skill at a disadvantage, and it has cheated, frustrated and disgusted hundreds of thousands of us who again and again have seen a first-class team disintegrated by alley tactics.

What do you think?

1. *Discuss the following statements:*
    (a) *"Hockey is naturally a violent sport and offers an opportunity for both players and spectators to vent their feelings of aggression."*

(b) "If you can't lick them in the alley, you can't lick them in the rink."

(c) "Crude violence has been deliberately encouraged by some businessmen who think it pays off at the box office."

3. VIOLENCE IN OUR NATIONAL SPORT

How violent is our national sport? What fosters this spirit?

PLAYERS STAGE FORUM FIGHT
Toronto Globe and Mail, *April 11, 1966.*

It was fight night at the forum Saturday, with some wrestling tossed in for good measure, and the purists will probably scream today that it had no business being on television.

DICK BEDDOES COMMENTS ON THE FIGHT
Toronto Globe and Mail, *April 11, 1966.*

"Take dead aim at 'em!" Mr. Clancy (assistant coach) hoarsely told the Toronto troops, "Let 'em know they're in a game where they've got to keep their heads up!"

Leafs were as combative as Clancy's inflammatory pep-talk and found, to the boisterous delight of 15,047 Montreal partisans, that Canadiens were in retaliatory mood. Oftener and oftener came the clash of sticks, the crash of padded bodies against the boards, the hunting cries of Quebec partisans sensing impending violence.

At 7:25 of the first period, Bob Pulford slammed Montreal's gangling Terry Harper headfirst into the fence. The wrath of the crowd sounded exclusively French "Le coude, le coude!" meaning the old, impious elbow.

Imlach contends that the noisy Montreal supporters intimidate the referees into calling penalties against opposing teams, instructions they might ignore in a sane rink. Referee Bill Friday did not, however, bench Pulford for dumping Harper.

"Choo! Choo!" erupted the Gallic booing form, "Get Pulford! Get Pulford!" Behind the lofty pigeon roost which serves as a press box in the old Forum, came the roar "Assomme le!" which is to say, "Slug him!"

DICK BEDDOES COMMENTS ON SPORTS VIOLENCE
Toronto Globe and Mail, *April 12, 1966.*

Getting knocked down is a normal hazard of a contact competition which players at every position except goal, must and do accept.

The blitz is the football equivalent of the duster or brush-back pitch in baseball, a muscular move similar to a hard check in hockey. None of these abuses, as a rule, are employed with personal malice, but are intended to impair a dangerous opponent's efficiency.

ROUGH PLAY CEMENTS RELATIONSHIPS WITH COACH
Toronto Globe and Mail, *April 12, 1966.*

Fontinato was asked what refined measures he would employ against Leafs if he were still with Canadiens.

"First of all Frank Mahovlich has a bad knee, eh? Now we know Toe wants to find out which knee it is, doesn't he?"

Fontinato said he would consider it his duty and also cement his relationships with his coach by knocking Mahovlich around.

THE GREEN—MAKI FIGHT

A vicious high-sticking fight between Ted Green of the Boston Bruins and Wayne Maki of the St. Louis Blues put Green into the hospital with a severe head injury. Green later sued for damages—creating a hockey precedent. This selection is from the Toronto Telegram of September 23, 1969.

Green will remain at Ottawa General Hospital for about two weeks, when he will probably be transferred to Massachusetts General Hospital in Boston for the second operation.

Inspector Conley said the assault is being investigated by Detective John Aldrich, but he had no idea when a report will be available.

Detective Aldrich will interview both hockey players and officials.

He added that a number of policemen also saw the attack.

Inspector Conley said it's possible a charge of assault causing bodily harm will be laid by the crown attorney's office.

Under the Criminal Code of Canada, assault causing bodily harm is defined as someone who unlawfully causes bodily harm to any person, or commits an assault that causes bodily harm to a person.

The offence is punishable by a two-year prison term.

More than $1,700 in automatic fines are pending as a result of a violent weekend in the NHL's pre-season schedule.

NHL president Clarence Campbell said today: "The civil jurisdiction is paramount and any time the police feel it's essential to intervene at a hockey game, they're clearly at liberty to do so.

"However, I have reservations against the advisability but it's up to the crown attorney if he should decide to press charges.

"The NHL won't try to influence anyone.

"I do feel we can take care of these things and our own system of discipline is adequate.

If the police press charges it would establish a precedent of almost 50 years in the NHL. There has never been an arrest leading to a prosecution in 50 years."

The Green-Maki incident was the second involving the Bruins in two days and both resulted in players leaving the benches to join the fights.

In Montreal Saturday night, the players' benches emptied when Dick Duff of the Montreal Canadiens and Jim Harrison of Boston fought.

League president Clarence Campbell said all members of both teams —with the exception of those on the ice at the time—will be fined $50 each.

Goalies Gerry Cheevers of Boston and Rogatien Vachon of Montreal both left their creases and are also subject to the $50 fines.

Green will also be fined $75 for arguing a minor penalty during Saturday's game.

And in Port Huron, Michigan, defenceman Carl Brewer of Detroit Red Wings was handed a misconduct penalty for arguing with a referee. He will also be fined $100.

Coach Scotty Bowman of St. Louis Blues said yesterday the National Hockey League has to get tough with stick-swingers to prevent injuries.

But he defended Wayne Maki, the Blues' player.

Bowman gave Maki's side of the incident at Ottawa, site of his team's training camp.

"When Green started swinging what else could Wayne do? He reacted naturally.

"I'll stake any of my players to a life suspension if they swing the lumber flagrantly. But where does it stop with Boston? They act like they are trying to live up to the clippings of Bobby Orr and the Animals."

Bowman, whose own playing career was ended by a fractured skull from a high stick while he was a 19-year-old forward with Montreal Junior Canadiens, added:

"The NHL hasn't explored enough avenues to control stick-swinging. Fines haven't stopped it. Suspending a guy for a few games is nothing.

"It might be different if a player was suspended a full year without pay.

"Players are well-warned for gambling in the NHL. If they are caught betting they know they are gone for life. Perhaps threatening lifetime suspensions would curb stick-swinging and clubbing referees."

Bowman described the incident "the way I saw it."

"Green hit Maki on the head with his stick and cut him a little. Then Maki gave Green a little jab on the temple. It wasn't a vicious two-hander like you might have heard. Green fell down, but he got up with help and skated to the clinic in the Ottawa Arena.

Neurosurgeon Dr. Michel Richard said yesterday Green was in satisfactory condition, and partial paralysis of the face and slight loss of feeling in one hand was clearing up. He will stay in hospital 10 days, and will return in about two weeks to have his skull patched with a plastic plate.

Toronto Globe and Mail, *October 3, 1967.*

"I like it when I see him get knocked down," Imlach said with pride yesterday. "He never stops getting up, does he? He gets up and scraps away. He kind of reminds me of myself, the way I used to play."

Ranger Harry Howell crunched young Imlach with a punishing body check against the boards on one occasion and Rod Seiling pinned him another time.

A few seconds later Imlach retaliated, putting all his 155 pounds into dumping Seiling at center ice. Later Imlach lined up the husky Jim Neilson and hit him with a hard check.

"Did you see him (Neilson) look around and see who'd bounced him?" said Punch.

What do you think?

1. *Do you feel that watching a violent sports contest or T.V. show increases the spectators' violent feelings, or helps to get rid of them harmlessly?*

4. COMMENTS ON THE MASS MEDIA: ITS ROLE IN VIOLENCE

How do the media influence our attitudes towards violence? How strong do you think this influence is? Desmond Morton's comments appeared in the Canadian Forum *of July 1969.*

The media do select. They do influence. They do develop attitudes. Who gave people the idea that politicians are crooks? Honest, clean-minded, unbelieving pompous reporters, that's who. Who says that all people who have grievances are cranks or deadbeats? And who decrees that people with troubles have to push their case to extremes of violence and disorder in hope of publicity?

PSYCHOPATHIC CRIMINALS MADE HEROES
Marshall Delaney reviewed Bonnie and Clyde *in* Saturday Night, *October 1967.*

Guns, violence, impotence, and cars—this is an American movie . . . I couldn't keep from asking myself whether Penn had not in fact contributed to the American violence-sickness he is analyzing; *Bonnie and Clyde* presents the psychopathic criminal as an American hero, and does so with great style and consistency. The message will be clear to all but the makers of the film: if life discourages you, if there's no hope in sight, then shoot your way out.

DEATH BROUGHT TO YOU LIVE BY U.B.S.

Michael Carreck satirizes the American networks' coverage of the Viet-nam war in Maclean's Magazine, January 1967.

We have the audience . . . I base this on the hunch that "Rat Patrol" and other like shows have conditioned the Folks Out There to take an interest in war. In this regard I have also to mention that the war-is-fun show, "Hogan's Heroes," had done more to make World War II swing than anything since Errol Flynn on the late show. . . . If the day comes for them to drop the Big One, we need to be palsy-walsy with the Boys in Blue if we want the Universal Broadcasting System to give our audience the from-the-bomb-bay coverage they're hoping for. . . .

What do you think?

1. (a) *In your opinion, does the mass media emphasize violence?*
   (b) *Do you think that the reporting of violent activities tends to create a climate of violence?*
   (c) *Does the mass media go beyond the mere reporting of violence and actually* create *it?*
2. *Many Canadians feel that the United States is a particularly violent country. Yet if the mass media reflect the attitudes and mores of the country which produces it, and since so much of our mass media is American-produced, does it follow that we may be as violent as the United States? Why or why not?*
3. *Analyze the elements of violence in athletics, movies, television, magazines and advertising. Do they encourage violence? If so, how?*

5. THE MACLEAN'S-GOLDFARB REPORT ON CANADIAN CULTURE AND VIOLENCE

Martin Goldfarb, a Toronto-based private consultant, collaborated with Maclean's Magazine *in publishing a report on the attitudes of Canadians towards violence.*

Mr. Goldfarb conducted his own survey. The results appeared in Maclean's Magazine, *August 1970.*

Attitudes about whether or not violence is natural vary widely by age, geographical area, education and income. The people most likely to regard a civil war as a natural development are those aged 25-34 (46%) with some university education (41%). A father and a mother not speaking to each other is considered most unnatural among French-speaking Que-beckers (83%). A high proportion of people aged 45-55 (47%) see nothing unnatural in a married couple's not sleeping in the same bed after an argument. However, only 26% of their more romantic sons and daughters, people aged 25-34, think it is natural to carry quarrels that far.

Goldfarb concludes from these figures that there is a fair amount of casual bickering, sometimes leading to major fights, going on daily in the average middle-class, English-speaking home. Most educated, well-to-do people are able to perceive this bickering as being wholly or partly an expression of love. But it indicates the degree to which violence creeps into the routine pattern of our lives, and is a symptom of the continued increase in the divorce rate.

TABLE 1

DO YOU THINK EACH OF THE FOLLOWING HAS OVERTONES OF LOVE OR VIOLENCE, BOTH OR NEITHER?					IS NATURAL OR NOT NATURAL?	
	Love %	Violence %	Both %	Neither %	Natural %	Not nat. %
Mother and son arguing over standing in school	48	4	20	26	90	10
Mother and father fighting over son's use of car	32	11	21	36	82	17
Sister and brother not speaking	15	17	24	42	70	29
Civil war	2	79	12	6	35	63
Parents not sleeping in same bed after an argument	10	22	24	43	35	65
Mother and father not speaking	16	22	28	33	50	48

WHAT MAKES A HEALTHY FAMILY?

Many Canadians apparently believe family relationships are phoney if they are based entirely on love. This attitude is particularly common among English Canadians. The population is evenly divided on the question of whether there is a need for violence and love in a healthy family—49% saying yes and 49% saying no. And nearly half of the people questioned (48%) believe the family environment is best when there is some violence and lots of love. Some sample comments:

—"When you bring up children in a loving home a few arguments don't matter. Never hit anyone fiercely."
(A laborer in Montreal).
—"Any child in a pampered state who has not had a normal family life that included a bit of violence will have a rude awakening when facing the world on its own."
(A young Vancouver executive.)

—"If there is no violence, somebody is bottling up an emotion. It is
bad for a healthy family."
(A male manager in Winnipeg.)
—"People need violence to see if they love each other."
(A grandmother in Quebec City.)

*   *   *   *   *

DO WE ENJOY SEEING VIOLENCE?

People are generally reluctant to admit they like seeing violence.
Table 2 suggests that many people certainly enjoy it. Analysis of this chart,
says Goldfarb, indicates that poorer people don'e become as upset by conflict as those who are better off. Almost all (92%) those making between
$10,000 and $12,000 are disturbed by pictures of war massacres. Of the
people making less than $6,000 only 76% react negatively to such pictures.
Goldfarb explains: "People in the lower-income groups are pragmatic about
conflict. They are less inclined to say violence is a basic human need but they
are also less timid about witnessing it. Violence is something they live with."

TABLE 2

WHICH OF THE FOLLOWING DO YOU OR DO YOU NOT LIKE TO SEE?			
	Don't like to see %	Like to see %	No comment %
Fighting at a hockey game	60	39	1
War-massacre pictures	83	17	–
Gangland shooting on TV	75	25	–
Picture of war in Vietnam	61	37	2
Two women fighting physically on TV	82	17	1

WHO ARE THE MOST VIOLENT PEOPLE IN OUR SOCIETY?

A majority of Canadians believe that violence is inevitable, sometimes even beneficial in our society. Asked whether violence is always bad
or evil, 55% of the respondents said no. More than half the population believe violence is in some way a basic human need; 15% are convinced of
this. A breakdown by income groups (see table 3) shows that people in the

$10,000 to $12,000 bracket favor violence most strongly. These make up the group Goldfarb calls "the strivers" in contemporary society, wage earners aggressively trying to get ahead in the world. They view life as a tough dog-eat-dog struggle, in which some violent behavior is necessary for survival. A sampling of comments confirms this:

—"People need violence, especially in 1970. They have to fight to get what they want."

(A young Montreal cartoonist.)

—"We are all animals and we also have some of the basic instincts of love and violence."

(A middle-aged Toronto salesman.)

—"A person has violent emotions that have to be released."

(A Winnipeg comptroller.)

TABLE 3

DO YOU THINK VIOLENCE IS A BASIC HUMAN NEED?			
	Agree strongly %	Agree somewhat %	Disagree %
INCOME			
under $6,000	16	40	44
$ 6,000– 8,000	10	46	44
$ 8,000–10,000	13	48	39
$10,001–12,000	34	25	41
over $12,000	21	49	30

*   *   *   *   *

CAN WE BRIDGE THE GULF BETWEEN OUR TWO CULTURES?

There are . . . profound differences between the two cultures in their attitudes to violence and family love. For instance, here's a breakdown into language groups of the people who think the following things should be sold or shown without restriction:

TABLE 4

	Eng %	Fr %
War toys	35	13
War movies	47	25
War stories on TV	51	29

Most French Canadians (61%) believe violence is always bad, while only 38% of English Canadians think so. And although 63% of the French reject the suggestion that both violence and love are needed for a healthy family relationship, a majority of English (52%) accept it.

"French-speaking Canadians are clearly more emotional and desire close family relationships," says Goldfarb. "These differences in attitude to violence inside and outside the family must affect life-styles and choices of pastimes. They help explain why understanding the other culture must involve more than merely learning the language."

*　　*　　*　　*　　*

SHOULD WAR TOYS BE BANNED?

A curious response emerges from table 5 below: nearly half of all Canadians believe war toys should be banned, but only one quarter favor outlawing real guns. We seem aware of the dangers of encouraging violence in children but less ready to deny the violent emotions in ourselves. . . .

TABLE 5

SHOULD EACH OF THE FOLLOWING BE RESTRICTED, NOT SOLD OR SHOWN, OR AVAILABLE TO EVERYBODY IN CANADA?				
	Restricted %	Not sold %	For everybody %	No comment %
Guns	67	24	9	–
War toys	28	42	29	1
War movies	42	16	42	–
War pictures in magazines	31	17	51	1
War stories on TV	39	14	46	1

What do you think?

1. *Do the findings of the Goldfarb survey surprise you? Why or why not?*
2. *What would your position be in table 3? Can we hope for a gentle society?*
3. *Goldfarb has shown that French Canadians are less inclined towards violence than English Canadians. How important do you think cultural influences are in forming a person's attitude towards violence?*

4

The Historical Experience

Canadians often describe their country's history as "non-violent," particularly when they compare it to the turbulent past of the United States. They frequently congratulate themselves on their civilized methods of effecting change, and assert the superiority and stability of their institutions and traditions.

This complacency was shaken as Canadians awoke to the turmoil of the 1960s, which demonstrated that Canadians are quite capable of radical and even violent actions. Surprised, many Canadians protested that "this type of thing doesn't happen in Canada."

They were wrong, as the following pages, dealing with violent episodes in Canada's history, will demonstrate. We have chosen seven incidents which reveal that Canadians have, for various reasons, chosen violence in the past to express their grievances for the purpose of remedying them.

(1) The Sons of Freedom Doukhobor Sect

(2) The 1930s

(3) Cape Breton Unrest

(4) The Winnipeg General Strike

(5) The Northwest Rebellion

(6) The Rebellion of 1837

(7) The Rebellion Losses Bill

Every issue facing us today has its historical roots as well as its present-day dimensions. Do the actions of those involved in present-day violence resemble those of past participants? Does the Canadian tradition in dealing with violence, be it repressive or tolerant, influence the attitudes of Canadians today? Does the study of the past reveal certain patterns behind events that can guide our actions in the present? Or is history merely a series of chance events that cannot illuminate our present problems at all? Have we learned from the past, or are we condemned to repeat it?

It is not our intention to answer these questions for you, but rather to stimulate you to examine them in greater detail so that you may see the relationship between the past and the present more clearly.

The Sons of Freedom

Late in the nineteenth century, the Doukhobors began to emigrate to Canada from Russia. They were members of a religious sect who, among other things, refused to be subject to any kind of civil government. They hoped that in Canada they would find complete freedom from governmental interference of any kind. Within the ranks of the Doukhobors were to be found a small extremist group called the Sons of Freedom. These fanatics were especially concerned about resisting modern Canadian influences particularly those their children would be subjected to in the educational system. And, moreover, the Sons of Freedom felt that the terroristic tactics they adopted to save their own unique way of life were, in themselves, an act of religious worship.

The first document is a description of the Doukhobors in 1970. The last three are newspaper items from 1962, when the Sons of Freedom terror reached its frightening climax in British Columbia.

1. HOW CANADA'S FIRST TERRORISTS WERE CRUSHED

On October 17, 1970 the Toronto Star *published an article about the Doukhobors, who were referred to in the article as Canada's "first" terrorists. Why was this article published during the October Crisis? Can you see a resemblance between the Doukhobors and the FLQ?*

On a lonely road overlooking Mountain federal prison, several hundred men and women who know more than anyone else in Canada about political terror are quietly preparing for winter.

Unlike almost everyone else across the nation, the pathetic remnants of the Sons of Freedom Doukhobor sect are unconcerned, and perhaps genuinely unaware, that governments in Ottawa and Quebec are facing their most serious threat in years, due to the tactics of the Front de Libération du Québec, a group not unlike themselves.

In the mountains just north of this village 75 miles from Vancouver, there is a strange collection of 200 shacks and cottages, where old men with a fantastic history of political sabotage are cutting wood and eating sunflower seeds.

Their language is Russian and their attitude is unhelpful, if not unfriendly. They profess to be poor peasants with no knowledge of anything in the world outside.

Yet this strangest of all Canadian sects, still living without benefit of electricity or running water, is the only group in Canadian history up until now to hold the power of government at bay by sabotage and terror. And hidden in its secret archives there may be a lesson in what happens when federal forces are arraigned against a radical minority.

The Freedomites are comparatively quiet now, although four of the terrorists were recently sentenced to jail for possession of explosives, four of their women are on trial for burning down the house of sect leader John J. Verigin, and one man was recently killed in a brawl.

To most Canadians east of British Columbia the Sons of Freedom Doukhobors are known somewhat hilariously for their habit of burning down shacks while simultaneously taking off their clothes.

This is the conduct which fascinates the wire services and the headline writers, but less well known and far more important, is the fact that an organized group of Freedomite terrorists, working in cells under fanatical discipline, less than ten years ago brought the whole economy of a large section of British Columbia to a standstill.

This may seem junior league compared with the current political kidnappings in Quebec; but over the years at least 20 people have died because of Freedomite activity; there have been about 1,200 bombings of public and private property; and the direct cost in property damage stands at around $20 million.

At one point in 1962 there was real danger of civilian vigilante action in much of southern British Columbia. Responsible authorities called for imposition of military law. Public buildings were floodlighted, armed guards prowled the streets and military-type roadblocks were everywhere.

In practical terms, there was some erosion of democratic rights. Most Doukhobor names end in the letters "off" and the RCMP painstakingly searched their cars while waving on the vehicles owned by people with names like "Smith" or "Jones."

In the background, members of a special Royal Canadian Mounted Police squad did a fantastic sleuthing job based on methods developed by the Security and Intelligence Branch. At one point they attempted to chronicle the history of every alarm clock and pocket watch sold in the Kootenays. Watches and clocks are vital to time bombs in both the Kootenays and Quebec.

In response to public demands that the Sons of Freedom should be summarily arrested, the RCMP eventually hit upon a plan. In March of

1962 a military-type operation involving 160 officers fanned out over the Kootenays. All 52 members of the Freedomite ruling body, the Fraternal Council, were arrested and charged with conspiracy to intimidate the Parliament of Canada, a Criminal Code offence closely related to sedition.

The arrests quieted public indignation although they touched off an unprecedented wave of arson and nudity. But in the end the conspiracy charge was thrown out on a technicality, and only those convicted of substantive offences of bombing or arson were jailed.

Even so, the trials and subsequent imprisonments prompted the Freedomites to leave their burned villages and travel en masse to Vancouver, and later to Agassiz, where they remain to this day.

Their weird little village still stands in the mountains, just as it did seven years ago. When they arrived in 1963, the Freedomites were stopped at the gates of Mountain prison. They climbed out of their bus and private cars and erected tents.

Over the years the tents have been covered with plywood and lumber, but essentially the Freedomites are still parked by the side of the road, waiting for a signal to do something. The land they occupy is owned by the municipality of Kent, which with some provincial assistance supplies schooling for the children and welfare for the indigents.

Freedomite men are good workers when the spirit moves them, and most now work on surrounding farms or in logging operations. The women tend the lamps and grow the gardens, the children go to school and mix fairly well with the non-Doukhobor community.

It's a strange resting place for the radical wing of the Doukhobors who came here from Russia at the turn of the century. Their first spiritual leader, Peter, the Lordly, Verigin, was killed with eight other people when a passenger train was bombed in 1924.

Of the 20,000 Doukhobors in Canada, most are remote but law-abiding. The radical wing, numbering about 2,500, has been engaged in endless strife with the authorities, much of it violent.

Although not as politically sophisticated as the FLQ, the Freedomites have many of the same characteristics. Their public utterances feature the same complaints, often concerning economic mistreatment.

The other similarity is that while there were only about 200 active terrorists, their activities were passively protected for years by thousands of sympathizers, who knew what was going on and kept silent until forced into the open quite recently.

At the moment they look and talk like harmless characters, some smartly dressed in leather coats, others in the flowing peasant clothes of old Russia.

What do you think?

1. *Compare the grievances of the Doukhobors with those of the Canadian Indian and the FLQ with respect to cultural, social, political, and educational aspirations.*

2. Compare the actions taken by the FLQ and the Doukhobors and the effects of these actions.

2. SEEK TROOPS TO HALT B.C. TERROR BOMBS

The Toronto Star of March 8, 1962 describes Doukhobor violence.

The Associated Chambers of Commerce of Southeastern British Columbia have sent a telegram to Prime Minister Diefenbaker and Premier W. A. C. Bennett urging "special measures, as in wartime, to be used if necessary, to end this destruction by fire and bomb."

The telegram followed the terror-bombing of a giant power tower here Tuesday that cut off power and forced the layoff of nearly 1,000 workers.

The mayors of Kimberley, Trail, Nelson and Creston and the associated chambers of commerce of the area called on the federal government for troops to end the terrorism.

In the House of Commons yesterday, the Prime Minister assured British Columbia M.P. H. W. Herridge that the federal and B.C. governments had discussed the situation and were considering steps toward "an effective solution" of the Doukhobor problem.

The British Columbia government has posted a reward of $10,000-a-head for information leading to the conviction of those responsible for the bombing of the power tower.

3. MARTIAL LAW URGED FOR B.C.

The Winnipeg Free Press of March 9, 1962, reports some of the public response to the violence.

Nelson, B.C. (CP)—A heated public meeting here called Thursday for drastic measures to end 30 years of terror in the southeastern B.C. Kootenays, stronghold of the radicals Sons of Freedom Doukhobors.

As a result, the citizens may place a motion before city council today insisting that a state of emergency exists and demanding that the east and west Kootenays be placed under the militia.

Attorney-General Robert Bonner said in Victoria he would not hesitate to ask for Canadian Army help if such action is needed.

Meanwhile, R.C.M.P. continued to investigate the Tuesday night bombing of a 300-ton, 266-foot power tower which crippled industry in the area and left 1,000 men without work.

The Consolidated Mining and Smelting Company said in a telegram to provincial and federal officials it feared future acts of terrorism may extend to other parts of the company's operations. The telegram asked for protection.

Suggestions at the public meeting ranged from martial law to sterilization of male terrorists. The 150 citizens agreed that the RCMP, bolstered by 17 additional officers since the pylon blast, are powerless to suppress the violence.

After the meeting one man hinted at an attack this weekend on the Freedomite headquarters of Krestova, a shacktown 25 miles west of here.

The unidentified man said: "All we do is talk, talk, talk. They better get the militia in here by Saturday. Some of the boys are going to drink Saturday night, and then, watch out Krestova."

Alderman B. C. Affleck called for martial law, armed guards and changes to the Canadian Criminal Code.

He also said it should be possible, if deemed necessary by two judges of the Supreme Court, to have twice-convicted saboteurs sterilized.

Earlier in the week the B.C. Government announced that $10,000 will be paid for information leading to the conviction of each of the pylon bombers.

More than 85 members of the stormy sect have been arrested since a fall RCMP crackdown on terrorism which has ranged from attempted church bombings to blasting sections of the Canadian Pacific Railway track.

Many have been convicted, and sentenced to prison terms ranging up to 28 years. Others are still awaiting trial.

The Doukhobors migrated to Canada in 1899 to escape persecution in Russia. In the Kootenays the group split into several factions. The Freedomites, who still cling to ancient teachings, became the most fanatic.

The orthodox Doukhobors are law-abiding, but the 4,000 Freedomites whose creed is non-violence and anti-militarism have been caught in terrorist activities many times in the last 30 years.

RCMP officers say the most recent outbreak of violence is probably in reprisal for recent jail sentences given Freedomites by a special assize court.

What do you think?

1. It has been suggested that the public often reacts hysterically when threatened by violence. In this light discuss the following extracts from the above document.
   (a) "All we do is talk, talk, talk. They better get the militia in here by Saturday. Some of the boys are going to drink Saturday night, and then, watch out Krestova."
   (b) "Alderman B. C. Affleck called for martial law, armed guards and changes to the Canadian Criminal Code. He said it should be possible . . . to have twice-convicted saboteurs sterilized."
2. How might the pacifist Freedomites justify their terrorist tactics? Why or why not would you agree?

4. IS THERE A PEACEFUL SOLUTION?

The editorial reaction of the Winnipeg Free Press *of March 14, 1962, to Doukhobor violence:*

The difficulty of finding a reasonable solution to the Sons of Freedom problem in British Columbia has led to demands for unreasonable solutions.

Following the recent blasting of a power transmission tower, assumed to have been done by sect members, there was talk of mob action. Nothing came of it, but further terrorist activity on such a scale could make necessary a heavy guard on the sect's settlement at Krestova.

Less violent proposals have included a demand by Mayor Shorthouse of Nelson that sect members be dispersed throughout Canada. Identity cards, curfews, and other violations of civil liberties on a group basis have been suggested.

The RCMP have been doing excellent work in tracking down the terrorists and their leaders. Arrests, trials, and convictions have been numerous. But building jails to house the convicted will not satisfy area residents. Understandably, they are more interested in prevention than in punishment. What can be done, short of walling off the Sons of Freedom, and making an internment camp of Krestova?

In the short run, the watchful presence of disciplined men, police and possibly soldiers, is clearly necessary. Their duties should be determined by strategic necessity, not by public sentiment.

But in the long run, the only hope is to encourage the Sons of Freedom out of their fanaticism. It is not necessary to make them full Canadians in the usual sense; if they can merely be drawn back into the peaceful fold of their fellow Doukhobors, the basic problem will be solved.

This is not impossible, but will require time and effort. Already Sons of Freedom children are being educated away from their parents; there is evidence that some of the young men are perturbed about sect leadership. Psychological knowledge of the nature of the sect's fanaticism should be sought and applied. Key points here include the inability of many Sons of Freedom to comprehend the law that brings them into Canadian courts, or to comprehend the incompatability of pacifism and violence.

But police state activities must be avoided, and civic officials must sooner or later take the lead in convincing the sect that the public wants to help them, not destroy them, once violence is ended.

What do you think?

1. Compare the reactions of the British Columbia and Ottawa governments during the Doukhobor terrorism with the steps taken by Quebec and Ottawa to combat the FLQ crisis in 1970.

2. *"But police state activities must be avoided. . . ."* What, in your opinion, is the best method for dealing with terrorists?
3. One of the grievances of the Sons of Freedom concerned their children's education. If a situation like the Doukhobor terrorism of 1962 arose again, what would you do if you were Chief of Police? Minister of Education?

The 1930s

In the 1930s Canada like every nation in the Western World experienced a prolonged and devastating economic depression. Thousands of men were unemployed and many families found themselves on the verge of destitution. Farmers, when they had crops to sell, could only obtain very low prices for their produce. All levels of government seemed incapable of handling effectively the crisis situation. There was a profound sense of disillusionment across Canada. And some desperate men began to look for radical solutions for the perplexing problems they were facing. It seemed to many that existing governments were both unwilling and unable to deal with the crisis situation. Leading those favouring a radical and revolutionary reshaping of Canadian society were the Communists. But the Communists, it should be pointed out, were only a tiny though noisy minority of the Canadian population. The vast majority of Canadians waited the Depression out.

1. A CONSERVATIVE JOURNAL: "RED" ACTIVITIES IN 1930-31.

The Canadian Annual Review, *1930-31 provides a brief description of Communist and radical left-wing agitation in Canada in 1930. The description comes from a non-radical, somewhat conservative publication.*

In times of economic stress, revolutionary agitation tends to be rife. The Dominion was not free from such during 1930, though no exceptional manifestations of the kind fail to be recorded.

"Red" activities at Toronto focussed attention, perhaps more than elsewhere, owing to the controversy which arose over the action of the police in suppressing Communistic demonstrations. A number of citizens took the view that undue severity had been exercised, and that there had been, in effect, an invasion of the right of free speech and assembly. A long-drawn out newspaper discussion followed. On January 15, 1931, there appeared a "manifesto" signed by 68 professors of the University of Toronto, urging that full opportunity for the expression of political views be permitted, provided they were neither seditious, blasphemous, nor indecent. The Chancellor of the University, the veteran Chief Justice of Ontario, Sir William Mulock, on the other hand, in a public address shortly after, delivered an impressive warning against permitting Communistic doctrine to enter into the body politic, further advocating that anyone disseminating such principles should be excluded from Canada.

*   *   *   *   *

At various points during the Summer and Autumn of 1930, clashes occurred between Communists and police. At Montreal a raid was conducted by the police upon Communist offices, and materials of an alleged seditious character seized. Communist demonstrations at Niagara Falls on August 1 were broken up by the crowd and the leaders compelled to leave. At Port Arthur, where a Finnish Communistic organization was effected in August, collisions between the civic authorities, Communists and unemployed occurred during October, 1930. Street disturbances on October 21, accompanied by attacks on the police and threats that shops would be looted, led to an augmenting of the police force which succeeded in maintaining order. On October 28 the premises of the Canadian Labour Defence League at Port Arthur were raided by city and Provincial police and the papers of organizations, whose headquarters were there, were seized. A detachment of Royal Canadian Mounted Police assisted in these movements. Threats of a similar demonstration at Sudbury about the same time were met by increased police activity. At Hamilton on November 7, a "Red" parade was halted and eight arrests made. The Winnipeg police on November 22 raided the headquarters of the Communist Party, and at Vancouver similar action took place on December 23.

What do you think?

1. What forms of expression were denied to the Communists in 1930-31? What alternatives were left to them?
2. Are minority groups given more freedom of expression today?
3. Compare this article with the "legitimate" forms of protest discussed by Justice Minister Turner on page 103.

2. RED MEETINGS RESULT IN MAY DAY RIOTS

The authorities in Canada reacted violently to what they called Communist agitation. What particularly concerned the authorities was Communist propaganda advocating the overthrow of the government as well as the attempts made by the Communists and their supporters

to bring about violent confrontation. *But many law enforcement officers and the governments they served refused to distinguish between
the Communists, who were in favour of the violent overthrow of government, and the socialists and others who favoured a democratic and
peaceful restructuring of Canadian society. Furthermore, it should be
realized that in some of the more violent confrontations it was the
police who began the bloodshed and who forced hitherto peaceful
demonstrators or strikers to lash back in self defence.*

*The first of May was a day of celebration for Communists and
Marxists all over the world. The following five news reports of some of
the May Day activities which occurred across the country in 1931 catch
something of the flavor of the agitation. They were compiled in the
Montreal Gazette of May 2, 1931.*

Port Arthur, May 1.—Using their batons freely, smashing banners
bearing revolutionary utterances, and tearing red tags from the coat lapels
of May Day demonstrators, a squad of about 20 city and provincial police
and 10 Royal Canadian Mounted Police prevented an attempt of the unemployed to form a parade this afternoon.

Following a number of speeches and a short band concert, in a
vacant lot in the presence of more than 1,000 people, including the Royal
Canadian Mounted Police detachment, and their squads of about seven men
each of the city and provincial police, the 200 or so demonstrators moved
down Lake Street and made an attempt to get into parade formation.

A parade without a permit is illegal and the police took about half
a dozen of the principals to the police station. It will be decided during the
night how many are to be actually charged and taken before the magistrate
at tomorrow's court.

TORONTO CONSTABLE INJURED

Toronto, May 1.—One constable suffered injuries which necessi-
tated his removal to hospital for emergency treatment, another was slightly
injured, and three men were arrested as a result of a demonstration here
today by local Communists.

PLANS CHANGED AT SOO

Sault Ste. Marie, Ont., May 1.—Plans announced here yesterday for
demonstrations throughout the city to celebrate May Day failed to mature,
although an open-air meeting was held on a James Street vacant lot, attended
by several hundred people, most of them curious bystanders. Rev. W. J.
Cowherd, Ivan Petelka and two others whose names were not announced
addressed the meeting. Police were on hand to prevent disturbances, but

their services were not required. There was no parade in the city, but banners calling on the workers to band themselves against capitalism were displayed in the crowd.

Winnipeg, May 1.—Historic Market Square, scene of many a workers' meeting, tonight was crowded by thousands of men and women while leaders of the Communist Party of Canada made militant speeches.

Heavy detachments of police surrounded the square and were stationed along nearby streets, but Winnipeg's May Day demonstration was without riot or even minor disorder. Constables of the Royal Canadian Mounted Police and provincial police were in barracks, called from their posts in rural districts, but their services were not required.

Led by a band of little girls dressed in red, the Communists and thousands of unemployed marched from Market Square through the principal business section of the city. They returned to the square, where again prominent Communists addressed the crowd, denouncing in fiery terms the capitalist system and present-day governments.

SEVERAL INJURED IN CALGARY
Calgary, May 1.—Seven men were arrested and many suffered slight bruises during a clash between Communists and police in a May Day celebration here today. None of those injured was seriously hurt, but around 25 men, including police, received blows from sticks and billies.

What do you think?

1. *Based upon the evidence available in these articles who do you feel should shoulder the blame for whatever violence occurred?*
2. *Why do you think the situation was more volatile in Port Arthur for example, than in Sault Ste. Marie? Do the newspapers create, or merely reflect this impression?*

3. "COMMUNISTS" CAUSE TROUBLE

The original source of this editorial published in 1931 was the Cochrane Northland Post. *However, another editor inserted the word "Communist" into the original when he reprinted it. Why would he do this?*

The Cochrane *Northland Post* calls attention to a serious situation in Cochrane and other Northern Ontario cities due to Communist agitators taking advantage of the unemployment situation to spread dissatisfaction and foment disorder. Cochrane for many weeks has been the Mecca for hundreds of transients who have flocked into the city from all quarters, east and west. These men have lost their outside occupation in the woods, the mines and on the farms and have drifted into Cochrane in the hope of finding something to do, or, failing which, to be kept in food and lodging. The municipality has been looking after them as best it could, but the burden has become intolerable and demands for aid are being made on the Ontario Government. An impasse has been reached.

The townspeople realize the plight of the transients and are willing to help them as far as possible. But they are rebelling against the tactics of Communists who have come in to preach disorder and to lead demonstrations. On Monday of last week these agitators organized a big parade, which marched to the Town Hall, where they interviewed Constable McCulloch, of the Provincial Police, who informed them the Acting Mayor was out of town, but would be back the next day. The paraders later started to riot, attacking motorists and pedestrians alike, and when the police intervened they were driven off by superior numbers. In the skirmish several of the officers were injured, one so seriously that he had to be taken to the hospital. The mob then marched through the streets, shouting insults at residents of homes on their way and using foul and blasphemous language.

The citizens resented these tactics so much that they later poured forth into the streets, "literally seething with indignation and expressed the determination to 'mop up' the trouble-makers." According to the *Northland Post,* the town has since resembled an armed camp rather than a peaceful community. Provincial police have come in to assist the local authorities. The citizens point out that the trouble is due to certain transients who are unemployed and whom they are feeding to the best of their ability. They say that the limit has been reached and that the Communist leaders must be dealt with summarily by Government authority. Their attitude has reason behind it.

The troubles of Cochrane may be repeated in other communities if the agitators are not promptly suppressed. Municipal as well as provincial and federal authorities are trying to meet the transient unemployment situation in the towns. It is intolerable that their honest, practical, efforts should be interfered with by men whose only mission is to counsel destruction.

What do you think?

1. *"Canadian society in general, and the establishment newspapers in particular, reflected the popular fear of Communism that was present during the 30s." Why was Communism seen as such a severe threat in the 30s? Do you think it was a threat in the 30s?*

2. *In this document who exactly were guilty of violence? Is this true today?*

3. *"Canadian society is much less repressive today than it was during the 1930s." Discuss.*

4. WARFARE BREAKS OUT IN ESTEVAN

The next three documents concern the often bloody strike in the coal mining community of Estevan, Saskatchewan. The strike occurred because of the refusal of management to recognize the miners' union. Other factors were a cutback in wages, and poor living conditions. This news account has been taken from the Winnipeg Free Press of September 30, 1931.

Estevan, Sask., Sept. 29.—Warfare broke out in the town of Estevan Tuesday afternoon leaving in its wake a grim toll of death and destruction as police battled for three-quarters of an hour with a mob of striking miners.

Late Tuesday night it had been determined that two strikers had been killed by rifle bullets, five strikers gravely injured, five bystanders and twelve policemen injured during the fracas.

Nick Narwan, one of the dead, was shot through the heart as he mounted a fire truck which was used to play water on the rioters. Julian Jryshko, Dienfait, was shot in the abdomen as he was milling in front of the town hall with the rioters. He died as he was brought into the Estevan hospital waiting room.

One mounted police officer, Constable Sutherland, R.C.M.P., was gravely injured during the riot. One other had his arm fractured by a bullet, and others received scalp wounds from flying rocks and pieces of metal. Most of the policemen were able to carry on after emergency treatment.

The riot was precipitated when the strikers, four hundred in number, decided to hold a parade and demonstration in Estevan in defiance of an edict forbidding this. The total of arrests made by the police in the riot reached eleven men and three women.

The battle was all over in three-quarters of an hour. Terror reigned in the town Tuesday night, however, and police are waiting for reinforcements and preparing for another outbreak.

5. ESTEVAN'S BLACK DAY

This editorial is taken from the Winnipeg Free Press of October 1, 1931.

After three dragging weeks of dissension in the Estevan coal field two men have been killed and many injured in a pitched battle in the streets. Somebody has a lot to answer for. All over the world the development of coal fields has been accompanied by bloodshed and violence, and there will be many who think that it would be better to close up the Estevan field than to add still more loss of life to that staggering total.

The story as we have it is as old as the history of industry. The workers claimed grievances, and miserable working conditions. The mine owners denied that there is ground for these complaints and refused to meet the union formed by the strikers, claiming they were agitator-led and had Communist affiliations. The dispute dragged on, and even the appearance of a Dominion conciliator and the appointment of a Commission to investigate conditions had no result. Then the men decided to hold a parade through the town of Estevan. A permit was refused. The parade took place in spite of the refusal, and contact between police and strikers touched off the explosion.

It is fairly certain that, had the parade permit been granted, no loss of life would have resulted. This has been the usual experience in the past. Surely a parade is an absurd issue on which to stake life and death. The whole issue should have been grappled with many days ago. The Royal Commission had been appointed for some days. Why had its inquiry not been begun before? Now the investigation must be held under the shadow of Tuesday's tragedy, making the whole problem a more complicated one to handle.

6. ESTEVAN

This poem, signed "V.G." appeared in the Canadian Forum, *a journal of left-wing opinion, March 1932.*

Dig, dig,
For the fatted pig.

The story, Estevan, is in your scroll,
In writhing lines of lead and blood and coal.

Copper, pump 'em full of lead!
Slaves with a grudge are better dead.

        Dig, dig,
        For the fatted pig.

Coal in their blood as they paid the toll.
Give the owner blood in his coal.

Madam wants an exotic feather.
Lead and blood and coal together.

Dig, dig,
For the fatted pig.

What do you think?

1. List the moves and countermoves which led to violence at Estevan.
2. Was violent action by the miners, in your opinion, justified?
3. What positive or negative effects might the miners' actions have on their chances for winning reforms in their working conditions?

7. THE SENATE AND SECTION 98

The left-wing Canadian intellectual journal, the Canadian Forum, *though strongly anti-Communist, was angered at the way in which the members of the Communist Party, in 1931, were being arrested "without due process of the law." Section 98 of the Criminal Code, which had been enacted by the Canadian Parliament in 1919 to deal with the "seditious conspiracy" behind the Winnipeg General Strike, was being used to destroy the Communist movement in Canada. Section 98 would not be removed from the Criminal Code until the summer of 1936. The following article by F. R. Scott appeared in the January, 1932 edition of the* Forum.

It is shocking to realize that we very nearly had no law at all under which the Communist party could be declared an unlawful association. The totally inadequate criminal law which we inherited from England had nothing in it nearly so efficient as the present section 98 of the Canadian Criminal Code, in virtue of which the Toronto Communists were chiefly sentenced. There was only a vague rule about seditious conspiracies, which had hardly ever been enforced, which no one understood, and for which the maximum penalty was a paltry two years. It wasn't till 1919, after the world—and Winnipeg—had been made safe for democracy, that the new section was added. It was apparently invented by the State of New York, and it suited so well the famous American methods of repressing crime that we thought we had better copy it. But later it very nearly got taken off the statute book. Prosperity seemed to weaken the moral fibre of the public. On no less than five occasions the Canadian House of Commons passed a bill to amend the Criminal Code by repealing section 98. Five separate times—in the sessions of 1926, 1926-7, 1928, 1929, and 1930. If it had not been for our Senate of picked men, who manfully threw out the bill every time it came before them, we should have been in a pretty fix now. In the session of 1929 the bill failed to pass the Senate by only three votes. If two members had been a little sleepier that day, Canadian institutions might be tottering. No wonder we insist that every senator shall own at least four thousand dollars worth of property.

*   *   *   *   *

Our parlour Bolsheviks had better understand what they are in for if the present law is to be enforced to the full. Canada doesn't need to put up with their nasty new ideas if she doesn't want to. Section 98 creates so many new crimes and establishes so many presumptions of criminality that lots of people who are not actually Communists are liable to prosecution. It is a good red-blooded article, with 115 lines of definitions, offences, and penalties, all so obscurely worded that no one can be sure just how much liberty of speech and association survives—except that it is pretty small. The following examples of its provisions will show what the authorities could do if they really got on the warpath. After defining an unlawful association as one whose purpose is to bring about any governmental, industrial, or economic change within Canada by use of force, or which teaches or defends the use of force, to accomplish such change, or for any other purpose, the article goes on to say amongst other things:

(1) Any person who sells, speaks, writes or publishes *anything* as the representative or professed representative of such association;

(2) Any person who wears or displays *anywhere,* any badge, banner, motto, button, etc., indicating or intending to suggest that he is a member of or in *anywise associated with* such association;

(3) Anyone who solicits subscriptions or contributions for it or contributes *anything* to it or to anyone for it as dues or otherwise;

shall be guilty of an offense punishable by twenty years.

How about that for getting after friends and sympathizers of Communists? The italics are added to show the whole-hearted way in which Parliament tackled the job in 1919: lots of all-embracing *anywheres, anywises,* and *anythings.* Then comes a still better clause:

(4) In any prosecution under this section, if it be proved that the person charged has,

(a) attended meetings of an unlawful association;

(b) spoken publicly in advocacy of an unlawful association;

(c) distributed literature of an unlawful association by circulation through the Post Office mails of Canada, or otherwise;

it shall be presumed, in the absence of proof to the contrary, that he is a member of such unlawful association.

Just examine that for a moment, all you red college professors. None of your old-fashioned ideas that a man is presumed innocent until he is proved guilty. All the police need do here is to show that you once attended a Communist meeting, perhaps through curiosity, or spoke publicly in advocacy of the party, or distributed literature (presumably any kind of literature) of the party, and at once the Canadian legal machinery gets to work and says you are a criminal liable to twenty years. You won't escape gaol unless you can prove that you are not a member of the party. And think what it will be like trying to make this proof! Obviously no members of the party will dare to testify that you are a non-member, because by coming forward he would at once give notice to the police that he is a criminal. You will simply have to give your own word—and why should a college professor's red word destroy a legal presumption?

What is meant by?

"parlour Bolsheviks"
"red-blooded article"

What do you think?

1. How does Section 98 compare with the War Measures Act, invoked in 1970, in limiting the rights of Canadians?
2. What literary methods does the author use to emphasize his argument? Is this style more effective than a straightforward account? Why or why not?
3. Why does the author say "No wonder we insist that every senator shall own at least four thousand dollars worth of property"?
4. Do you feel that Section 98 was a valuable addition to the Criminal Code? Why or why not?

8. DETECTIVE KILLED IN REGINA RIOT

One of the most fascinating responses to the Great Depression in Canada, was the On-to-Ottawa-Trek of 1935. From the Pacific coast, a march of the unemployed, shrewdly led by a core of Communists, made its way to Ottawa where the protesters hoped to pressure the Conservative Government led by Prime Minister R. B. Bennett to do something about the plight of the unemployed. At Regina, there was a bloody confrontation and this incident led to the disintegration of the movement. The Ottawa Evening Citizen of July 2, 1935, provides an account of the Regina Riot.

Regina, July 2—Ominous quiet settled over Regina today after a day of rioting and bloodshed. One man, Plainclothes Detective Charles Miller lay dead, fatally pummelled when caught in the surging melee of an army of relief camp strikers and sympathizers who turned violently upon police as they broke up an open-air meetings in the city's market square.

Another man, identified as Dan McGee, a striker, was near death. He was found bleeding from head-wounds after the mob had been driven from the square by tear-gas, batons and bullets.

Five city constables were being treated for less serious injuries. Scores of strikers were in hospitals, treated by doctors called in to aid in the emergency.

Behind prison bars was tall, lank Arthur Evans, Toronto-born leader of the "On-to-Ottawa marchers," recruited from federal relief camps from the Pacific seaboard and the Prairies. Twenty-six other strikers are in custody.

For three hours after police charged the strikers' meeting, called to raise funds to keep the stranded camp deserters in Regina, fighting resumed through the city's streets. Dominion Day flags were ripped from buildings. Windows were broken. Property damage was heavy.

When dawn broke, the streets, strewn with debris, were almost deserted. Police continued to patrol all thoroughfares. Disorder had died.

Protected by steel helmets, wielding batons, Royal Canadian Mounted Police charged into the market-square meeting as one of the speakers began to tell of the necessity to raise funds for the marchers early in the night.

Some of those at the meeting fell upon the constables. A group of men attacked Detective Miller, an eye-witness told, beating him over the head with sticks until he lay on the street dead.

Tear gas bombs were hurled among the men, women and children who crowded the square. Eyes streaming from the stinging fumes, they fled. One woman fell. It was believed that her leg was broken in the crush.

Steel-helmeted R.C.M.P. and blue-coated city police kept the crowds moving but experienced no trouble after midnight. Police moved around in small squads. They stood in groups about every 150 to 200 yards and in same cases were closer together. They carried riding crops and batons and were armed with revolvers.

First warning of the raid on the meeting, called by the strike leaders to explain their negotiations with authorities and to ask for funds for food, was a quick sally of police from the vicinity of the police station.

First outbreak occurred when the helmeted Mounted Police swooped down upon the strikers and supporters meeting in the market square. They appeared as a spokesman began a plea for funds to aid the strikers, ordered by authorities to remain in Regina. They have camped here since June 14 when they were first halted on their "On-to-Ottawa" trek from western relief camps.

A score of men were taken into custody as police reinforcements were rushed by truck and on horse after the meeting broke up.

9. AN EYEWITNESS ACCOUNT OF THE REGINA RIOT

This report is by Richard Liversedge, from his Recollections of the On-to-Ottawa-Trek *(Vancouver: privately published, 1962).*

We rolled into Regina around the middle of the month, that is, June, 1935, and if there is any truth to this premonition business, then that is what most of us must have felt, because every one of us thought that something different would happen there, and of course, later on, something did happen.

Our entry into Regina was something of a triumph. We had been successful up to now, had built our forces up, and we were a proud little army. As we marched through the city streets, throngs of people lined the sidewalks to give us a rousing welcome. At the Exhibition Grounds where we were to stay as usual, an official welcome had been prepared for us.

*   *   *   *   *

There was lots of unemployment poverty on the prairies, and the people of Regina understood our struggle, and made it their own. There was understanding and cordial relations between the camp workers and the people of Regina, for the whole of the time that we were there.

*   *   *   *   *

[*While the trekkers were in Regina they received word that Prime Minister Bennett wanted to negotiate with them. Fearing that Bennett was only buying time in order to move Mounties into Regina, the strikers wanted to refuse the offer. But realizing that public opinion would turn against them if they did refuse, the strikers voted to send a delegation to Ottawa.*]

From that day on the trek took on a different complexion and a different tone. The men drew closer together, there was a new awareness, a new alertness. All seemed to be aware of and preparing for some kind of a crisis.

Before the delegation left for Ottawa, a small committee from our central strike committee contacted the Saskatchewan Premier, Mr. James Gardiner, his attorney-general, Mr. Davies, and some members of the cabinet. We apologized for our continual presence in Regina, but assured the premier and his colleagues that there was no cause for alarm regarding our conduct and that we could guarantee the good behaviour of every single man on the trek. This was the first of a series of meetings between the Saskatchewan cabinet and our committee. The meetings were always cordial, and Premier Gardiner and Mr. Davies were always courteous and friendly whenever we met them.

*   *   *   *   *

The delegation of eight from the trek had left by train for Ottawa. . . .

In Regina we tightened up our regulations, as we were receiving authentic news of police reinforcements arriving steadily, and being stationed around Regina. Militia being warned to be ready for call. Ominous signs. We were having routine marches around town, but one division now was always left at the Exhibition Grounds on guard. . . .

[The trekkers heard that the Ottawa negotiations as expected, had been an utter failure.]

In Regina we awaited the return of our delegation, and upon its arrival, a public meeting was held to report. It was a big meeting, and a condemnation of the boorish conduct of the Prime Minister. It was felt by the majority of the trekkers that we would have to retreat. The leaders of the trek were in daily contact with the Saskatchewan cabinet, and beginning to arrive at an agreement for calling off the trek.

Evans constantly warned Premier Gardiner and his ministers of the danger of allowing the federal authorities to usurp provincial autonomy in the field of law enforcement. The cabinet in Regina were fully alive to the danger, and all, from Premier Gardiner down, knew that the trek posed no threat to law and order in Saskatchewan. They accepted our pledged word as sacred. We knew that with the hundreds of police reinforcements we could not continue east on the railroad without severe strife and bloodshed.

We made a token run of three trucks, loaned by sympathizers, with a few men in each, on the provincial highway from Regina to the east. On the outskirts of Regina the trucks were stopped by the R.C.M.P. and the men thrown in prison. The sole purpose of this token run was to show the people of Saskatchewan that their province was being taken over by the federal police.

Then came the federal order-in-council, directed to the people of Regina, stating that any person who from that date, gave aid or succour to the "On to Ottawa" trekkers, would be prosecuted under section 98 of the Criminal Code.

By the first of July, 1935, our plans were made to call off the trek. Most of that day our committee had been in the Parliament Building conferring with premier and cabinet, and a public meeting was scheduled for the evening, on Regina Market Square, to acquaint the public of our decision. All that was left to do was the working out of details of our retirement. The Saskatchewan government had promised their help, but the Federal government had other plans.

Dominion Day, 1935, our country's birthday, and what a birthday celebration it turned out to be. The meeting that evening on Market Square, while not being as big as most meetings we had held, still had a substantial audience. . . .

There were probably four or five hundred of us [*trekkers*] on the Market Square, and there would be two or three hundred still having supper, or walking around town. The vast bulk of our men were watching two ball games out at the Exhibition Grounds.

The meeting wasn't long under way. Evans was speaking, when four large furniture vans backed up, one to each corner of the Market Square. A shrill whistle blasted out a signal, the backs of the vans were lowered and out poured the Mounties, each armed with a baseball bat.

They must have been packed very tightly in those vans, there were lots of them. . . . In less than minutes the Market Square was a mass of writhing, groaning forms, like a battlefield.

As we retreated I saw one woman standing over an upturned baby carriage, which had been trampled by these young Mounties, and I saw four Mounties pulling at the arms and legs of one of our men, whom they had on the ground, while a fifth Mountie continued to beat viciously at the man's head. This man they had down spent the next year in the mental institution at Prince Albert.

The surprise was complete, and it was a victory for the Mounties, the only one they had that night. Even at that, they were unable to follow up, as there were also not a few Mounties writhing on the ground. . . .

The word went around quickly, for the trekkers to assemble on one of the main streets to march back to the stadium. . . . Here is where our long stress on organization and discipline paid off.

A couple of men were dispatched to thumb a ride out to the stadium, to warn all trekkers there to stay in the Exhibition Grounds, not to come down town, but to post strong guards at all entrances. On that street in Regina, we assembled under group leaders. . . . . We had just started our march when somebody in a car coming towards us told us that there were two hundred horsemen lined across the street ahead of us, and then unmistakeably from away behind came the clop-clop of a large body of horsemen.

It was to be a squeeze play. We were not going to be allowed to get out of town. We were to be smashed up. How incredibly stupid. Immediately orders were given us to build barricades, and there was plenty of material to work with.

The street was lined with parked cars and we simply pushed them into the streets, turned them on their sides, and piled them two high. . . .

It was then, before the first futile charge was made by the Mounties, that the miracle happened. The young boys, and even some girls, of Regina, organized our ammunition column. Without being asked, they came riding bicycles in from the side streets, their carrier baskets loaded with rocks, and then rode off for another load.

The Mounties never reached the first barricades, that is, the ones at each end of the street, and the attempts which they made to get behind and in between the barricades from the side streets were all beaten back. . . .

There were casualties in every charge, and the horses couldn't face the heavy rock barrages, and always turned down the side street in front of us, often with the rider laying on the horse's neck.

*　　*　　*　　*　　*

The police must have had orders to beat and rout us thoroughly that night, for there can be no other explanation for the senseless continuation of those stupid horse charges.

We were not a rabble. We refused to be beaten up. We had tried desperately to avoid combat, even after the first unprovoked police attack. Whatever order was brought out of the chaos that night, then it was us, and not the police, who brought the order.

*　　*　　*　　*　　*

At one intersection where some of our men with lots of rocks were keeping at bay a squad of Mounties on foot, the Mounties tried tear gas, but they fired them into the wind, and the boys picked the gas shells up and lobbed them back at the Mounties.

It was here that the police fired the first revolver fire, the first casualty being an innocent bystander, or passer-by. He was a hospital orderly on his way to work at the general hospital, when he got shot through the stomach, and was still in a serious condition some months later, the last I heard of him.

It was a terrible night, downtown Regina a shambles. Not a store with a window left in, the streets lined up with rocks and broken glass, dozens of cars piled up in the streets with no glass in them, and twisted fenders and bodies.

*　　*　　*　　*　　*

It was decided that we break up into groups, scatter out, make for the suburbs, and by circling around the city, get back to our headquarters at the Exhibition Grounds, as there was no possible chance to get there by the main route, which was heavily guarded by cordons of police.

This plan was carried out, and most of the men got back. The people in the suburbs who were all out in their yards were very helpful, pointing out the best routes to take, and warning of which streets were being patrolled.

The group with which I started out had one more fight to face before we got them out of town. Circling around we came to an intersection, crowded by a large body of our men. . . . The strangest sight of all, to us, . . . were two lines of police, ordinary city police, in blue uniforms and helmets, shoes brightly polished, and very fresh looking.

*　　*　　*　　*　　*

Behind them were two lines of our old acquaintances, the Mounties, on horses. All was very quiet as we arrived, but, there was plenty of evidence that heavy fighting had taken place.

Like the rest of downtown Regina, the street here was ankle deep in rocks, our men breathing hard, but standing relaxed although each had an armful of rocks. The Mounties on their horses looked droopy and dejected. Only the city police looked fresh. The boys told us that the blue-coats had just arrived, something new was going to be tried.

All at once they started to come, and our group leaders gave the order, "Line up, boys, here they come!"

As the cops drew quite near, with nobody running, and no missiles coming yet, they showed some uneasiness. Then came the command from our leader. "Now, boys, and make it good!"

The blue coats tried to keep coming, but as one and then another went down they broke, and our first rank went after them. To escape our attack, the retreating bobbies drew their revolvers and opened fire. It was the heaviest gunfire of the night, and half a dozen of our boys were wounded. (That night forty of the trekkers received gunshot wounds.)

Then came the Mounties. It was a vicious attack, but was beaten back. The men of the trek were in a dangerous and resentful mood, bitter, and fighting mad. The mood to be, "You, the police, started this madness, you won't let us withdraw, so all right, come and get it." As it turned out, that unsuccessful attack of the city and Mounted Police was the last big skirmish of the night.

After the police withdrew . . . there came towards us . . . a solitary figure.

That he was coming to parley was clear and as he drew closer to the intersection we saw that the man was a City Police Inspector, or captain. He came right up to us and said, "Are you men going to disperse?"

One of our leaders answered, "Where have you been all night? And what the hell do you think we have been trying to do all night?"

"Never mind that now," this man said, "I'm in charge here at the present time, and this nonsense has gone on long enough. I'm giving you a chance to get out. From now on it's going to be all bullets. I'm going to clear the streets, and I'll clear them with gunfire if it's necessary, but I'm giving you time to clear out of town."

And turning to the Regina folks who were crowding the foyer of a cinema, he said, "And you people can go home if you do it right away, or otherwise go back into the theatre and stay there until you're told to go home."

We on our part said, "That's all we've been waiting to hear all night, and goodnight to you, Captain."

*   *   *   *   *

July 2nd, 1935, we arose from our straw to the gabble-gabble of excited comment, and on emerging into the open, a truly marvelous, almost unbelievable sight met our gaze.

The Exhibition Grounds at Regina were fenced in by that strong, industrial fence, with entrances at intervals all around the grounds, and at every entrance was a squad of Mounties with mounted Vickers machine guns facing into the grounds.

Along the whole side of the grounds was a railroad spur, which must have been for the purpose of unloading cattle and grain exhibits at the yearly fair. Here along this track were boxcars, and on top of the boxcars were Mounties, with Vickers guns facing into the grounds.

It was the first Canadian concentration camp. . . .

What do you think?

1. *This article presents the police as instigators of violence in Regina. What articles in the contemporary section of this book make similar charges? What reply might a police force make to these charges?*
2. *What controls should a democratic society place on its policemen to ensure that they will be responsible in their use of force?*

10. PRIME MINISTER BENNETT COMMENTS ON THE REGINA RIOT

During a debate in the House of Commons, recorded in Hansard, *July 2, 1935, concerning the Regina incident Bennett commented on the origins of the riot.*

I am infomed and I believe that this movement is, as the Minister of Justice has said, not a mere uprising against law and order but a definite revolutionary effort on the part of a group of men to usurp authority and destroy government. Those who are familiar with what happened in one city of this dominion at one time will appreciate how there may be a partial realization of their hopes and expectations in that regard, for no one who has read of what took place at that time, of the taking possession of government, the endeavour to police the city and to order its activities, to control the feeding of the people with a system of cards under allotments, can fail to realize the danger that confronts us in such a revolutionary movement as that. Some of these telegrams that come are signed with very strange names, such as the Junior Band of Communists. They now openly call themselves communists, no longer disguising themselves under some fictitious name, but glory in calling themselves communists and indicate clearly what their purpose is. Declarations were made by the leaders of this group in Regina, gathered together in the manner I have stated. I have stated as clearly as possible that they were not only those who came from the camps, with them I shall deal presently, but they were an aggregation of all those who had been attracted to this movement, some as a lark, an adventure, some for the purpose of finding opportunity to give effect to their opinions by the destruction of organized authority.

What do you think?

1. *How has Bennett substantiated his argument? If you were a member of the Opposition how might you reply to him?*

11. EDITORIAL: MR. BENNETT A HYPOCRITE

An editorial from the Ottawa Evening Citizen, *July 4, 1935, condemns Mr. Bennett's statements about the riot.*

Many Canadian people will continue to regard the talk about an organized revolutionary effort throughout Canada as grossly exaggerated. Experience in the past has demonstrated repeatedly that evidence of red revolutionary plotting is sometimes manufactured by police agents. They provide employment for themselves by persuading the government that sedition is rampant.

It is notorious too, as Mr. Woodsworth pointed out in debate last Tuesday, that police spies are employed to work inside the Communist organizations. Whether in Poland or in Canada, wherever this method is employed, one certain result has been to breed the agent provocateur. Revolutionary plots are hatched by some of the very agents of the government who are supposed to be working to save the country from revolution.

However exaggerated the fear of red revolution may be in Canada, members of the government have at least convinced themselves that the danger is real. When they argue in this manner, however, they indict themselves of having allowed the Communist menace to grow until it has contaminated the Canadian unemployed.

In 1930, before the Conservatives took over the government, Mr. Bennett's public utterances gave no hint of seeing signs of rampant Communism. He spoke of the unemployed only as the unfortunate victims of government incompetence at Ottawa. When he incited the unemployed against the government, he could hardly have believed that the men were red revolutionaries, but it would have been difficult to find any words more calculated to undermine respect for constituted authority than Mr. Bennett's address to the distressed people in Western Canada when he described the government at Ottawa as follows:

> This group of mercenaries, holding office by sham and subterfuge, look upon them as treacherous to you, self-confessed, deserving of your passionate condemnation.

In the years since, Mr. Bennett's administration has built up an enormous police organization across the country. When the unemployed have passionately condemned the government, they have been denounced as Communist agitators.

What do you think?

1. Throughout these documents there is evidence that an intense fear of communism existed in the 1930s. Has such a fear been repeated in Canada since then? Does it exist today? What conditions would prompt a "big Red scare"?

2. *Why does it appear necessary in times of stress that the establishment find a scapegoat? Who or what are the scapegoats today?*

12. PUBLIC BUILDINGS OCCUPIED IN VANCOUVER

In Vancouver in 1938, the unemployed organized a sit-down to bring public attention to the problems of the jobless in British Columbia. This sympathetic editorial appeared in the Vancouver Sun, May 26, 1938.

Since last Friday certain public and semi-public buildings in Vancouver have been invaded and occupied by a host of unemployed men who have drifted into Vancouver from many Canadian points.

This invasion and this occupation were not unforeseen. Ever since the forestry camps closed and jobless men, disinherited by the Federal Government whose responsibility they are, commenced to gather in this city, it has been plain that, unless Ottawa awakened to its obvious duty, some form of lawlessness was bound to ensue.

So far these men have exhibited amazing restraint. They have demonstrated, of course, a deep contempt for Government and their actions have given Vancouver much unfavorable publicity throughout the continent.

But the contempt for Government they have exhibited is not very much greater than that felt by the average citizen. What the foreign news services and foreign broadcasting stations have been saying about this situation is not very much stronger than what Vancouver people have themselves been saying about Ottawa.

The point is that issue has been joined, openly and even bitterly, between these drifting unemployed and the Government of Canada which refuses to do anything for them.

One of them must be right and the other must be wrong.

If Ottawa is right in its stand and these men are rebels, then Ottawa should have cleared them out of the Post Office and the Art Gallery, etc.

Ottawa has not done this. Ottawa has done nothing at all.

If Ottawa is wrong in its stand and these men are right, then work should have been found for them long since. Land should have been made available for them to support themselves. Construction works totalling more than the pitiful $40,000,000 provided in the estimates should have been planned to an extent that would absorb all Canada's idle labor.

But again Ottawa has done nothing. There is no land scheme. There is no adequate plan of public works. There is no attempt to enforce the law relating to illegal assemblies.

These "sit-down" demonstrations of the unemployed have symbolized:

(1) A breakdown in our economic machinery for dealing with labor.
(2) A breakdown in our natural machinery for protecting society against the wilful obstruction of malcontents.

Whichever way you look at it, Ottawa has simply failed to function.

The writer of this article has been a Canadian for five generations. Like thousands of others, he has behind him a century and a half of pioneering and hardship and adventure and a tradition of sacrifice and work devoted to the proposition of a brave new country arising out of a wilderness of fabulous new wealth and molded according to the ideals of freedom and democracy and active progress.

And what is the fruition of these five generations of Canadianhood, the flowering of this century and a half of pioneering effort?

Nothing but a feeling of shame and frustration at the total incapacity, the criminal neglect and the disgraceful indifference of Canadian leaders to the condition that has been permitted to develop here.

We have less real government in Canada today than prevails in any Hottentot village in darkest Africa. We have less governmental efficiency than prevails among the Negroes of the Gold Coast. We have less real leadership than was enjoyed by the captive Jews in Egypt before Moses was chosen to carry them out of bondage.

A century and a half of striving has been in vain. Generations of pioneers have worked and died to accomplish exactly nothing.

What do you think?

1. What do the following reveal about the author and his style?
   (a) "One of them must be right and the other must be wrong."
   (b) "pitiful $40,000,000"
   (c) "The writer of the article has been a Canadian for five generations."
   (d) "We have less real government in Canada today than prevails in any Hottentot village in darkest Africa."

Cape Breton Unrest

In the early 1920s, the coal-mining and steel-producing area of Cape Breton Island experienced tremendous union-management friction. There were frequent strikes and considerable bloodshed. Militant trade unionists found themselves in bitter conflict with intransigent management. The *Maritime Labour Herald* was a union-backed newspaper, while the Sydney *Post,* though sympathetic to big business, was very objective in its reporting and in its editorial comment during the period of labor-management turmoil on Cape Breton.

1. RIOTERS STONE TROOPS

The Sydney Post *of July 17, 1925, described a clash between strikers and troopers.*

The detachment of Royal Canadian Dragoons, which were forwarded here from Sydney last night were met on their arrival by a mob, which attacked the Mounted Men with sticks and stones. The troopers rode through a fusillade of flying missiles, one of which found serious target, a Dragoon being put out of business. His injuries were, however, not serious, and, after a short period, he was able to join his comrades.

The clash was of short duration, the troopers dispersing the mob without resorting to violence.

Early this morning the Dragoons returned to the city, and at the moment are in quarters at the steel plant.

During the melee plate glass windows in Anthony's brick block and McLellan's barber shop were wrecked.

Late reports from the Scotian area are to the effect that order prevails.

2. AFTERMATH OF BATTLE

An editorial from the Maritime Labour Herald, *June 18, 1925*

. . . In New Waterford particularly, where men in groups talk the battle over and re-enact every phase of it, all feel that while the men were only partly responsible for the beginning of the scrap, it was certainly they who finished it. While the men are duly elated at their victory nearly all of them are ashamed of the destruction and looting which followed all over the mining centres. The general public have ceased to sympathize with us. They now fear us. The calling out of the troops Saturday together with all the police and defensive forces of the city in order to defend it from assault by the Waterford warriors makes the Waterford men smile. The writer wishes to reassure the good people of Sydney, and promises to advertise any contemplated action against the city one week ahead. This from ordinary humanitarian motives and in order that woman and children and the Besco police may be removed to a place of safety.

3. TROOPS CALLED IN FOR CAPE BRETON STRIKE

Sydney Post, *June 19, 1925*

A troop train carrying some 400 officers and men and about 150 horses, arrived in the city this morning at 5 o'clock, and detrained at the steel plant, where they will go under canvas, and be ready for action should their services be needed in the strike zones to the north or south.

Two batteries comprised the section: that of the Royal Canadian Horse Artillery and of the Royal Canadian Artillery. They came direct from Petawawa camp, where they had been in quarters. This morning field guns were unloaded from the train.

Reports from the various strike areas this morning said that no violence of any kind was noted during the night, and it is believed generally that further outbreaks will not be precipitated.

What do you think?

1. (a) How do you account for the fact that organized labor which underwent such trying struggles in the early part of this century is so unsympathetic to the student protesters of to-day?
   (b) What are the similarities and differences between the aspirations and techniques of the student protesters today and of the labor people in the past?

4. STEELWORKERS SURROUNDED BY ENEMIES

An editorial follows from the pro-strike paper, the Maritime Labour Herald *dated August 4, 1923. John L. Lewis was the fiery leader of the United Mine Workers. Armstrong was the premier of Nova Scotia; King was at that time in power in Ottawa.*

After a heroic struggle that has lasted since the 27th of June the steel workers of Sydney have decided to return to work with their demands still unattained. That such a fight could be made by the steel workers against such forces lined up against them is in itself a great thing. The steel workers return to work conscious of the fact that the strike was a test of strength of their young union and that it stood the test. They go back to work knowing that they fought an unequal struggle and if they have to retreat at this time, at some time in the future they will be able to take up the fight for a better standard of living and, in that future struggle, the experience of this strike will stand them in good stead.

*   *   *   *   *

"Law and Order" has triumphed! It took both the provincial and federal governments, the troops and provincial police, the desperate lying of the capitalist press, the arrest of over a hundred workers, men and women, to prevent these steel workers gaining a few cents more a day in wages. What a victory for the Armstrong and King governments! They did their duty by Roy Wolvin and the shareholders of the corporation. John L. Lewis must also be given credit as a fine fighter in the interests of the corporation. By his treacherous action he forced the miners back to the mines leaving the steel workers battling alone against the labor-skinning corporation. No doubt the gratitude of Wolvin and Company will be expressed in gifts of great value to their faithful servants.

What do you think?

1. What is meant by the statement "Law and Order has triumphed" as it has been used in the above article?
2. Examine your initial reaction to the editorial. What is it exactly about this article that prompted your response?

The Winnipeg General Strike

The Winnipeg General Strike of June, 1919 was one of the most important and influential incidents in twentieth-century Canadian political and labor history. The strike began as a battle over whether or not certain workers should be represented by a trade union. When management proved intransigent, the labor movement decided to use the general strike—or general sympathy strike on the part of all workers— to pressure management into recognizing the right of workers to be represented in collective bargaining by a union of their own choice. The strike triggered an unprecedented anti-union backlash in Winnipeg and the rest of Canada. Many people opposed to the strike were convinced that a Bolshevik take over of Canada was imminent. But the strike, it should be emphasized, was certainly not controlled in any way by the Winnipeg Communists. Only a few were involved and they were far from the levers of power. Nevertheless, the strike was seen by those people who had traditionally controlled all levels of Canadian government as a very real threat to their influence and power by ordinary workingmen.

The *Morning Bulletin* and the *Manitoba Free Press* were the Winnipeg organs of the anti-strike forces who had organized the Committee of One Thousand to oppose the strikers. The *Strike Bulletin* was the mouthpiece of the strikers. Largely because of the activities of the Committee of One Thousand and the growing frustrations of the strikers, violence broke out on June 10 and continued for another eleven days.

Violence probably reached its peak on June 21. Some of the strike leaders were arrested, one of whom was the Reverend J. S. Woodsworth, a Methodist minister and the man who would be the first leader of the C.C.F. (the forerunner of the N.D.P.). In response to the strike the then Conservative Government under Robert Borden introduced a significant amendment to the Criminal Code—section 98—which, it was hoped, would help to deal more effectively with what many Canadians felt to be seditious behaviour. A discriminatory amendment to the immigration legislation was also passed during this time.

1. THE GREAT UNREST

An editorial appeared in the anti-strike paper the Morning Bulletin *of May 1, 1919.*

The threat of a police, fire department, street railway and building trades strike in Winnipeg is serious enough in itself, but even more serious is the evidence it affords that the sense of crime and social responsibility has largely given way to the idea that power held should be power used for the direct and special benefit of whoever holds it. Unless there is a recognition of the principle of individual responsibility for the welfare and safety of organized society, the organization of society cannot continue and civilization ceases to exist.

Civilization is built on the principle of the division of labor. Division of labor carries with it inequality in the measure of service rendered, and therefore inequality in the reward of service. There is no possible equality of service under the system of a division of labor. Therefore there cannot be equality of conditions or of reward of service.

Civilization as it is, is the result of the efforts of untold generations of men and women. It is not the work of the people of today. They did not make it. But they may destroy it. A cathedral that took a century to build may be burned down in a few hours. It is always hard to climb up. It is always easy to fall down. Former civilizations as great as this, have been swept away in waves of savagery.

As matters stand, there are inequalities in the burdens borne and in the rewards received for services rendered or work done. It is the duty of every one to aid in securing as fair an equalization of burden and reward as is humanly possible. The frequent and far-reaching changes of world conditions may make what was fair yesterday unfair today. There must be continual readjustment. That every readjustment shall be with a view to the best interests of all is the best that can be done in this world of many limitations.

In heaven it may be different and better, but for the present we have to deal with conditions as they are on earth. We did not make our own limitations or fix those by which we are surrounded. We can only do our best to better conditions as we find them. When we undertake to make over world conditions for our own special and sole benefit, the contract is too large to be successfully handled. Bolshevism can destroy. It cannot create.

What do you think?

1. *How would you describe the political stance of the writer? Why?*
2. *The writer states that "the sense of social responsibility has largely given way to the idea that power held should be power used for the direct and special benefit of whoever holds it."*
   (a) What does the writer mean by "a sense of social responsibility"?
   (b) Can an impartial sense of social responsibility ever exist? Why or why not?
   (c) ". . . world conditions may make what was fair yesterday unfair today." Are these changes in condition brought about by a sense of social responsibility or through an adjustment in the balance of power? Discuss.
3. *Why would the author say that the workers were trying to make over "world" conditions?*

2.   MAYOR GRAY ASKS CITIZENS TO AVOID VIOLENCE

A statement by the Mayor of Winnipeg appeared in the Manitoba Free Press *on May 1, 1919.*

TO THE CITIZENS OF WINNIPEG:

During the last few days the premier and myself have done all humanly possible to bring about a settlement of the untoward conditions at present pertaining between employers and employees We urged arbitration. When that was rejected we got the parties together several times for consultation to see if some agreement could be arrived at. This failing, we made suggestions of our own that might appeal to both sides, but all to no avail.

The strike will possibly be on by the time that this is in print, or soon after. It is likely to be the biggest strike in the history of our city. It will vitally affect every citizen and I want to make an earnest appeal to all, the employees, the striking members of all the unions, and to that great body of the public who have no responsibility, no say, in causing this tremendous struggle, but who will suffer as a consequence.

Citizens of Winnipeg: History has taught us that men only learn wisdom under the pressure of calamity—calmness, patience and British fair play are the salient attributes that must and will guide us safely through this trying hour in our city's life.

I firmly believe that no one individual would willingly cause suffering to another, but the psychology of the mass, or mob, as it is more commonly called, is hard to fathom. Law and order must be the fundamental basis of our social structure, and if that one basic point is observed all others follow in its even tenor as night follows day.

As mayor of this city, by the suffrage of the people, I wish to state most emphatically that I will not allow myself to be stampeded by any particular section of society, but will act and will only act as the occasion warrants in the interests of the people.

I appeal earnestly for co-operation and calmness under all conditions. I firmly believe that all those various factions of employers and employees involved in this unfortunate affair will be constitutional and law-abiding.

Should any acts be committed that savor of lawlessness I will act swiftly and surely and will use to the full the powers vested in me by the voice of the people.

Citizens, go about your business quietly.

Do not congregate in crowds.

Make no provocative statements.

And at all times realize that the constituted authorities will take all the necessary steps to ensure no radical departure from the normal, law-abiding conditions of community life.

What do you think?

1. *Mayor Gray was to harshly repress the Winnipeg strikers "in the interests of the people." How would Mayor Gray define "the people"? How would the strikers?*

2. *"Law and order is the fundamental basis of our social structure." Discuss.*

3. STRIKERS REASSURE CITIZENS OF WINNIPEG

The Manitoba Free Press of May 15, 1919 included a bulletin from the Central Strike Committee. It was in response to a statement by the War Veterans' Associations alleging that labor was trying to hurt the public good.

We, the central strike committee, having had brought to our attention the statement made over the signatures of J. O. Newton, G.W.V.A. [*Greater Winnipeg Veterans' Association*]; John Hay, A. & N.V. [*Army and Navy Veterans*]; and C. J. F. Wheeler, I.V. and C. [*Imperial Veterans in Canada*], which would make it appear that there is a desire on the part of organized labor to violate law and order, deem it necessary at this time to issue a statement setting forth our position.

In the first place, we would draw to the attention of those who express fears of disorder that the Trades & Labor Council of this city conducted a general strike last year without any disorder or violation of the law; we would further remind them that the present strike of the Building and Metal Trades workers has now been in progress for two weeks, and as Chief McPherson has stated in the press, not one case of disorderly conduct has been reported.

In order to demonstrate our desire and also show to the citizens that we can, as in the past, conduct our actions constitutionally, we hereby publicly announce that we are in possession of a solid strike vote from the Policemen's union with full authority to call upon them should we deem it necessary, but have decided to instruct the Policemen's union to remain at work, thereby proving that we have no other motive than to maintain peace and order in the community.

We have also made arrangements to have each organization on strike detail a number of their members off to assist the authorities should the occasion arise.

Measures such as these are sufficient answer to the baseless aspersions that have been cast upon organized labor through the press recently, which have a tendency to incite rather than allay any disorder.

Realizing the hardship and increased suffering that would accrue to the inmates of the hospitals through the withdrawal of the operators, we have arranged to leave sufficient to provide for the requirements; we have also arranged that for the present a supply of water for domestic purposes not to exceed 30 lbs. pressure shall be continued in order to eliminate undue hardships.

Recommendations shall be made to the city authorities to provide suitable quarters and proper equipment for an emergency squad which will be provided from amongst the members of the Fireman's union for the purpose of attending all fires with a view to saving life that may be in danger.

What do you think?

1. The Central Strike Committee qualified the "general" in general strike. Were these qualifications adequate for the life and welfare of the community?
2. In your opinion, was the general strike an act of violence on the part of the strikers against the people of Winnipeg?

4. "NO RIOTS!" VETERANS DECLARE

The Winnipeg General Strike occurred only six months after the armistice of 1918 had been declared. Consequently there were thousands of returning soldiers in Canada, many of whom were uprooted and jobless. Like the workers, they were looking for a "solution." This description of their rally appeared in the Bulletin *of June 5, 1919.*

This was a bad day for the Bolsheviki in Winnipeg Three thousand returned soldiers marched through the streets today to the parliament buildings and to the city hall to announce their intention to uphold law and order and constituted authority. The Labor Temple strikers organized a counter-parade of large proportions, but they kept away from the line of march of the returned soldiers.

At the parliament buildings Premier Norris addressed the soldiers in reply to a resolution they submitted in which they said they were with him and all constituted authority. Norris in reply assured the men he would do all in his power to meet their demands to deport alien enemies, destroy the high cost of living and bring to justice the men who had attempted and partially succeeded in putting a Soviet government into force in Winnipeg.

"I feel better today than yesterday" said Norris amid cheers, "and to know you boys are with us makes a big difference." He stood between two sergeant majors who bore great Union Jacks and surrounding the steps were literally thousands of uniformed men and other returned soldiers with buttons on. Thousands of citizens were on the outskirts and added to the cheers of the men, while autos by the thousands were all around the building. It was a different scene from yesterday, when the strikers were out in force. Banners confronted Norris reading in three-foot letters "We Stand for Constituted Authority," "Down with the High Cost of Living," "To Hell with the Aliens," "Fall in you Canadian Corps," "Down with Bolshevism."

Vice President Wheeler, of the Imperial Veterans also spoke and said he wanted to see all the alien enemies sent to Quebec and forced to swim the river, amid vast cheers, then after three cheers for the government, the parade four deep and a mile long swung into Kennedy Street and north to Portage into Main and surrounded the city hall where Mayor Gray addressed the crowd.

What do you think?

1. What tactics did Premier Norris use to oppose the strikers? In your opinion can they be justified?

2. Are charges that demonstrations are led by "outside agitators" attempts to avoid confronting specific injustices? Or is it true that all demonstrations attract "all-purpose disidents"?

3. "Down with the high cost of living." What does this slogan reveal about the situation of the soldiers?

4. Why would veterans be particularly aroused by a "big Red scare"?

5. AN ACT TO AMEND THE IMMIGRATION ACT

The Canadian government felt that foreigners or recent immigrants had played key roles in organizing the Winnipeg General Strike and other radical outbursts. It was therefore decided by the government

to establish machinery which would get rid of troublesome immigrants quickly.
(Statutes of Canada, 9-10 Geo. V, chap. 26, June 6, 1919.)

41. (1) Every person who by word or act in Canada seeks to overthrow by force or violence the govt. of our constituted law and authority in the United Kingdom of Great Britain and Ireland, or Canada, or any of the provinces of Canada, . . . or who in Canada defends or suggests the unlawful destruction of property or by word or act creates or attempts to create any riot or public disorder in Canada, or who without lawful authority assumes any powers of government in Canada or in any part thereof, or who by common repute belongs to or is suspected of belonging to any secret society or organization which extorts money from or in any way attempts to control any resident of Canada by force or threat of bodily harm, or by blackmail, or who is a member of or affiliated with any organization entertaining or teaching disbelief in or opposition to organized government shall, for the purposes of this Act, be deemed to belong to the prohibited or undesirable classes, and shall be liable to deportation in the manner provided by this Act. . . . Provided that this section shall not apply to any person who is a British Subject, either by reason of birth in Canada, or by reason of naturalization in Canada.

What do you think?

1. *What do you think the government wished to accomplish by the passage of this act?*
2. *Do you think that the passage of this act was justified?*
3. *"Every person . . . who is . . . affiliated with any organization . . . in opposition to organized government . . . shall be liable to deportation . . . this section shall not apply to any person who is a British subject. . . " How would this legislation affect troublemakers who were:*
   (a) newly arrived Britons?
   (b) Ukrainians who had enjoyed a long residence in Canada?
4. *Do you feel that Canada's immigration laws have helped Canadians to preserve their national myth of racial tolerance? Why or why not?*

6. FREE PRESS WARNS OF VIOLENCE

Three weeks after the strike was called no action had been taken by the government to meet with the workers or to respond to the workers' demands. Consequently the Central Strike Committee decided to tighten the strike by removing workers in vital industries, hoping to force the government into action. An editorial from the Manitoba Free Press, June 6, 1919, is an interpretation of this move.

Winnipeg has presumably settled down to the process of slowly starving the strikers, while the wealthy men stand by in stolid semi-indifference, or rub their hands in glee. That must change. It was the strikers who made arrangements for bread and milk and ice, to run on. This has been taken by the Committee of 1,000 to mean "Business as Usual."

Therefore, it was decided to withdraw all workers who had been allowed to return to what we regarded as vital industries. If Norris says he will not budge, then he must be made to budge. It is the business of the government to feed the people, and the strikers will see that they assume this responsibiity. If they refuse, and the people through hunger, rebel, then so much the worse for the government.

Labor will not call off the sympathetic strike. It will intensify it. It is time for the government to wake up from its Rip Van Winkle sleep and grasp the meaning of the industrial chaos of this hour. It is time for them to quit whining about calling off the sympathetic strike. Labor has patiently and magnificently waited for three weeks. Its self-restraint has been admirable. But if the governments intend that labor shall continue along this line and gradually starve, then most assuredly they would have one more guess coming.

None who attended the strike committee on Tuesday night could possibly misunderstand the new temper that was manifesting itself.

The Strike Bulletin, in place of beating about the bush, might as well have said what was in its mind bluntly, because the meaning of the article is quite plain.

This is an admission that the strike committee knows that the methods by which it expected to bring this city to its knees in two or three days at the most, have utterly failed. They have not been able to coerce or bludgeon the citizens into submission: and they are now confronted with the problems of what to do next.

It is quite obvious that there are only two alternatives before them.

One is to abandon the sympathetic strike which has been so colossal and costly a failure. But admission of defeat is too bitter a draught for the leaders who have manoeuvred their following into this desperate position.

The other course is a resort to violence; and the article in the Strike Bulletin is a perfectly plain warning to the authorities that if they do not submit forthwith to the dictators at strike headquarters, there is to be an attempt to subvert authority by force. The words have no other possible meaning.

The authorities are not responsible for the sad plight of the people to whom the Strike Bulletin makes reference. That responsibiity is borne wholly by the leaders of the strike committee, Russell, Robinson & Co. They deprived these people of their positions; they shut off their supplies; they are responsible for the suffering that has ensued. Further, it is within their power to mitigate the plight of the great majority of the people; if they refuse to do this theirs is the responsibility.

If instead of doing this they carry out their threat of resorting to violence, they will be called to a sudden, swift and terrible accounting alike by the authorities which they are defying and the followers whom they have betrayed.

What do you think?

1. According to the Manitoba Free Press, the alternatives open to the strikers were to completely abandon their strike, or to resort to violence. Were these in fact their only alternatives?

7. ALIENS AND COMMUNISTS RESPONSIBLE FOR WINNIPEG STRIKE

A classified advertisement sponsored by the Citizen's Committee of One Thousand appeared in the Manitoba Free Press of June 12, 1919. The Citizens' Committee was an anti-strike group which raised and organized volunteers to man the public services and special constables to maintain the peace. How would this advertisement affect the climate of violence?

CANADIAN, OR REVOLUTIONIST—WHICH?

On Tuesday afternoon, blood was freely spilled at the principal corner of Winnipeg, in the worst riot in the history of this city or country.

Sergeant Fred Coppins, V.C., officer of the Law, engaged with his companion returned heroes in the discharge of of his sworn duty, while momentarily isolated, was dragged from his horse by a group of aliens and dangerously wounded. On Wednesday a riot occurred on Main Street, at Higgins Avenue and T. S. Morrison, a returned soldier and a police officer, attacked by aliens, was shot and wounded.

These riots were not the ordered demonstrations of sincere, loyal Trades-Unionist citizens of Winnipeg; but were perpetrated and kept going by alien enemies—blood-kin of the men our Soldiers have been battling in Europe. They were CARRIED OUT by the Alien; but the responsibility for inspiriting and inciting them must rest upon the Autocrats of the Strike—the little group of Revolutionaries who, after moiling for years to gain "control" of Union Labor, now consider the time ripe to unfurl the red insignia of Bolshevism in this land of Canada.

THE RIOT WAS BORN OF REVOLUTION

Do you not believe this? Do you not agree that the Autocrats of the Strike are entirely responsible for these riots in Winnipeg, planned and forecasted to be the Overt Act that would usher in their Red Revolution and make them Dictators of a Bolshevikied Canada?

What do you think?

1. *In previous articles we have noted that, during crisis periods, people usually look for a scapegoat to assume the blame for what is happening. Often the search for a scapegoat arouses the racial antagonisms of the populace. What techniques has the author here used to play upon these inclinations? How does he clarify or confuse the issue?*

2. *35,000 of Winnipeg's 200,000 citizens were on strike in 1919. Examine the conspiracy theory with these figures in mind.*

8. ONE KILLED AS MOB ATTACKS MOUNTED POLICE

Violence broke out in Winnipeg on June 10, and reached a peak Saturday, June 21. The Manitoba Free Press of June 23, 1919, reported some of the incidents.

Mike Sokolowski, a Registered Alien Shot Through Heart and Instantly Killed, Presumably While Stooping to Pick up Missile—Thirty of Injured, Including Several Members of R.N.W.M.P. [*Royal Northwest Mounted Police*], Taken to Hospital, But Ten Were Sent Home After Minor Wounds Had Been Treated—Believed All of Injured Will Recover—Police Did Not Open Fire Until Several Minutes After Riot Act Was Read, and In Majority of Cases Fired Into Pavement Or Into Air—Police Fired On From Roofs and Windows—Military Called Out to Help Suppress Riot

---

One Rioter shot dead—Mike Sokolowski, 552 Henry Avenue.

Between 60 and 70 persons injured; 30 treated in hospitals and scores in drug stores.

Upwards of 100 arrests, and many more pending.

These three brief sentences give the effect of the rioting in Winnipeg on Saturday afternoon, when Main Street, opposite the City Hall, was the scene of the culmination of the disturbances which have disfigured the history of the city since the general sympathetic strike began over five weeks ago. The Riot Act was read on the steps of the City Hall by Mayor Gray about 2:30.

What is meant by?

"reading the Riot Act"

9. LABOR NEWS BANNED—EDITOR ARRESTED

J. S. Woodsworth was jailed for printing inflammatory material in his newspaper. A prominent strike leader in 1919, Woodsworth later became an M.P. The report of Woodsworth's arrest and a transcription of his material appeared in the Manitoba Free Press of June 24, 1919.

The *Western Labor News,* published by the strike committee has been suppressed, and the acting editor, J. S. Woodsworth is under arrest on a charge of sedition.

The sheet was printed on the premises of The Voice Publishing company and the building of this firm, 211 Rupert Street, was raided by members of the Royal North West Mounted Police force last evening. A quantity of type-set matter, and of copy ready for the printers, and evidently intended for use in the issue of the paper today, was seized.

Shortly after the raid had been completed, J. S. Woodsworth, formerly a Methodist minister, who had taken the position of editor during the enforced absence of William Ivens, was taken into custody by the city police. He will probably appear before the police court this morning.

It is presumed action was taken because of an inflammatory article published during the progress of the riots, culminating in the reference to Saturday's riots printed yesterday.

Monday's issue of the *Western Labor News, Special Strike Bulletin, No. 32,* in reporting the riots of Saturday has the following to say, under the heading "Bloody Saturday":

> One is dead and a number injured, probably thirty or more, as result of the forcible prevention of the "silent parade" which had been planned by returned men to start at 2:30 o'clock last Saturday afternoon. Apparently the bloody business was carefully planned, for Mayor Gray issued a proclamation in the morning stating that "Any women taking part in a parade do so at their own risk." Nevertheless a vast crowd of men, women and children assembled to witness the "silent parade."
>
> The soldiers' committee, which had been interviewing Senator Robertson, had not returned to their comrades when the latter commenced to line up on Main Street, near the city hall.
>
> No attempt was made to use the special city police to prevent the parade. On a previous occasion a dozen of the old regular city police had persuaded the returned men to abandon a parade which had commenced to move.
>
> On Saturday, about 2:30 p.m., just the time when the parade was scheduled to start, some 50 mounted men swinging baseball bats rode down Main Street. Half were red-coated R.N.W.M.P., the others wore khaki. They quickened pace as they passed the Union bank. The crowd opened, let them through and closed in behind them. They turned and charged through the crowd again, greeted by hisses, boos, and some stones. There were two riderless horses with the squad when it emerged and galloped up Main street. The men in khaki disappeared at this juncture, but the red-coats reined their horses and reformed opposite the old post office.
>
> Then, with revolvers drawn, they galloped down Main street,

turned, and charged right into the crowd on William Avenue, firing as they charged. One man, standing on the sidewalk, thought the mounties were firing blank cartridges until a spectator standing beside him dropped with a bullet through his breast. Another standing nearby was shot through the head. We have no exact information about the total number of casualties, but there were not less than thirty. The crowd dispersed as quickly as possible when the shooting began.

When the mounties rode back to the corner of Portage and Main, after the fray, at least two of them were twirling their reeking tubes [*sic*] high in the air in orthodox Deadwood Dick style. Some individuals, apparently opposed to the strike, applauded the man-killers as they rode by.

Lines of special police, swinging their big clubs, were then thrown across Main street and the intersecting thoroughfares. Dismounted red-coats lined up across Portage and Main declaring the city under military control. Khaki-clad men with rifles were stationed on the street corners.

What do you think?

1. *What differences do you note between Woodsworth's description of the riot and the one in the previous article?*

2. *Do you consider the article to be inflammatory? Does it constitute sedition? Why or why not?*

10. GOVERNMENT REACTS WITH EMERGENCY MEASURES

In response to the violence which occurred in Winnipeg on Saturday June 21, the Canadian government passed an amendment to the Criminal Code—section 98. (Statutes of Canada, 9-10, Geo. V, Chap. 46.) This emergency measure was repealed in 1936; and it is an irony of history that J. S. Woodsworth, who was jailed in 1919, was the MP who was instrumental in the repeal.

1.   Any association, organization, society or corporation, whose professed purpose or one of whose purposes is to bring about any governmental, industrial or economic change within Canada by use of force, violence or physical injury to person or property, or by threats of such injury, or which teaches, advocates, advises or defends the use of force, violence, terrorism, or physical injury to person or property, or threats of such injury, in order to accomplish such change, or for any other purpose, or which shall by any means prosecute or pursue such purpose or professed purpose, or shall so teach, advocate, advise or defend, shall be an unlawful association. . . .

2. Any person who acts or professes to act as an officer of any such unlawful association, and who shall sell, speak, write or publish anything as the representative or professed representative of any such unlawful association . . . or wear, carry or cause to be carried any badge, insignia, emblem, banner, motto, pennant, card, button or other device whatsoever, indicating or intended to show or suggest that he is a member of or in anywise associated with any such unlawful association, or who shall contribute anything as dues or otherwise . . . or who shall solicit subscriptions or contributions for it, shall be guilty of an offense and liable to imprisonment for not more than twenty years.

*   *   *   *   *

4. In any prosecution under this section, if it be proved that the person charged has,—

    (a) attended meetings of an unlawful association; or,

    (b) spoken publicly in advocacy of an unlawful association; or,

    (c) distributed literature of an unlawful association by circulation through the Post office mails of Canada, or otherwise;

it shall be presumed, in the absence of proof to the contrary that he is a member of such unlawful association.

What do you think?

1. There is a tradition in law that a person is to be considered innocent until proven guilty. To what extent does paragraph four of section 98 contravene with this tradition?

2. Compare the circumstances which prompted the passing of section 98 in 1919, the War Measures Act in 1939, and the War Measures Act in 1970.

11. VIEWS ON THE 1919 WINNIPEG GENERAL STRIKE

TWO YEARS LATER

(a) J. S. Woodsworth, in a letter to a cousin dated August 25, 1921. This letter is found in Grace Woodsworth MacInnis's book: J. S. Woodsworth: A Man to Remember (Toronto: MacMillan and Co., 1953).

The strike has been entirely misrepresented. I know the details intimately. Without hesitation I say that there was not a single foreigner in a position of leadership, though foreigners were falsely arrested to give colour to this charge. . . .

In short, it was the biggest hoax that was ever "put over" any people! Government officials and the press were largely responsible. . . .

(b) *H. A. Robson, K.C., author of the* Report of Commission to Enquire into the Causes and Effects of the General Strike, *which was brought out in November of 1919. (Winnipeg. Public Archives of Manitoba.)*

It is too much for me to say that the vast number of intelligent residents who went on strike were seditious or that they were either dull enough or weak enough to be led by seditionaries . . . but the cause of the strike . . . was the specific grievance [*the refusal of collective bargaining*] . . . and the dissatisfied and unsettled condition of Labour at and long before the beginning of the strike.

. . . it is more likely that the cause of the strike is to be found under the other heads [*other than unemployment*], namely, the high cost of living, inadequate wages . . . profiteering. . . .

. . . If Capital does not provide enough to assure Labour a contented existence with a full enjoyment of the opportunities of the time for human improvement, then the Government might find it necessary (to step) in and let the state do these things at the expense of Capital.

What do you think?

1. (a) *According to Mr. Robson what were the causes of the strike?*
   (b) *Compare this opinion with Prime Minister Bennett's apparent view at the time of the strike.*
2. *How do you account for the contradictions between Woodsworth's and Robson's reports of the strike, and the newspaper accounts of the strike?*
3. *To what extent can "government officials and the press" influence:*
   (a) *public opinion?*
   (b) *the course of events?*
   (c) *the atmosphere of crisis?*

The Northwest Rebellion

The name of Louis Riel is closely linked to the two rebellions in the Northwest but, for the purposes of this volume, we have chosen to refer only to the events which took place in Saskatchewan in 1884 and 1885. The earlier rebellion in 1870 was harshly put down by the Macdonald Government, and Riel was exiled to the United States. However, that rebellion did win provincial status for tiny Manitoba, thus assuring the fearful Métis of the same minority guarantees which the Quebec constitution possessed.

By 1884 many of the Métis, or French-speaking half-breeds, and some of the Indians residing in present-day Saskatchewan were becoming increasingly concerned about advancing European civilization. White settlers, and the Canadian Pacific Railway (to be completed in 1885) threatened their traditional way of life. In the spring of 1884 the Métis invited the leader of the 1870 rebellion, Louis Riel, to return to Canada.

1. A LETTER TO RIEL

A spokesman for the Saskatchewan Métis wrote Riel, who was then living in the United States, inviting him to return to Canada. (Ottawa. Public Archives of Canada. Macdonald Papers., cited in J. H. Stewart, Kenneth McNaught and Harry S. Crowe: A Sourcebook of Canadian History [Toronto: Longmans, Green and Co., 1959], pp. 183-184.)

. . . We may say that the part of the North-West in which we are living is Manitoba before the troubles, with the difference that there are more people, that they understand things better, and that they are more determined; you will form an idea as to the conditions upon which the people base their claims, for the reason that there are many people in the North-West whom the Government have recognized less than Indians; and yet it is these poor half-breeds who have always defended the North-West at the price of their blood and their sacrifices for a country which is stirring up the whole world to-day. They have been petitioning for the last ten years. I suppose the Government have looked upon the matter as mere child's play; despite formal documents and Acts of Parliament as a guarantee, the whole matter has been a farce; the honor of Parliament and of the Government has been trampled under foot when justice was to be done to the poor half-breeds. My dear cousin, I think the solemn moment has come. For my part, I have closely watched the people of the North-West, as well as the Indians, and the one cry resounds from all, it is the spark over a barrel of powder. It is late, but it is the time now more than ever, for we have right and justice on our side. Do not imagine that you will begin the work when you get here; I tell you it is all done, the thing is decided; it is your presence that is needed. It will, in truth, be a great event in the North-West; you have no idea how great your influence is, even amongst the Indians. I know that you do not like the men much, but I am certain that it will be the grandest demonstration that has ever taken place, and the English are speaking about it already. Now, my dear cousin, the closest union exists between the French and English and the Indians, and we have good generals to foster it. . . . The whole race is calling for you!

What do you think?

1. *Is this letter a call for violence? Explain.*
2. *Compare the complaints of this Saskatchewan Métis with those of modern Indians.*

2. RIEL ANSWERS

Louis Riel answered the invitation of the Saskatchewan Métis. (Ottawa. Public Archives of Canada, Macdonald Papers., cited in R. C. Brown and M. E. Prang: Confederation to 1949 [Scarborough, Ontario: Prentice-Hall of Canada Limited, 1966], p. 47.)

. . . The communities in the midst of which you live have sent you as their delegate to ask my advice on various difficulties which have rendered the British North-West as yet unhappy under the Ottawa Government. Moreover, you invite me to go and stay amongst you, your hope being that I for one could help to better in some respects your condition. . . .

To be frank is the shortest. I doubt whether my advice given to you on this soil concerning affairs on Canadian territory could cross the borders and retain any influence. But there is another view. The Canadian Government owe me two hundred and fifty acres of land, according to the thirty-first clause of the Manitoba treaty. They owe me also five lots valuable on account of hay, timber, and river frontage. These lots were mine according to the different paragraphs of the same thirty-first clause of the above-mentioned Manitoba treaty. It is the Canadian Government which have deprived me, directly or indirectly, of those properties. Besides, if they only pay attention to it a minute, they will easily find out that they owe me something else.

Those my claims against them are such as to hold good notwithstanding the fact that I have become an American citizen. Considering, then, your interest and mine, I accept your very kind invitation. I will go and spend some time amongst you. By petitioning the Government with you perhaps we will all have the good fortune of obtaining something. But my intention is to come back early this fall.

What do you think?

1. *Why did Riel agree to return?*
2. *What course of action for the redress of grievances is he suggesting here? Is there a threat of violent action?*

3. RIEL SPEAKS TO HIS PEOPLE

Riel travelled through Saskatchewan rallying the Métis, in the early months of 1885. (Ottawa. Public Archives of Canada, Macdonald Papers., cited in G. F. G. Stanley: The Birth of Western Canada: A History of the Riel Rebellions [Toronto: University of Toronto Press, 1931], p. 318.)

DEAR BROTHERS IN JESUS CHRIST

The Ottawa Government has been maliciously ignoring the rights of the original half-breeds during fifteen years. The petitions which have been sent to that Government on that matter and concerning the grievances which our classes have against its policy are not listened to: moreover, the Dominion has taken the high handed way of answering peaceable complaints by dispatching and reinforcing their Mounted Police. The avowed purpose being to confirm in the Saskatchewan their Government spoliation and usurpation of the rights and liberties of all classes of men, except their resident oppressors the Hudson's Bay Company and land speculators, by threatening our liberty and our lives. The aboriginal half-breeds are determined to save their rights or to perish at once. They are supported with no doubtful energy by a large number of able half-breeds, who have come to the Saskatchewan, less as emigrants than as proscripts from Manitoba. Those of the emigrants who have been long enough in this country to realize that Ottawa does not intend to govern the North-West so much as to plunder it, are in sympathy with the movement. Let us all be firm in the support of right, humane and courageous, . . . just and equitable in our views, thus God and man will be with us, and we will be successful.

What do you think?

1. In what ways are the frustrations which plagued the Métis similar to those experienced by the people in "The Time for Singing Is Past"?
2. What parallels may be drawn between the actions taken by these two groups and the effects of these actions?

4.   EDITORIAL: MACDONALD IS TO BLAME

The Toronto Globe, although an anti-Macdonald newspaper, was one of the earliest crusaders for the acquisition of western lands by Canada. This editorial on the Northwest Rebellion is taken from the Globe of March 24, 1885.

It is now reported that the Métis in the Saskatchewan district, who believe that they have been unjustly dealt with, are in open revolt, under the leadership of Sir John's old friend RIEL; that some of the Indian tribes make common cause with them, and that bloodshed is to be feared. We hoped that these rumours would prove untrue, and that the dissatisfied Métis intended nothing more by anything they have done than to make a decisive demonstration. But the admission of SIR JOHN MACDONALD yesterday afternoon, that the rising actually had taken place, that the wires had been cut, and the telegraph operators imprisoned, gives only too much ground for the supposition that the reports are under rather than over stated.

The Halfbreeds some time ago adopted a series of resolutions in which their grievances were set forth, and their wishes were expressed. They have frequently held public meetings since. They have employed all the usual constitutional means of gaining the attention of the Government, and obtaining redress of what they believe to be intolerable grievances. We are not prepared to say that everything they asked in those resolutions should be done, although it does seem that when lands were set apart for the Métis in Manitoba, the Métis in other parts of the North-West should have had as much done for them. But we do say that if the Government had pursued a wise policy in their regard, a people whose brethren in Manitoba were found so tractable would not be so discontented, and it would not be necessary to concentrate a large force of the mounted police to subdue or overawe them. If MR. DEWDNEY [*Lieutenant-Governor of the Northwest Territories and former Indian Commissioner*] were a man mindful of his duty, and capable of dealing with the Métis and the Indians in such a way as to secure their confidence and respect, and if SIR JOHN MACDONALD and his Minister of the Interior knew what their duty was, and made an honest effort to do it, the discontent might easily have been allayed long ago, if, indeed, it had ever existed.

What do you think?

1. *Where do the sympathies of this writer lie?*
2. *How does he feel the rebellion could have been avoided?*

5.   EDITORIAL: LAW AND ORDER MUST BE MAINTAINED

This editorial, dated March 30, 1885, is also from the Toronto Globe.

The news which we published on Saturday morning shocked the whole community inexpressibly. It was difficult to realize that by Canadians the blood of Canadians had been shed on Canadian soil, and for the first time the gravity of the situation was fully felt. Although we had given repeated warnings of the danger that threatened, few could believe that bloodshed was possible. But now they saw that a conflict was begun which may last for weeks, or even for months, in which many lives may be lost, in which may be engendered feelings that would work mischief for many years to come; by which, even were the revolt suppressed within a few days, incalculable injury is done to Canada.

The first feeling was that of profound regret. The next was that law and order must be maintained at any cost, and that the insurgents, no matter what their grievances may be, must be taught that armed resistance to the supreme authority is a crime so great as to deprive them of all claim to sympathy.

The insurrection must be quelled at once. The people of Canada demand that the Government take the most prompt and energetic measures for its immediate suppression. If the force already ordered to the Saskatchewan is not undoubtedly sufficient to overcome at once any possible combination of Halfbreeds and Indians, a larger force should be despatched immediately. In a case like this half measures are unwise, unjust to the country, and unjust to the deluded men who may imagine that success is possible for them if the force sent to deal with them is not sufficient to crush them at once.

When they have been crushed, when the men who have so madly risen have been routed or imprisoned or driven out of Canada, the people will enquire, who is responsible for all that has happened; whose hands are stained with the blood of the Canadians who have fallen on either side? The responsibility is awful.

We have charged SIR JOHN MACDONALD with the responsibility when we hoped that at worst the country would see only some threatening demonstrations. Such explanations as he has given have gone to prove that the responsibility is his. He knew that there was danger of an outbreak, yet he did nothing more than station some Mounted Police at Carleton. He admits now that it would have been advisable to send commissioners to settle the claims of the Métis, but although he had the whole season to determine what should be done, and to do it, the commissioners were not sent. LOUIS RIEL, he says, has invited these people to revolt. He knew what RIEL was. He knew that RIEL was invited to come from the United States into Canada to lead men who openly declared that they had despaired of obtaining redress without RIEL's assistance. He was warned then of what might happen. But he neither redressed the grievances complained of nor dealt with RIEL as prudence dictated. So dangerous a man should have been closely watched, and as soon as he began to invite these people to revolt he should have been arrested and treated as his crime deserved. Nothing was done, and under the policy of "masterly inactivity" Canada finds herself face to face with rebellion, and sees her sons shot down on her own soil by the score.

What do you think?

1. The authors of the two preceding editorials deplore the course of action which the rebels took yet they also hold Sir John A. Macdonald responsible for this turn of events. How can you account for this position?

2. Compare the position of the editorial here to Prime Minister Trudeau's speech on the proclamation of the War Measures Act on page 76. How does the editorial compare with your own views during the October Crisis?

3. Was the danger represented by Riel the same as the danger represented by the FLQ kidnappers? Why or why not?

6. BLOOD STAINS THE SOIL

An anti-rebel editorial from the Saskatchewan Herald *of April 23, 1885, shows the Anglo-Saxon community's response to the rebellion.*

One short month ago the fairest field in Canada was the Saskatchewan country; to-day it is the most desolate. And brightest and most prosperous in all her settlements was the Battle River Valley, whose sons hailed the opening of Spring with joy and thankfulness, rejoicing in the prospects of the coming year, impatient to begin the labors that were to bring them their reward. But in one brief day their hopes were blasted; instead of being the masters of peaceful and happy homes they were at one blow bereft of everything but manhood—reduced from a condition of plenty to one of absolute penury; houseless, homeless and penniless.

Blood stains the soil, and the air is thick with the smoke of desolation. Nearly a score of our citizens have been slain without a moment's warning by ingrates whose interests they guarded as carefully as they did their own, and whose hands were daily opened in charity to the men they looked upon as unfortunate and to be pitied. In the town itself, or that part of it lying south of Battle River, there is only enough left to remind the sufferers of their once comfortable homes, and to recall the fact that many things of peculiar value are irretrievably lost and can never be replaced.

Their crime was that they were white; the penalty imposed was death.

Of all their fair farms that covered the land but few remain—some of these lie under the guns of the fort, while the others are held by men in alliance with the Indians; for on no other grounds can their owners hope for exemption from the universal ruin. With the exception of these there is not a home that has not been raided, scarcely a house that has not been burned.

It has always been the boast of this district that taking their numbers all through their horses and cattle were better bred than in any other district on the Saskatchewan; the people were generally well off, and made improved stock a specialty in their system of farming; but to-day they are not owners of a hoof. They are afoot and the marauders mounted; their dairies are bare while their herds are being ruthlessly slaughtered by the thieves. The work of extermination has begun, evidently without a thought for the morrow.

And yet in the face of these awful facts—in spite of the ruin wrought upon an industrious people—men are to be found and some of them in high positions, who characterize these crimes as a "mistake," and suggest that their perpetrators come in and acknowledge it, make new promises as to the future, and resume their old position as petted and pampered wards of the crown.

It is too late for any such suggestions. The Government and the people of Canada have been deceived as to the civilization of these wild tribes. They have shown themselves incapable of gratitude; their apparent tractability was cunning; their civilization but a cloak to hide their hellish plans. They have thrown down the gauntlet, and now that it has been taken up the issue must be pressed until the fullest justice has been done.

But while punishment must be meted out to the Indians what shall we say to those white men and nominally civilized Half-breeds who have instigated this rising? On them rests a fearful responsibility, and on them the penalty must lie. Those who, knowing better, incited to these murders and devastations, put themselves on a level with the savages in all save their animal courage, and as their light was greater so must their punishment be exemplary.

The work will not be done in a day, but it must be done thoroughly, and we have confidence that the people of Canada who have so long ungrudgingly given the vast sum of money spent in feeding the Indians while apparently settling down to a new mode of life, will, now that the feeding scheme has proved a failure, cheerfully give whatever men and money may be required to fight them, and re-establish peace and order on such foundations as shall not again be shaken.

What do you think?

1. *What methods does this author use to persuade his readers? What is he trying to achieve?*
2. *". . . the issue must be pressed until the fullest justice has been done."*
   (a) What does the author mean?
   (b) Under what circumstances does he justify the use of violence?
   (c) Do you agree with him? Why or why not?

7. LOUIS RIEL AT HIS TRIAL

Riel's treason trial began on July 20, 1885, after his Métis forces had been crushed at Batoche. He was executed on November 16, 1885. (Canadian Sessional Papers, Volume 12, No. 43.)

The only things I would like to call your attention to before you retire to deliberate are: 1st. That the House of Commons, Senate and Ministers of the Dominion, and [*those*] who make laws for this land and govern it, are no representation whatever of the people of the North-West.

2nd. That the North-West Council generated by the Federal Government has the great defect of its parent.

3rd. The number of members elected for the Council by the people make it only a sham representative legislature and no representative government at all.

British civilization which rules to-day the world, and the British constitution has defined such government as this is which rules the North-West Territories, as irresponsible government, which plainly means that there is no responsibility, and by all the science which has been shown here yesterday you are compelled to admit if there is no responsibility, it is insane.

Good sense combined with scientific theories lead to the same conclusion. By the testimony laid before you during my trial witnesses on both sides made it certain that petition after petition had been sent to the Federal Government, and so irresponsible is that Government to the North-West that in the course of several years besides doing nothing to satisfy the people of this great land, it has even hardly been able to answer once or to give a single response. That fact would indicate an absolute lack of responsibility, and therefore insanity complicated with paralysis.

The Ministers of an insane and irresponsible Government and its little one—the North-West Council—made up their minds to answer my petitions by surrounding me slyly and by attempting to jump upon me suddenly and upon my people in the Saskatchewan. Happily when they appeared and showed their teeth to devour, I was ready: that is what is called my crime of high treason, and to which they hold me today. Oh, my good jurors, in the name of Jesus Christ, the only one who can save and help me, they have tried to tear me to pieces.

If you take the plea of the defence that I am not responsible for my acts, acquit me completely since I have been quarrelling with an insane and irresponsible Government. If you pronounce in favor of the Crown, which contends that I am responsible, acquit me all the same. You are perfectly justified in declaring that having my reason and sound mind, I have acted reasonably and in self-defence, while the Government, my accuser, being irresponsible, and consequently insane, cannot but have acted wrong, and if high treason there is it must be on its side and not on my part.

What do you think?

1. *Riel had been advised to plead not guilty by reason of insanity. He refused, even though the plea could have saved his life. Why did he refuse?*
2. *Discuss the validity of Riel's defense of his actions?*
3. *How do you account for the fact that today Riel is considered by many Canadians to be a national hero?*
4. *What lessons of the Northwest Rebellion might be applied to the situation of the Canadian Indian or the Quebec separatist?*

The Rebellions of 1837

In 1837 two rebellions broke out in British North America: one in Upper Canada, and the other in Lower Canada.

Louis-Joseph Papineau, an aristocratic lawyer and politician, led the rebellion in Lower Canada. A severe economic recession combined with racial animosities created a rebellious mood among Lower Canadian dissidents who wanted to have effective political control not only over the legislative arm of government, but also over the executive arm which was, in 1837, firmly in the grip of the English-speaking minority of Quebec.

In Upper Canada the rebellion was led by the Scottish firebrand, William Lyon Mackenzie, newspaper editor and politician. For Mackenzie and his followers, a violent overthrow of the Family Compact—the small, elite group which controlled executive government in Upper Canada—was the only effective way to ensure that many Canadians, not merely a select few, be involved in the decision-making processes of government. Here too, an economic recession, plus American political influences and an arrogant Tory administration encouraged the resort to arms.

The documents immediately following relate to the rebellion in Lower Canada.

1. WILL THE CANADIANS SHOULDER THEIR MUSKETS?

Some English-speaking rebels in Upper Canada reacted with enthusiasm to the news about Papineau's rebellion. The following is taken from William Lyon Mackenzie's Constitution, *July 5, 1837.*

It gives us great pleasure to learn that the Hon. Mr. Papineau experienced the most cordial reception on his arrival to attend the meeting of the Counties of Bellechasse and L'Islet, about 25 miles below Quebec. The people turned out in large numbers, not with colors nor flags, but with something more significant—*with muskets.* We are happy to learn that the people are thus exhibiting a proper sense of their situation. From England they have nothing to expect but insult and robbery.

Two or three thousand Canadians meeting within 25 miles of the fortress of Quebec, in defiance of the proclamation . . . with *muskets* on their shoulders, and the Speaker of the House of Commons [Lower Canada] at their head, to pass resolutions declaratory of their abhorrence of British Colonial Tyranny, and their determination to resist and throw it off, is a sign not easily misunderstood. . . .

Yes! with the exception of the fortress of Quebec, the Canadians, whenever they see fit to do it, can make the power of their Downing Street Tyrants vanish instantaneously in every part of Lower Canada, and that too forever.

What do you think?

1. John A. Macdonald once remarked, "I carried my musket in '37."
   (a) Does this surprise you?
   (b) How do you imagine Macdonald might have replied if Louis Riel had reminded him of his participation in an earlier Canadian rebellion?

2. LOUIS-JOSEPH PAPINEAU TO THE PEOPLE OF LOWER CANADA

In order to gather followers and to explain what he was advocating, Papineau issued the following proclamation, "An Address from the Confederation of Six Committees to the People of Canada" on October 24, 1837.

Fellow Citizens:

When a people find themselves invariably exposed to a series of systematic oppositions [*objections*], in spite of their expressed desires for all manners [*customs*] recognized by constitutional useage, by popular meetings and by their representatives in Parliament after mature deliberation; when their governors, instead of redressing the various grievances which they themselves brought about by their misrule, solemnly recorded and proclaimed their guilt-ridden determination to undermine and shake to the foundation civil liberty; it becomes the urgent duty of the people to address themselves seriously to the consideration of their unfortunate position, the dangers which surround them, and, through a well-planned organization, to make the arrangements needed to preserve intact their civil rights and their dignity as free men.

The wise and immortal authors of the American Declaration of Independence set forth in that document the principles on which alone are based the Rights of Man. Fortunately, they insisted on establishing the institutions and the form of government which alone would guarantee permanently prosperity and the social well-being of the inhabitants of this continent, and demanded a system of government entirely dependent on the people and those directly responsible to them.

In common with the various nations of North America and South America that have adopted the principles contained in that Declaration, we regard the doctrines which it contains as sacred and self-evident = That God created no artificial distinctions between man and man; that government is nothing more than a simple human institution formed by those who ought to be liable for its good or bad operations, that government is consecrated for the benefit of all those who will consent to come or remain under its protection and control, and that as a result the form of it can be changed as soon as it ceases to accomplish the ends for which this government was established; that the public authorities and men in power are only the executors of desires legitimately expressed by the community, honoured when they have the confidence of the people and respected so long as they enjoy public esteem, people who should be removed from power as soon as they cease to give satisfaction to the people, the sole legitimate source of power.

In accordance with these principles and on the faith in the treaties and capitulations transacted with our ancestors and in the imperial parliament's guarantees, the people of this province have not, during long years, ceased through respectful requests to complain of the intolerable abuses which taint their lives and paralyze their industry. As far back as the time when reparations were conceded to our humble forefathers, aggression followed aggression, until finally we no longer appear to cling to the British empire for our well-being and prosperity, our liberties and the honour of the people and of the English crown; instead we look only with a view to fatten a horde of useless officials who, not content to enjoy salaries enormously disproportionate in respect to their responsibilities and the country's resources, have combined in a faction solely motivated by private interest in opposition to all reforms and designed to defend all the ingenuities of a government which is the enemy of the rights and liberties of this colony. . . .

What do you think?

1. Summarize Papineau's position with regard to grievances and remedies.
2. Compare his position to those of Louis Riel, Stanley Gray, Rocky Jones, and the FLQ.

3. BRITISH CONCILIATORY POLICY RESPONSIBLE FOR REBELLION

The Montreal Gazette of November 25, 1837, expressed the English, Tory, anti-French Canadian point of view.

Should Her Majesty's Government in England or the Executory of this Province, be desirous of witnessing a practical illustration of that line of policy, which it has hitherto been their object to pursue in respect to

LOWER CANADA, let them go to the banks of the Richelieu river and there they will find it indelibly written in characters of blood. There will they also find a scene worthy of the serious contemplation of the ruler and statesman; especially of such rulers and statesmen as have for some time past wielded the destinies of LOWER CANADA. There they may gather the bitter fruits of a timid and conciliatory Administration. There they may behold the brave troops and loyal subjects of their Royal Mistress, bleeding to the core by the hands of those rebel ruffians, whom it has been their pleasure to treat with the highest political consideration and respect, even at a period when these ungrateful and abandoned wretches presumed to approach the very footstool of the Throne with a menace of treason up their lips. The sight is a deplorable one. But, as to the ultimate cause, who can reflect upon it, without shuddering at the responsibility incurred by those who have reduced the Province to its present condition, and turned it into a common slaughter-house, rather than swerve from a vain-glorious system of government, as unwise and unmanly in its conception as it has been ruinous in its consequences. We know not the human punishment that is adequate to such moral and political delinquency. But we can assure the British Ministry, and the Parliament which submitted to be dictated to by such a set of drivellers, that the whole of their conduct, with respect to this Province, has aroused a feeling among the loyal and Constitutional inhabitants, which nothing can eradicate but their dismissal and disgrace from the Queen's counsels and services. Nor can they plead ignorance on the score of this conduct. They were frequently warned of the danger which they incurred, by the prosecution of their vain attempts to bring about harmony and peace, by means of conciliating the good will of a revolutionary party. They were informed that such a party existed, and they would not believe it. They were told that the only way of governing this province, so as to render it a happy and prosperous Colony, was not by indulging and conceding every new grievance proclaimed by the rebellious faction in the House of Assembly; but by enforcing the laws, and asserting the fundamental principles of the Constitution. But still they persevered in their folly and blindness. The Governor was told—and no one can deny that he acted up to his instructions—that "conciliation and a reconcilement of all past differences are studiously presented as the great object of your mission." What was this, but surrendering into the hands of the enemies of good government and the supremacy of the Mother Country, the very keys of the ideal of the Constitution? Not only so; but they were indulged, pampered, and caressed with every favour and blandishment that could possible be conferred upon the best and primest friends of the country. What has been the result? In two words—Treason and Rebellion. The Province resounds with the cry, "to arms"; and the bloody and accursed flag of a sanguinary revolution waves insolently over our heads—polluting the very air that British freemen breathe! The thought is harrowing, and the sight distracting. Nothing can possibly be more galling to every loyal and constitutional subject of Her Majesty, than the reflection, that it is, almost to a man, the very individuals upon whom her Ministers and Representative in this Province, conferred so many hopes, favours, and honours, who are now combined against her person, dignity, and laws. It is almost equally gallingly to reflect, that it was from the polluted hands and debased intellects of the same individuals, that the loyal and peaceable people of this Province, have for many years been under the necessity of accepting such a system of jurisprudence and policy, as savoured, in every sentence and object, of the present infamous design. Our former rulers and representatives in the Legislature are now our adversaries in the field of battle. The transition from one capacity and character to another, is, indeed, great and sudden; but to those who could read the signs of the times, it was neither unnatural nor unexpected. They must be more than judicially blind, who did not perceive the distorted lineaments and features of a revolutionary project, in those prolonged and incessant efforts made by the leaders of the faction, to change from time to time the basis of the Constitution; and the dexterity with which they contrived to erect one pretended grievance in the room of another, the moment that they found that their wishes had been anticipated by a weak and wavering Government.

What do you think?

1. (a) *Who does the writer blame for the troubles?*
   (b) *Compare this reaction with the* Globe *editorials on the Northwest Rebellion pages 176 and 177.*
2. *The great French political observer Alexis de Tocqueville remarked that it is the lessening of repression and hardship that leads to revolution. What are the similarities and differences between de Tocqueville's argument and that of the author of this document?*
3. *How would Papineau reply to the allegation of this author that the British government was "weak and wavering"?*
4. *Do you think that many Canadians would say that the FLQ activities in Quebec were aided and abetted by a "weak and wavering government"?*

4. TO THE HABITANTS OF THE DISTRICT OF MONTREAL

Not all French Canadians were ardent rebels. Many were opposed to the violence of the rebels. A petition signed by Lower Canadian magistrates appeared in the Brockville Recorder, November 30, 1837. It reflects the moderate, French-Canadian, anti-Papineau position.

As Magistrates and preservers of the peace of Her Majesty our gracious Queen, in this District, we think that it is our duty to proceed in advance of the events which threaten the public tranquility, and to advise you paternally of the danger you incur, in allowing yourselves to be longer misled, and also of the punishment which will come upon you, if you continue a strife as parricidal as unequal.

Officers of Justice in the discharge of their painful duties have been fired upon. Prisoners, lawfully arrested, and who ought to be subjected to the justice of the country, have been rescued. These crimes are heavy, and bring the most severe punishment upon them who are guilty of them.

It is not you, inhabitants of the country, who have voluntarily placed an obstacle in the way of justice: but it is certain perfidious men, who have pushed on isolated individuals to commit acts unworthy of men who know how to respect the public peace and the law.

We exhort you, not only to abstain from every violent proceeding, but, futher, to return peaceably to your firesides, to the midst of your families, in whose bosom you will never be molested. It is by trusting yourselves to the protection of the law and the British Government, that you will succeed in restoring peace and prosperity within your country. Already we are informed, that several parishes which had been excited have returned from their errors and repent of them sincerely.

Should our language be misunderstood, should reason be slow to make itself heard, it is still our duty to warn you, that neither the military force nor the civil authorities will be outraged with impunity, and that the vengeance of the laws will be equally prompt. The aggressors will become the victims of their rashness, and will owe the evils that will fall upon their own obstinacy. It is not those who push you on to excess, who are your true friends. Those men have already abandoned you, and would abandon you again at the moment of danger, while we, who call you back to peace, think ourselves to be the most devoted servants of our country.

What do you think?

1. *Compare this statement with that of Prime Minister Trudeau's on the proclamation of the War Measures Act.*

5. PROCLAMATION OF MARTIAL LAW

In response to the rebellion, the Governor of Lower Canada, the Earl of Gosford, instituted martial law in early December. The announcement appeared in the Montreal Transcript, December 9, 1837.

Whereas there exists in the District of Montreal a traitorous conspiracy by a number of persons falsely styling themselves Patriots, for the subversion of the Authority of Her Majesty, and the destruction of the established Constitution and Government of the said Province; And whereas the said traitorous conspiracy hath broken out into acts of the most daring and open Rebellion; And whereas the said Rebellion hath very considerably extended itself, insomuch that large Bodies of Armed Traitors have openly arrayed themselves, and have made and do still make attacks upon Her Majesty's Forces, and have committed the most horrid excesses and cruelties; And whereas in the parts of the said District in which the said conspiracy hath not yet broken out into open Rebellion, large numbers of such persons so calling themselves Patriots, for the execution of such their wicked designs, have planned means of open violence, and formed public arrangements for raising and arming an organized and disciplined Force, and in furtherance of their purposes have frequently assembled in great and unusual numbers; And whereas the exertions of the Civil Power are ineffectual for the suppression of the aforesaid traitorous and wicked Conspiracy and Rebellion and for the protection of the lives and properties of Her Majesty's loyal subjects; And whereas the Courts of Justice in the said District of Montreal have virtually ceased, from the impossibility of executing any legal process or warrant of arrest therein.

Now, therefore, I, ARCHIBALD, EARL OF GOSFORD, GOVERNOR IN CHIEF, and Captain General in and over the said Province of Lower Canada, by and with the advice and consent of her Majesty's Executive Council for this Province, have issued orders to Lieutenant General Sir John Colborne, commanding Her Majesty's Forces in the said Province, and other Officers of Her Majesty's Forces in the same, to arrest and punish all persons acting, aiding, or in any manner assisting in the said Conspiracy and Rebellion which now exist within the said District of Montreal, and which have broken out in the most daring and violent attacks upon her Majesty's Forces, according to MARTIAL LAW, either by DEATH, or otherwise, as to them shall seem right and expedient for the punishment and suppression of all Rebels, in the said District; of which all Her Majesty's subjects in this Province are hereby required to take notice.

What do you think?

1. "Often it is necessary to suspend certain human liberties and free-doms in order to maintain them." Discuss.

6. THE BURNING OF ST. BENOIT

St. Benoit was a small village twenty-eight miles west of Montreal. The village was burned by British troops on December 16, 1837. This account of the burning appeared in the Montreal Transcript of the same day.

We are sorry to state that we have reason to fear the humane intentions of the Commander of the Forces have been in part frustrated, as regards the respecting of the property of those who had returned to their allegiance. In saying this, we do not mean to convey the slightest reproach to the brave troops under his command; these, of course, implicitly obeyed the orders of their General. But we are very credibly informed, that no sooner had Sir John taken his departure from St. Benoit, than the village was set on fire in several places. When our informant looked back upon the place, it appeared he said one sheet of livid flame, and the fire appeared to be issuing from the windows of the church. We have too much reason to fear that the excessive zeal of many of the ultra-loyalists, not on duty, hurried them into acts of vengeance, both at St. Eustache and St. Benoit, and that some of them even stooped to appropriate what they could not mistake for their own, and which the troops had spared.

What do you think?

1. *Who burned the village of St. Benoit?*
2. *Whom would you hold responsible for this act? Why?*

7. AFTERMATH OF THE REBELLION IN LOWER CANADA

Steward Derbishire, a London barrister who became a journalist, though not connected with the Durham mission sent Durham a report of conditions in Lower Canada. Below is an excerpt from a conversation Derbishire had with Denis Viger, Papineau's cousin. The document is dated at Quebec, May 24, 1838. (Ottawa. Public Archives of Canada. Durham Papers.)

. . . He (Viger) told me that the spirit of persecution and lawless vengeance had run so high against all of the french party who had been conspicuous in politics that he had not ventured to leave his house for several months. I had noticed that the plate bearing his name had been taken down from the street door. He cautioned me to be discreet . . . as . . . the "Volunteers' . . . at present dragooned the City & exercised summary jurisdiction upon whomsoever they pleased to consider as enemies to the State. I did not need the caution; for I had already seen enough of these gentlemen to know that they permitted no man to hold an opinion different from theirs. He told me that the outrages, insults, and destruction of property by the "Volunteers" had left wounds in the minds of the Canadians that would never be healed.

. . . The Disorders complained of to me were the shooting of men as they stood in the door ways of their wooden dwellings long after all opposition had ceased; the firing of houses and barns by parties of Volunteers . . . The most exaggerated statements of these matters are spread through the Country for the purpose of inflaming the minds of the *habitants.* . . . I . . . heard a Volunteer state at a public dinner table at Montreal that he had with

his own hand fired fifteen (dwellings) . . . however . . . for weeks prior to the
. . . military operations against the places above named, the "Patriots" had
lived at free quarters in the houses of the Royalists, driving away the Owners,
whose lives they sought, & appropriating their property of every description
to the supply of bands which were gathering and arming as they alleged for
the extirpation of the British race in Canada.

What do you think?

1. *On page 179, in the section on the Northwest Rebellion, the
Saskatchewan Herald in an editorial said of the white settlers,
"their crime was that they were white; the penalty imposed was
death." In the above document Derbishire reported that the Volunteers believed that the rebels wanted "the extirpation of the British
race in Canada." What are the similarities between these two beliefs? How reasonable do you think such beliefs are? What are their
effects likely to be?*
2. *"The Disorders complained of to me were the shooting of men as
they stood in the door ways of their wooden dwellings long after
all opposition had ceased." How can you account for such wanton
behaviour?*
3. *"Violence is a deeply ingrained human trait in all of us. It only
needs an excuse to manifest itself." Discuss.*

8. MACKENZIE'S CALL TO REVOLUTION

*Beginning the readings on the rebellion in Upper Canada is an excerpt
from a pamphlet written by Mackenzie and published in Toronto on
November 27, 1837. (J. M. Bliss: Canadian History in Documents
[Toronto: Ryerson Press, 1966], pp. 46-48.)*

*There have been Nineteen Strikes for Independence from European
Tyranny, on the Continent of America. They were all successful! The Tories,
therefore, by helping us will help themselves.*

The nations are fallen, and thou still art young,
The sun is but rising when others have set;
And tho' Slavery's cloud o'er thy morning hath hung,
The full tide of Freedom shall beam round thee yet.

BRAVE CANADIANS! God has put into the bold and honest hearts of
our brethren in Lower Canada to revolt—not against "lawful" but against
"unlawful authority." The law says we shall not be taxed without our consent
by the voices of the men of our choice, but a wicked and tyrannical govern-

ment has trampled upon that law—robbed the exchequer—divided the plunder—and declared that, regardless of justice they will continue to roll their splendid carriages, and riot in their palaces, at our expense—that we are poor spiritless ignorant peasants, who were born to toil for our betters. But the peasants are beginning to open their eyes and to feel their strength—too long have they been hoodwinked by Baal's priests—by hired and tampered with preachers, wolves in sheep's clothing, who take the wages of sin, and do the work of iniquity, "each one looking to his gain in his quarter."

CANADIANS! Do you love freedom? I know you do. Do you hate oppression? Who dare deny it? Do you wish perpetual peace, and a government founded upon the eternal heaven-born principle of the Lord Jesus Christ—a government bound to enforce the law to do to each other as you would be done by? Then buckle on your armour, and put down the villains who oppress and enslave our country. . . .

That power that protected ourselves and our forefathers in the deserts of Canada . . . will be in the midst of us in the day of our struggle for our liberties, and for Governors of our free choice, who would not dare to trample on the laws they had sworn to maintain. In the present struggle, we may be sure, that if we do not rise and put down Head [*Governor of Upper Canada*] and his lawless myrmidons, they will gather all the rogues and villains in the Country together—arm them—and then deliver our farms, our families, and our country to their brutality—to that it has come, we must put them down, or they will utterly destroy this country. If we move now, as one man, to crush the tyrant's power, to establish free institutions founded on God's law, we will prosper, for He who commands the winds and waves will be with us—but if we are cowardly and mean-spirited, a woeful and a dark day is surely before us. . . .

CANADIANS! It is the design of the Friends of Liberty to give several hundred acres to every Volunteer—to root up the unlawful Canada Company, and give *free deeds* to all settlers who live on their lands—to give free gifts of the Clergy Reserve lots, to good citizens who have settled on them—and the like to settlers on Church of England Glebe Lots, so that the yeomanry may feel independent, and be able to improve the country, instead of sending the fruit of their labour to foreign lands. The fifty-seven Rectories will be at once given to the people, and all public lands used for Education, Internal Improvements, and the public good. £100,000 drawn from us in payment of the salaries of bad men in office, will be reduced to one quarter, or much less, and the remainder will go to improve bad roads and to "make crooked paths straight"; law will be ten times more cheap and easy—the bickerings of priests will cease with the funds that keep them up—and men of wealth and property from other lands will soon raise our farms to four times their present value. We have given Head and his employers a trial of forty-five years—five years longer than the Israelites were detained in the wilderness. The promised land is now before us—up then and take it. . . .

. . . the prize is a splendid one. A country larger than France or England; natural resources equal to our most boundless wishes—a government of equal laws—religion pure and undefiled—perpetual peace—education to all—millions of acres of lands for revenue—freedom from British tribute—free trade with all the world—but stop—I never could enumerate all the blessings attendant on independence!

Up then, brave Canadians! Get ready your rifles, and make short work of it; a connection with England would involve us in all her wars, undertaken for her own advantage, never for ours; with governors from England, we will have bribery at elections, corruption, villainy and perpetual discord in every township, but Independence would give us the means of enjoying many blessings. Our enemies in Toronto are in terror and dismay —they know their wickedness and dread our vengeance . . . now's the day and the hour! Woe be to those who oppose us, for "In God is our trust."

What do you think?

1. *Summarize the arguments Mackenzie uses to justify a resort to violence.*
2. *Compare his arguments with other Canadians who have called for the same type of action.*

9.   REBELLION IS FOLLY

The Reverend Anson Green was a Methodist minister living in Upper Canada in 1837. Like most Methodist ministers of the time, Green was opposed to the rebellion. His views are given in an extract from his biography, The Life and Times of Reverend Anson Green, *(Toronto: Methodist Book Room, 1877).*

That the people of Upper Canada have grievances to redress, no one who reflects, can for a moment doubt. But one after another these grievances are being removed in a constitutional way, and only for a few hot heads, on both sides, our country would now be at rest. To appeal to arms under these circumstances is folly and madness. It is true that much patience, humility, and grace are necessary to submit quietly to be deprived of our rights, and snubbed and tyrannized over by a few selfish men; but rebellion is the last thing to be thought of; and especially when we have the House of Assembly with us, and the Home Government on our side.

What do you think?

1. *If all men shared the views of the Reverend Anson Green would change still take place?*
2. *Compare the religious appeals made by the Reverend Green with those of Mackenzie. How does each interpret the Christian ethic? Why do you think these contradictions occur?*

10. WILLIAM LYON MACKENZIE JUSTIFIES THE REBELLION

The fiery editor wrote the following article in his newspaper, The Constitution, November 29, 1837.

. . . We have before said, and we here repeat the opinion, that neither 1,000 men—no, nor 10,000 men would be able to stand a month against the Canadian people, united and determined to be free. They have waited 60 years longer than the rest of America, for British justice, and have met with injury and insult. . . . As Ireland was coerced for 1,000 years so would they now coerce, first Lower Canada, and us next. But, thank God for inspiring the Canadians with valour in an honest and heavenly cause—they know the value of FREEDOM, and they will make that greatest of blessings theirs. . . .

Some say, "We are reformers—but not revolutionists." This is foolish talking. They ask for reform—60 years, perhaps, like our Lower Canadian brethren—and meet continued oppression. Is not revolution in such a case a bible duty? Is not the whole scripture, given for our use and example, full of authorities for revolt against wicked rulers? We know that it is. There was slavery and bondage in old times—there is so now. Was it wrong then to seek for freedom?—The scriptures say it was praiseworthy—Is it wrong now? Ask our fellow men whose color is different from ours. Would it be justifiable in them to revolt against the established authority of the northern states? Egerton Ryerson and his brother George may reply, if they can. We say that we would glory in such a revolt, and rejoice in its success. . . .

What do you think?

1. Mackenzie's rebellion was considered at the time to be a failure, and yet it led to permanent reforms.
   (a) What were those reforms, and why did they occur?
   (b) To what extent can we evaluate the possible future significance of FLQ violence?
   (c) List the strengths and weaknesses that an implicit threat of violence gives to a reform movement.

11. TORONTO IN ARMS

The Christian Guardian *editorial of December 13, 1837, may be regarded as the official policy of the Upper Canadian Methodist Church towards rebellion.*

While writing the foregoing article, little did we think that it would be our painful duty to state that Mackenzie's measures were so far ripened into revolution as to lead already to armed opposition to the constituted authorities.

THIS IS THE FACT. An armed force is collected on Yonge Street, and is threatening an attack upon the city. The Governor, like a brave representative of his youthful Queen, is under arms at the head of loyal men. The streets are being barricaded, the garrison and the market buildings are placed in the best possible state of defence that the short notice would admit. Unless Divine Providence interfere, much blood will be shed.

Canadians of every class! Canadian REFORMERS!—Are you prepared to shed the blood of your countrymen? Can any thing Mackenzie can offer you compensate for the guilt you must incur if you enrol under his revolutionary banner, and deluge your fruitful fields with blood? For God's sake pause! Frown down the propagators of discord! Lift up your voices in prayer, and exert all your energies, to save your fireside and families from the untold horrors of civil war. The Royal Standard of Britain yet waves triumphantly, and invites the loyal and the good to unite in its defence, and still avail themselves of its PROTECTION against aggression.

What do you think?

1. *What points in this editorial might Mackenzie quarrel with?*
2. *How effective would this kind of appeal be today? Why?*

12. PROCLAMATION BY WILLIAM LYON MACKENZIE

Mackenzie issued his Proclamation, taken here from the Montreal Transcript, January 2, 1838, to the people of Upper Canada asking that they join his movement. But, in spite of his rhetoric, few did; his rebellion was considered, at that time, to be a failure.

INHABITANTS OF UPPER CANADA!—For nearly fifty years has our country languished under the blighting influence of military despots, strangers from Europe, ruling us, not according to the laws of our choice, but by the capricious dictates of their arbitrary power.

They have taxed us at their pleasure, robbed our exchequer, and carried off the proceeds to other lands—they have bribed and corrupted ministers of the Gospel, with the wealth raised by our industry—they have, in place of religious liberty, given rectories and clergy reserves to a foreign priesthood, with spiritual power dangerous to our peace as a people—they have bestowed millions of our lands on a company of Europeans for a nominal consideration, and left them to fleece and impoverish our country—they have spurned our petitions, involved us in their wars, excited feelings of national animosity in countries, townships and neighbourhoods, and ruled us as Ireland has been ruled, to the advantage of persons in other lands, and to the prostration of persons in other lands, and to the prostration of our energies as a people.

We are wearied of these oppressions, and resolved to throw off the yoke. Rise, Canadians, rise as one man, and the glorious object of our wishes is accomplished.

BRAVE CANADIANS! Hasten to join that standard, and to make common cause with your fellow citizens now in arms in the Home, London and Western Districts. The opportunity of the absence of the hired red coats of Europe is favourable to our emancipation. And short sighted is that man who does not think that although his apathy may protect him from it, yet it must end in INDEPENDENCE and freedom from European thraldom for ever!

Until Independence is won, trade and industry will be dormant, houses and lands will be unsaleable, merchants will be embarrassed, and farmers and mechanics harassed and troubled; that point once gained the prospect is fair and cheering, a long day of prosperity may be ours.

What is meant by?

"hired red coats of Europe"

What do you think?

1. *If the major issue in the Rebellion of 1837-38 was "representation" and "participation," is it much the same issue that the dissident groups of today are talking about? Explain.*
2. *Most of us would agree that the position of the Family Compact and the Château Clique amounted to a government by elite. Are we still governed by elite?*

13. ANTI-REBEL SONG

Oh, now that the rebellion's o'er,
Let each true Briton sing:
"Long live the Queen in health and peace,
And may each rebel swing."
And good Sir Francis Head, may he
With health and power by crowned;
May earthly happiness to him
For evermore abound.
God prosper, too, my own loved land,
Thy sons so brave and true,
A heavy debt of loyalty
Doth England owe to you.
But still for Mac there's one more step
To end his life of evil:
Soon may he take the last long step
From gibbet to the devil.

Anon.

What do you think?

1. Compare the techniques used by this song to appeal to an audience with those of the Reverend Green's on page 192. Which is likely to be more effective? Why?

14. ARISE CANADIANS

This poem appeared in Mackenzie's Gazette of May 19, 1838, when Mackenzie was in American exile and the rebellion seemed to have been a complete failure. Rebels Lount and Matthews were hanged for treason.

Arise—Canadians, arise, and battle for the right;
Fair liberty's the glorious prize, awake then to the fight.
Oh, why do ye thus meanly kneel, nor dare your country save;
Arise!—gird on th' avenging steel, and tyrant minions brave.
And know ye not ye weakly frail, that ye yourself must free;,
Then why send forth that coward wail, dare ye not freemen be?
And heard ye not that shout of scorn, your tyrant masters send?
O'er the Atlantic wave 'tis borne—awake, your chains to rend.
Have Lount and Matthews vainly borne for you a Felon's death?
Their graveless bones now grin in scorn, they ask a bloody wreath.
Rise! swear by Jove's eternal name, swear by your fathers' graves:
To avenge their death in blood and flame, and crush your Tyrants—
    slaves.
Awake! Canadians arise, 'tis freedom calls to fight;
He nobly lives or nobly dies, who battles for the right.

What do you think?

1. Who is to determine what is "right"? How is it to be determined?
2. Where can you find in Canadian society today the glorification of arms indicated in this poem?

The Rebellion Losses Bill

In the wake of the Rebellions of 1837-8, a bill was introduced into the Canadian legislature to reimburse certain of the so-called "rebels" in Lower Canada for some of the losses and damages which they had incurred during the vigorous suppression of that rebellion by the English forces. Great controversy surrounded the passage of the bill, since many English-speaking inhabitants of Lower Canada and Upper

Canada could not understand why those people who had unsuccessfully revolted against constitutional authority should be compensated for their losses. The problem was compounded by the racial tension existing between French and English Canadians.

1. OPPOSITION TO REBELLION LOSSES BILL

The intense opposition to the bill, along with the underlying racial friction, is revealed in this document. The "Governor" referred to here is Lord Elgin then Governor General of the United Canadas. (Ottawa. Public Archives of Canada. Elgin-Gray Papers.)

During the present session of Parliament, measures have been brought forward that have greatly agitated the community, but none more so than the bill recently passed by both houses for the payment of the "Rebellion losses" in Canada East, or as it is expressed "the payment of rebels of Lower Canada." This bill passed the Lower House by a majority of only four, and now awaits the signature of the Governor General. Large meetings have been held by those opposed to the measure, and violent resolutions have been adopted. In publishing the proceedings of one of these meetings, the Montreal *Courier* holds the following language:

The resolutions were received with tremendous cheers. But one feeling animated the meeting, and is shared by the whole country; and that is, never to submit to the payment of the rebels. Let the parliament pass the bill, let the Governor sanction it if he pleases, *but while there is an axe and rifle on the frontier, and Saxon hands to wield them, these losses will not be paid.*

What do you think?

1. What would have been the attitudes of the "Saxon hands" towards Mackenzie and Papineau?

2. Do you agree that there has been a change in views regarding the use of violence? If so, how can you account for it?

2. INDEMNITY SANCTIONED BY ELGIN

After the Rebellion Losses Bill had been passed by the Assembly, Lord Elgin's carriage was stoned as he returned home. This report is taken from La Minerve, *April 26, 1849*

The sanction to thirteen or fourteen bills which came before the indemnity bill would have been given amidst perfect silence. When approval was pronounced on the latter, those discontented held silent for a moment, one of them gave the signal cry, murmurs and grumblings commenced, then they left the gallaries [*sic*] and went to assemble in the streets where His Excellency had to pass after completing his functions in the name of the Sovereign. You could certainly expect some insults on their part, in view of their conduct inside, but who would have ever believed that they have the effrontery and audacity to go so far as throwing eggs and ice on His Excellency and his Aides-de-Camp? The driver stopped the horses to evade this little shower that was more disgusting than dangerous; but the illustrious personages that he was driving seemed impassive and unperturbed in the middle of everything, they even made fun of this fanatical outrage. Nevertheless they continued to feel a little sorry to see their compatriots completely forgetting reason to indulge in assault and battery, in frenzied acts of so vile a nature that one has probably never seen among civilized people. It is impossible to believe that the populace went to such excesses on their own volition. Ordinarily the people understood very little about government affairs, but let themselves be moved by those they are accustomed to regard as their friends. It is possible, you will say, that informed and intelligent men counsel or approve a conduct so ferocious and savage? We will reply, no, if we didn't have before our eyes proof to the contrary.

What do you think?

1. Why do you think the illustrious personages here are so impassive and unperturbed? Would they be so today? Why or why not?

3.   THE BURNING OF THE PARLIAMENT BUILDINGS

The evening after the passing of the Rebellion Losses Bill, the House of Assembly in Montreal was burned by a Tory mob. The event was described in the Montreal Gazette, *April 27, 1849.*

The writer of this Report, on proceeding to the House of Assembly, on Wednesday evening, at about nine o'clock, to take his place in the Reporter's Gallery, fell in with a crowd of persons marching towards the House. The crowd advanced on the House by different streets, from the direction of the Place d'Armes. It speedily surrounded the House, and commenced throwing stones through the windows. The crowd was large but not very dense; the writer was able to walk about through every part of it. The excitement appeared to be intense. A party of the more violent among the crowd proceeded to burst open the hall door . . . smashing the door to atoms. They then rushed up the main stairs into the Hall of the Assembly, a few members only having remained, among whom were Messrs. Stevenson, Galt, McConnell, and Dr. Fortier,—the first named, with great coolness planted themselves in such a manner as to escape the volleys of stones, and, like philoso-phers, coolly surveyed the scene; the last screaming and yelling from very fear. The mob proceeded to demolish everything in the Hall. One fellow took possession of the Speaker's Chair, and declared, in a solemn voice, that he dissolved the Parliament in the Queen's name, and that the members had better take themselves off, or he would not answer for their lives. The remaining members, together with other individuals and four or five ladies, had in the meantime taken refuge behind the Speaker's Chair.

The writer proceeded round the House on the outside. The crowd appeared to be composed, as far as he was able to observe, of merchants and other respectable citizens of Montreal for the most part.

The number of persons inside the House was not very large; there was a party in the lobby, engaged in breaking up the Committee Rooms, Clerks Offices, and knocking windows out. . . . A few boys were throwing stones through the windows. The writer heard some expressions to the effect that it was not improbable that the mob in the building would set it on fire. . . . The men then fired these loose papers and threw them about the room. The wind was high and in a very few moments the wooden gallery and a canvas covering above it were enveloped in flames. The crowd stood at some distance watching in an apparently impassive manner the progress of this handful of incendiaries. The anxiety of the moment was painful. . . . The writer's first impulse was to hasten for the police; he did not take this step, as the wild fire rapidity, with which the flames spread rendered it useless. . . .

All this occurred in the space of ten or fifteen minutes. The wooden part of the building was now blazing with intense brightness. A dense smoke was visible inside the main building. A moment more and it belched through the windows and chimneys with awful fury. . . . In a little time more, the whole building, from one end to the other, was enveloped in one sheet of living flame. It was now impossible to approach near the building, for the intense heat; the belching flames now burst through the roof as it fell in. And the sight became awfully and magnificently beautiful! The night was clear and cold; and the high wind lashed the flames to maddening fury.

. . . The next morning. The House lies in smoking ruins. The stone of which it was built being blue limestone, the walls are whitened, crumbled, and tottering in a very dangerous state.

What do you think?

1. *How does this writer explain the violence that took place? Do you agree with his view?*

2. *What is the symbolic significance of the attack on the House of Assembly? What is the usual justification for such an attack? What do you think can be accomplished by it?*

3. *Compare this event with the sacking of the computer centre at Sir George Williams University.*

4. THIS SHAMEFUL ACT

This document and the one following are editorial comments on the burning. They both condemn the act, but for different reasons. Would these commentaries still apply today? The first editorial appeared in the Methodist paper, the Christian Guardian, *May 2, 1848. The second is from the* Examiner, *May 9, 1848.*

Too strong language can hardly be used in expressing our disapprobation of this shameful act. Nothing can justify it. However indignant the people might feel, on the passage and sanctioning of the Indemnity Bill, no justification at all can be found for the senseless, lawless, and incendiary act of destroying property to the amount of two-thirds of the sum appropriated to pay the Rebellion Losses. Soon, however, the building may be erected again; but documents have been destroyed which can never be replaced; and beyond all this, a stain has been fixed upon our Colonial character which may not easily be effaced; and passions have been awakened which perhaps will not soon be allayed.

What do you think?

1. *Would the author of this editorial agree with the findings of the Goldfarb Report regarding the culture reinforcement of violence?*

5. THE LAST DESPERATE STRUGGLE OF TORYISM

Whoever regards with the eye of a statesman and the feelings of a patriot the late barbarian outrages in Montreal, will find in them greater causes of indignation and regret than the mere destruction of property, however wanton the act or irreparable the loss. This outrage was only a means, of which the end was to rob the people of this Province of their most sacred right—that of local self-government. The outrage was planned by tyrants, and executed by barbarians. Every people to whom the right of self-government is denied are either the vassals of a foreign power or the slaves of a domestic despot. The free spirits of Canada are willing to occupy neither of these degrading positions. The rights of British subjects have been solemnly guaranteed to them by the Home Government. Our Commons House of Assembly is freely elected by the people; and the second branch of the Legislature is no longer in a position to neutralize or stifle public sentiment. The majority rules. The measures of the present Legislature are passed by no narrow majorities, obtained by the concurrent influence of bribery, trickery, and corruption. The infamy of these means belongs to the predecessors of the present Government. The laws passed by the existing Legislature bear the stamp of the public will. But there is a faction in the state that sets itself above the laws, the legislature, and the constitution. This is the same faction that resisted the introduction of popular government; and for half a century ruled the people with a rod of iron. That people, now admitted to their legitimate share in the government, have taken from this despotic faction the means of wealth, corruption, and tyranny. We now witness that faction attempting, by unconstitutional means, to regain its lost position, and that power which it so long abused. Thrown upon their own resources, the members of the old bureaucratic system find themselves rapidly descending in the social scale. These men of desperate fortunes with whom politics was a trade, and the public purse their constant exchequer, find no hope in constitutional opposition to the government of the day and the measures passed by the representatives of the people. They have therefore resorted to the desperate expedient of violence. We have their own admission that the Parliament House was burnt "by men with good coats on their backs"—men whose fortunes decay under a popular system of government. The question with them was not whether "rebels should be remunerated," for they are not ignorant that this was never intended; but whether the people of Canada are to be deprived of the inestimable right of local self-government, that a few incapable and corrupt men may again fatten on the hard earned revenues of an industrious people. Disguise it as they may, that is the real question. With the hope of obtaining their object they sought to coerce the Representative of Her Majesty into vetoing a measure passed by a large majority of the people's representatives. Lord Elgin is too practiced a statesman not to understand his position and duty, and too firm and honorable a man to degrade the dignity of his station by abdicating the functions of his high office, at the voice of faction and the attitude of menace. His Excellency's sin is, to have upheld the constitutional rights of the people, by refusing to oppose the wishes of their representatives, and to have preserved unsullied the dignity of the sovereign whom he represents, by scorning to yield to menace and threats. . . .

. . . Toryism is but consistent with itself in seeking for selfish purposes, to crush popular liberty, and reduce a free people to a state of degrading vassalage. The destruction of our liberties was the object sought to be secured by the destruction of the parliament buildings.

It is alleged by the calumniators of Lord Elgin, who excuse the outrages of the 25th April, that the Indemnity Bill was a measure of "unusual Character," and being such that Lord Elgin should have refused it the Royal sanction. But the truth is, far from being of an unusual character, the measure was considered so much a matter of course that it was deemed unnecessary to make special reference to it in the Royal speech. The proposal to indemnify the sufferers in Lower Canada had been before Parliament and the country, for four years, without encountering the opposition of any party. The initiatory steps taken by the Tories, unopposed by the Liberals, had bound all parties, and pledged the faith of the Government, to carry to completion what had, with such singular unanimity, been begun. A similar measure for Upper Canada had been passed without opposition. It is well known that the measure had been regarded as a matter of course, ever since the Upper Canada Rebellion Losses were paid; and no party would have dreamt of opposing its passing, had not the Tories, prostrate and disorganized as a party, discovered in it the materials of political capital, in which, before this (to them) fortunate discovery, they were hopelessly bankrupt.

The truth is but too evident that the Tories only wanted a pretext for attempting the destruction, by violence, of that principle of popular government, of which, for years, they opposed conspiracy, planned by the bankrupt leaders of the Tory faction, to effect this object, there is sufficient evidence, patent to the public: to say nothing of that which, from prudential motives, is for the moment withheld. A reference to our quotations, in previous numbers from the Montreal *Gazette*, the *Courier* and several prints of that stamp in Upper Canada, threatening and predicting violence as the penalty of Lord Elgin's assenting to the bill, can scarcely fail to convince any one that the writers must have been cognizant of the existence of some willing agency ready to carry the threats into effect. . . .

What is meant by?

"Toryism"

What do you think?

1. "The Tory violence surrounding the Rebellion Losses Bill serves to underline the fact that even the establishment, so enamored of law and order, will resort to illegal action if their interests are seen to be threatened." Discuss.
2. Compare the attitude of the Tories during the events described above to the attitudes of some contemporary groups.

5

Conclusion

What do you think?

1. The North York Daily Mirror published a news item on December 6, 1970 which conveyed the following information.
   —About 400 people marched for the aid
     of the Moatfield Foundation in celebration
     of the anniversary of the March of the Upper
     Canadian rebels on Montgomery's Tavern in
     1837.
   —Leading politicians, including a Member of
     Parliament, a Member of the Provincial Legis-
     lature, and several North York aldermen partic-
     ipated in the event; some to the extent that
     they wore period costumes, carried muskets
     and jokingly posed for photographers while
     "arresting" or "capturing" one another.
   —A letter from the Prime Minister was read to
     the group.
   (a) How is it that the rebels and traitors of yesterday can become the heroes of today?
   (b) Conduct a survey in your school and/or neighbourhood to determine present attitudes towards:
       —Louis-Joseph Papineau
       —William Lyon Mackenzie
       —Louis Riel.
   (c) Is there a discernible difference between those attitudes presented by your neighbourhood as opposed to those of your school? If there is how do you account for it?
   (d) Is it fair to say that the rebels and traitors of today will become the heroes of tomorrow?
   (e) If you answer "yes" to the above, then do you think that this will apply to those presently in the FLQ?

2. (a) *Either as an individual, or as a group, decide upon some change that you would like to see come about. (This proposed change could relate to your family relationships, your school and its structure, your community, etc.,—in other words, virtually anything.)*

   (b) *Either as individuals, or as groups:*
   —*Sketch out a plan for implementing the change*
   —*Include alternative approaches*
   —*Indicate which approaches you would prefer to utilize*
   —*Render an opinion as to which tactic or approach you would expect to be the most successful*

3. *Discuss the role and effectiveness of the following in the implementation of change.*
   —*the political party*
   —*the petition*
   —*the mass media*
   —*individual action*
   —*elections*
   —*collective bargaining*
   —*the Royal Commission*
   —*civil disobedience*
   —*demonstration*
   —*pressure group*
   —*violence*

4. *Suggest a number of ways in which a mass demonstration can turn into a riot. Who is responsible for the riot in each case? When this situation occurs, who is most likely to be blamed for causing the riot?*

5. *Discuss the following:*
   "Private property is the cornerstone of our system, and all dissent must stop short of any infringement upon it—thus the establishment defines the limits of dissent so as to effectively preclude its challenging the system in any real way."

6. *Debate the proposition: "All those who profess to support violent revolution in our democratic society are either unbalanced misfits or hopeless romantics born into the wrong age."*

Suggested Readings

General

BINGHAM, JONATHAN B.: *Violence and Democracy* (New York: World Publishing, 1970).

COOK, RAMSAY, ed.: *Politics of Discontent: Essays by H. J. Schultz and Others* (Toronto: University of Toronto Press, 1967).

CRITCHLEY, THOMAS ALAN: *The Conquest of Violence: Order and Liberty in Britain* (London: Constable, 1970).

DEMARIS, OVID: *America the Violent* (Baltimore: Penguin, 1971).

GRAHAM, HUGH DAVIS: *Violence in America: Historical and Contemporary Perspectives* (New York: New American Library, 1969).

GRANATSTEIN, J. L. AND R. D. CUFF, eds.: *War and Society in North America* (Toronto: Nelson and Sons, 1971).

IRWIN, JOHN, ed.: *Great Societies and Quiet Revolution* (Toronto: CBC Publications, 1967).

MANN, WILLIAM E.: *Social and Cultural Changes in Canada* (Vancouver: Copp Clark, 1970).

MCNAUGHT, KENNETH: "Violence in Canadian History," in Moir, John S. ed.: *Character and Circumstance* (Toronto: MacMillan, 1970).

OSSENBURG, RICHARD J.: *Canadian Society: Pluralism, Change, and Conflict* (Scarborough, Ontario: Prentice-Hall, 1971).

PORTER, JOHN: *The Vertical Mosaic* (Toronto: University of Toronto Press, 1965).

ROBIN, MARTIN: *Provincial Politics in Canada* (Scarborough, Ontario: Prentice-Hall, 1972).

SKOLNICK, JEROME H.: *The Politics of Protest* (New York: Simon and Schuster, 1969).

THORBURN, HUGH: *Party Politics in Canada* (Scarborough, Ontario: Prentice-Hall, 1972).

UNDERHILL, FRANK H.: *The Radical Tradition: A Second View of Canadian History* (Toronto: CBC Publications, 1960).

Youth

BLACK, DAVID, ed.: *Getting On With It: or, Riel, Reports to an Allegorical Meeting of Shades Near Moose Jaw* (Canadian Union of Students, 1969).

CARD, B. Y.: *Trends and Change in Canadian Society: Their Challenge to Canadian Youth* (Toronto: Macmillan, 1968).

DALY, MARGARET: *The Revolution Game: The Short Unhappy Life of the Company of Young Canadians* (Toronto: New Press, 1970).

REICH, CHARLES: *The Greening of America* (New York: Bantam Books, 1970).

The Indian

BURNFORD, SHEILA: *Without Reserve* (Toronto: McClelland and Stewart, 1969).

CANADIAN BROADCASTING CORPORATION: *The Way of the Indian* (Toronto: CBC Publications, 1962).

CANADIAN CORRECTIONS ASSOCIATION: *Indians and the Law* (Ottawa: Indian Affairs Branch, 1967).

CARDINAL, HAROLD: *The Unjust Society* (Edmonton: M. J. Hurtig, 1970).

HAWTHORNE, HARRY B.: *A Survey of the Contemporary Indians of Canada* (Ottawa: Indian Affairs Branch, 1966-67).

INDIAN-ESKIMO ASSOCIATION: *Native Rights in Canada* (Toronto, 1969).

ROBERTSON, HEATHER: *Reservations Are For Indians* (Toronto: Copp Clark, 1970).

WAUBASHEGIG, ed.: *The Only Good Indian* (Toronto: New Press, 1970).

The Black Canadian

WINKS, ROBIN W.: *The Blacks in Canada* (Montreal: McGill-Queen's, 1971).

The Radical Left

HOROWITZ, GAD: "The Role of a Canadian Political Party: Toward the Democratic Class Struggle," *Journal of Canadian Studies*, 1967.

ROUSSOPOULOS, DIMITRIOS: *The New Left in Canada* (Montreal: Our Generation Press, 1970).

RYERSON, STANLEY: *The Open Society: Paradox and Challenge* (New York: International Publishers, 1965).

The Separatist

BAIN, GEORGE: "The Making of a Crisis—Quebec 1970," *Canadian Forum*, January 1971.

BERGERON, LÉANDRE: *The History of Quebec: A Patriote's Handbook*, trans. by Baila Marcus, (Toronto: New Canada Press, 1971).

CORBETT, EDWARD M.: *Quebec Confronts Canada* (Baltimore: Johns Hopkins University Press, 1967).

GELINAS, GRATIEN: *Yesterday the Children Were Dancing* (Toronto: Clarke, Irwin, 1967).

HAGGART, RON: *Rumours of War* (Toronto: New Press, 1971).

LÉVESQUE, RENÉ: *Option for Quebec* (Toronto: McClelland and Stewart, 1968).

MACLENNAN, HUGH: *The Return of the Sphinx* (Toronto: Macmillan, 1967).

MORF, GUSTAVE: *Terror in Quebec: Case Studies of the FLQ* (Toronto: Clarke, Irwin, 1970).

PORTAL, ELLIS: *Killing Ground: The Canadian Civil War* (Toronto: Peter Martin Associates, 1968).

RIOUX, MARCEL: *Quebec in Question*, trans. by James Boake, (Toronto: J. Lewis and Samuel, 1971).

ROTSTEIN, ABRAHAM, ed.: *Power Corrupted: The October Crisis and the Repression of Quebec* (Toronto: New Press, 1971).

SMITH, DENIS: *Bleeding Hearts, Bleeding Country: Canada and the Quebec Crisis* (Edmonton: M. J. Hurtig, 1972).

STEWART, JAMES: *The FLQ: Seven Years of Terrorism* (Montreal: Montreal *Star* with Simon and Schuster, 1970).

TAYLOR, CHARLES: "Behind the Kidnapping: Alienation too Profound for the System to Contain," *Canadian Dimension*, December 1970.

VALLIÈRES, PIERRE: *White Niggers of America*, trans. by Joan Pinkham, (Toronto: McClelland and Stewart, 1971).

The Poor

ADAMS, IAN: *The Poverty Wall* (Toronto: McClelland and Stewart, 1970).

Canada, Senate, Special Committee on Poverty, *Submissions*, January 19, 1969.

CANADIAN WELFARE COUNCIL: *Urban Needs in Canada* (Ottawa, 1965).

FOGELSON, ROBERT M.: *Violence as Protest: A Study of Riots and Ghettos* (Garden City, N.Y.: Doubleday, 1971).

MANN, WILLIAM E.: *Poverty and Social Policy in Canada* (Vancouver: Copp Clark, 1970).

The Establishment

BERTON, PIERRE: *The Smug Minority* (Toronto: McClelland and Stewart, 1968).

MCGRATH, W. T., ed.: *Crime and its Treatment in Canada* (Toronto: Macmillan, 1965).

MORTON, DESMOND: "Aid to the Civil Power: The Canadian Militia in Support of Social Order," *Canadian Historical Review*, December 1970.

Our Culture and Violence

CLARKE, SAMUEL D.: *Urbanism and the Changing Canadian Society* (Toronto: University of Toronto Press, 1961).

IRVING, J. A., ed.: *Mass Media in Canada* (Toronto: Ryerson Press, 1962).

LARSEN, OTTO N., comp.: *Violence and the Mass Media* (New York: Harper and Row, 1968).

WEINHAM, BENJAMIN: *Seduction of the Innocent* (New York: Rinehart, 1954).

The Sons of Freedom

HAWTHORNE, HARRY B.: *The Doukhobors of British Columbia* (Vancouver: Doukhobor Research Committee, 1955).

HOLT, SIMMA: *Terror in the Name of God: The Story of the Sons of Freedom* (Toronto: McClelland and Stewart, 1964).

WOODCOCK, GEORGE: *The Doukhobors* (Toronto: Oxford University Press, 1968).

The 1930s

BLISS, MICHAEL, ed.: *The Wretched of Canada* (Toronto: University of Toronto Press, 1971).

HORN, MICHIAL: *The Dirty Thirties* (Toronto: Copp Clark, 1972).

LIPSET, SEYMOUR MARTIN: *Agrarian Socialism* (Berkely: University of California Press, 1959).

WILBUR, JOHN AND RICHARD HUMPHREY: *The Bennet New Deal: Fraud or Portent?* (Toronto: Copp Clark, 1968).

YOUNG, WALTER D.: *Democracy and Discontent: Progressivism, Socialism, and Social Credit in the Canadian West* (Toronto: Ryerson Press, 1969).

Cape Breton Unrest

The People's History of Cape Breton (Halifax, 1971).

RAWLYK, G. A.: "The Farmer—Labour Movement and the Failure of Socialism in Nova Scotia," in *Essays on the Left* (Toronto: McClelland and Stewart 1971).

The Winnipeg General Strike

ALLEN, RICHARD: *The Social Passion: Religion and Social Reform in Canada 1914-1928* (Toronto: University of Toronto Press, 1971).

BALAWYDER, A.: *The Winnipeg General Strike* (Vancouver: Copp Clark, 1967).

HOROWITZ, GAD: *Canadian Labour in Politics* (Toronto: University of Toronto Press, 1968).

MAGDEN, BEATRICE: *The Winnipeg General Strike: Management—Labour Relations* (Toronto: Maclean-Hunter, 1969).

MASTERS, DONALD C.: *The Winnipeg General Strike* (Toronto: University of Toronto Press, 1950).

MCNAUGHT, KENNETH: *A Prophet in Politics: A Biography of J. S. Woodsworth* (Toronto: University of Toronto Press, 1959).

PENTLAND, H. C.: "Fifty Years Afterward: The Winnipeg General Strike," *Canadian Dimension*, July 1969.

ROBIN, MARTIN: *Radical Politics and Canadian Labour 1880-1930* (Kingston: Industrial Relations Centre, 1968).

The Northwest Rebellion

ANDERSON, FRANK: *"1885": The Riel Rebellion* (Calgary: Frontiers Unlimited, 1962).

BOWSFIELD, HARTWELL, comp.: *Louis Riel: Rebel of the Western Frontier or Victim of Politics and Prejudice?* (Toronto: Copp Clark, 1967).

——————: *Louis Riel: The Rebel and the Hero* (Toronto: Oxford University Press, 1971).

COULTER, JOHN W.: *Riel: A Play for Two Parts* (Toronto: Ryerson Press, 1962).

HOWARD, JOSEPH KINSEY: *Strange Empire: A Narrative of the Northwest* (New York: Morrow, 1952).

LAMB, ROBERT E.: *Thunder in the North: Conflict over the Riel Rising* (New York: Pageant Press, 1957).

OSLER, EDMUND BOYD: *The Man Who Had to Hang: Louis Riel* (Toronto: Longmans Green, 1961).

SILVER, A.: *The Northwest Rebellion* (Vancouver: Copp Clark, 1967).

STANLEY, G. T. G.: "The 'Half-Breed' Rising of 1885," *Canadian Historical Review*, 1936.

——————: *The Birth of Western Canada: A History of the Riel Rebellions* (London: Longmans Green, 1936; Toronto: University of Toronto Press, 1961).

——————: *Louis Riel* (Toronto: Ryerson Press, 1963).

The Rebellions of 1837

ARMSTRONG, F. H.: "William Lyon Mackenzie: Persistent Hero," *Journal of Canadian Studies*, 1971.

CLARK, SAMUEL D.: *Movements of Political Protest in Canada 1640-1840* (Toronto: University of Toronto Press, 1959).

GATES, LILLIAN: "The Decided Policy of William Lyon Mackenzie," *Canadian Historical Review*, 1959.

KILBOURN, WILLIAM: *The Firebrand: William Lyon Mackenzie and the Rebellion in Upper Canada* (Toronto: Clarke, Irwin, 1956).

LINDSEY, CHARLES: *The Life and Times of William Lyon Mackenzie* (Toronto: Coles Canadiana Collection, 1971).

MACKENZIE, WILLIAM LYON: *The Mackenzie Poems* (Toronto: Silver, 1966).

OUELLET, FERNAND: "Papineau dans la Révolution de 1837-8," *Canadian Historical Association Report*, 1958.

OUELLET, FERNAND: *Louis Joseph Papineau: A Divided Being*, Canadian Historical Association Booklet, No. 11.

PARKER, W. H.: "A New Look at Unrest in Lower Canada in the 1830s," *Canadian Historical Review*, 1959.

REA, J. E.: "William Lyon Mackenzie—Jacksonian?" *Mid-America*, 1968.

SCHULL, JOSEPH: *Rebellion: The Rising in French Canada, 1837* (Toronto: Macmillan, 1971).

The Rebellion Losses Bill

FOSTER, JOSEPHINE: "The Montreal Riots of 1849," *Canadian Historical Review*, 1951.

Films

Flowers on a One-way Street (60 min., NFB).
> The award-winning documentary which examines the conflict that resulted when a group of citizens (mostly young people) attempted to have Yorkville Avenue in Toronto closed to motor traffic.

L'Acadie, L'Acadie (90 min., NFB).
> A powerful and controversial documentary chronicling the student troubles at the University of New Brunswick in 1970. The film was produced by the French-language section of the National Film Board and deals with the question of French-language rights at the university.

Prologue (90 min., NFB)
> A feature film that has won wide acclaim both in Canada and abroad. In documentary style, the film deals dramatically with the options open to those who disagree with the "system."

Riel and the National Dream (28 min., OECA)
> This particular television drama deals primarily with the problem of Canadian expansion into the West. It also probes the nature of Métis response, especially in regard to the 1885 Riel Rebellion. The program consists of interviews with Riel, Gabriel Dumont and John A. Macdonald.

Saul Alinsky (Part I) (28 min., NFB).
> This is a particularly provocative and useful film since it deals with the well-known American organizer, Saul Alinsky. He talks to members of the Company of Young Canadians as they discuss the nature of social protest and the boundaries of legitimacy.

Saul Alinsky (Part II) (28 min., NFB).
> Here Alinsky deals with Duke Redbird and other Indian residents of the Rama Indian Reserve as they discuss, sometimes quite heatedly, the methods by which the Canadian Indian can achieve his goals.

Saul Alinsky Goes to War (60 min. NFB).
> This film details the fight of the labor force with the Eastman Kodak Company in Cleveland, Ohio. The workers hired Alinsky as their organizer.

Violence and Order (28 min., OECA).
> A surrealistic examination of Canadian attitudes as they relate to the question of violence in the process of social and political change. It is a television drama, and uses the rebellion of 1837 in Lower Canada as a focus.

Filmstrips

Law and Order (37 frames, NFB).
Rebellion in Lower Canada (29 frames, NFB).
Rebellion in Upper Canada (39 frames, NFB).